JOURNAL FOR THE STUDY OF THE OLD TESTAMENT
SUPPLEMENT SERIES
144

JSOT Press
Sheffield

AMONG THE PROPHETS

Language, Image and Structure in the Prophetic Writings

Edited by
Philip R. Davies
and
David J.A. Clines

Journal for the Study of the Old Testament
Supplement Series 144

Copyright © 1993 Sheffield Academic Press

Published by JSOT Press
JSOT Press is an imprint of
Sheffield Academic Press Ltd
343 Fulwood Road
Sheffield S10 3BP
England

Typeset by Sheffield Academic Press
and
Printed on acid-free paper in Great Britain
by Biddles Ltd
Guildford

British Library Cataloguing in Publication Data

Among the Prophets: Language, Image and
Structure in the Prophetic Writings.—
(JSOT Supplement Series, ISSN 0309-0787;
No. 144)
I. Davies, Philip R.
II. Clines, David J.A. III. Series
224

ISBN 1-85075-361-x

CONTENTS

Part III
MINOR PROPHETS

PREFACE

The papers presented in this volume were originally offered to the *Journal for the Study of the Old Testament* and accepted by its editors for publication. In view of the growing pressure on space in the *Journal*, it was subsequently decided, with the consent of the contributors, to issue them in the *JSOT* Supplement Series, in the belief that such a volume also affords a more convenient format for the reader interested in the themes and directions of current research into the prophets.

The Editors

ABBREVIATIONS

AB	Anchor Bible
AnBib	Analecta biblica
ANET	J.B. Pritchard (ed.), *Ancient Near Eastern Texts*
BDB	F. Brown, S.R. Driver and C.A. Briggs, *Hebrew and English Lexicon of the Old Testament*
BETL	Bibliotheca ephemeridum theologicarum lovaniensium
BHS	*Biblia hebraica stuttgartensia*
Bib	*Biblica*
BibOr	Biblica et orientalia
BKAT	Biblischer Kommentar: Altes Testament
BN	*Biblische Notizen*
BZ	*Biblische Zeitschrift*
BZAW	Beihefte zur *ZAW*
CBQ	*Catholic Biblical Quarterly*
CML	J.C.L. Gibson, *Canaanite Myths and Legends* (Edinburgh: T. & T. Clark, 2nd edn, 1978).
GKC	*Gesenius' Hebrew Grammar*, ed. E. Kautzsch, trans. A.E. Cowley
FRLANT	Forschungen zur Religion und Literatur des Alten und Neuen Testaments
HAR	*Hebrew Annual Review*
HAT	Handbuch zum Alten Testament
HDR	Harvard Dissertations in Religion
HTR	*Harvard Theological Review*
HUCA	*Hebrew Union College Annual*
Int	*Interpretation*
JBL	*Journal of Biblical Literature*
JETS	*Journal of the Evangelical Theological Society*
JQR	*Jewish Quarterly Review*
JSOT	*Journal for the Study of the Old Testament*
JSOTSup	*Journal for the Study of the Old Testament*, Supplement Series
NCB	New Century Bible
NEB	*New English Bible*
NJPSV	New Jewish Publication Society Version
OTL	Old Testament Library
RHPR	*Revue d'historie et de philosophie religieuses*
SBL	Society of Biblical Literature
SBLDS	SBL Dissertation Series
SBT	Studies in Biblical Theology

ST	*Studia theologica*
TDNT	G. Kittel and G. Friedrich (eds.), *Theological Dictionary of the New Testament*
TDOT	G.J. Botterweck and H. Ringgren (eds.), *Theological Dictionary of the Old Testament*
TSK	*Theologische Studien und Kritiken*
UT	C.H. Gordon, *Ugaritic Textbook* (Rome, 1965)
UUÅ	Uppsala Universitetsårsskrift
VT	*Vetus Testamentun*
WBC	Word Biblical Commentary
WMANT	Wissenschaftliche Monographien zum Alten und Neuen Testament
ZAW	*Zeitschrift für die alttestamentliche Wissenschaft*

LIST OF CONTRIBUTORS

K.T. Aitken
Department of Hebrew & Semitic Languages, Aberdeen, Scotland

Leslie C. Allen
Fuller Theological Seminary, Pasadena, California, USA

Michael L. Barré
St Mary's Seminary and University, Baltimore, Maryland, USA

Athalya Brenner
Oranim College of Education, Tiv'on, Israel

Alan Cooper
Hebrew Union College, Cincinnati, Ohio, USA

John B. Geyer
Dundee Congregational Church, Dundee, Scotland

Francis Landy
University of Alberta, Edmonton, Alberta, Canada

James Nogalski
The Southern Baptist Theological Seminary, Louisville, Kentucky, USA

John F.A. Sawyer
Department of Religious Studies, Newcastle-upon-Tyne, England

M.G. Swanepoel
Lunnonroad 211, Pretoria, South Africa

Marvin A. Sweeney
University of Miami, Florida, USA

Timothy L. Wilt
United Bible Societies, Kinshasa, Zaire

Part I
ISAIAH

Hearing and Seeing:
Metamorphoses of a Motif in Isaiah 1–39

K.T. Aitken

Abstract

The motif '(not) hear/see'/'(not) know/understand' occurs in four forms. Rhetorical and thematic connections between the forms map out a series of transformations in the movement from judgment to salvation. A negative/negative (didactic) form presents Israel's lack of knowledge as the result of a perverse refusal to hear Yahweh's words and see his works. This is transformed into a positive/negative (theological) form, whereby Israel is disabled from attaining knowledge through hearing and seeing, and its judgment is sealed. However, within the context of salvation, the negative/negative form is transformed into a positive/positive (didactic) form, as Israel now responds to Yahweh, while the positive/negative form is likewise transformed into a negative/positive (theological) form as the disabilities that had prevented knowledge are removed.

The words 'hear' and 'see', together with 'know' and 'understand', are frequently used in First Isaiah (chs. 1–39) as summarizing terms for Israel's responsiveness or lack of responsiveness to Yahweh and its consequences, and together they may be said to form one of the central motifs of the book. Besides its frequency, the centrality of the motif is also suggested by the commission of Isaiah in 6.9-13, where the prophet is told to go and say to the people, 'Hear indeed, but do not understand, and see indeed, but do not know' (v. 9). This formulation of the motif clearly lays great stress on the positive–negative relation in which the terms stand to one another. Equally clearly, this is only one of a set of four possible relations between the terms:

A.	not hear/see	—	not know/understand	[– –]
B.	hear/see	—	not know/understand	[+ –]
C.	hear/see	—	know/understand	[+ +]
D.	not hear/see	—	know/understand	[– +]

Each of these forms finds more or less explicit expression in a number of passages in the book. It is reasonable to assume that they stand in some kind of relation to one another, and that these relations centre on the negative and positive values variously assigned to the terms. Accordingly, this set of potential relations between 'hear/see' and 'know/understand' may be taken to form a structural matrix within which the motif has significance, and within which its forms are transformed.

The matrix itself already points towards a certain degree of organization and patterning of relations between the individual forms of the motif. First, from the perspective of the second term, the forms clearly fall into two contrasting pairs: those which do not result in knowledge/understanding (A, B), and those which result in knowledge/understanding (C, D). Secondly, between the pairs there is an inversion between a negative/negative (A) and a positive/positive (C) form, and between a positive/negative (B) and a negative/positive (D) form. This implies that 'C' is a transformation of 'A', and 'D' is a transformation of 'B'.

It remains to be seen whether and in what way these relations and transformations suggested by the matrix at this fairly abstract level are articulated through the expressions of the various forms of the motif within the present literary form of the book.[1]

A. *Not Hear/See—Not Know/Understand*

1. *Isaiah 1.2-20*

These verses form a well-rounded rhetorical and kerygmatic unit within the chapter. They comprise two panels of complaint followed by appeal: vv. 2-4, 5-8(9); vv. 10-15, 16-20. Both panels are introduced by שמע // האזין (vv. 2, 10), and are linked to each other by the repetition סדם // עמרה (vv. 9, 10), and by the inclusion כי דבר (פי) יהוה (vv. 2, 20). There is also a close thematic correspondence between the opening complaint and the closing appeal concerning Israel's sin and rebellion. Thus, מרעים (v. 4), רע מעלליכם and חדלו הרע רע (v. 16) pick up חטאיכם (v. 18) picks up גוי חטא (v. 4), and the verbs מאן and

---

1. On connections between the motif in chs. 1–39 and chs. 40–55, see R.E. Clements, 'Beyond Tradition-History: Deutero-Isaianic Development of First Isaiah's Themes', *JSOT* 31 (1985), pp. 101-104; R. Rendtorff, 'Jesaja 6 im Rahmen der Komposition des Jesajabuches', in J. Vermeylen (ed.), *The Book of Isaiah* (Leuven: Leuven University Press, 1989), pp. 73-82.

מרה (v. 20) echo פשע, עזב and נאץ (vv. 2, 4).

The theme of the divine complaint in vv. 2-3 is Israel's lack of knowledge (לא ידע // לא התבונן) resulting from their rebellion (פשע) against Yahweh. The perversity of Israel's condition is emphasized through the contrast with the ox and ass. In v. 4 the complaint is expanded in prophetic speech in terms of Israel's sinfulness (חטא // עון), having rejected (עזב) and despised (נאץ) Yahweh.

The form and language of v. 2 recall the legal charge brought by parents against a rebellious son (בן סורר ומורה) in Deut. 21.18: 'he will not listen (איננו שמע) to our voice'. Though the verb used in v. 2 is מרה, פשע is found in 1.20, 3.8 and 30.9 (מרי). This last passage is particularly significant, since it looks back to vv. 2-4 and explicitly describes Israel as 'sons who are not willing to hear the instruction (תורה) of Yahweh' (cf. בנים סוררים, 30.1).[1] Furthermore, the elaboration of the charge in v. 4 appears to be equivalent to refusing to hear Yahweh's voice. This is suggested by the parallel in 5.24, where Israel have forsaken (מאס) the instruction (תורה) of Yahweh,[2] and despised (נאץ) his word. Israel's lack of knowledge is therefore rooted in their refusal to hear Yahweh's instruction.

Accordingly, the second panel begins with a summons to Israel to hear Yahweh's instruction (תורה, v. 10), and ends with the choice confronting Israel either to be willing to hear (שמע) or to refuse (מאן) to hear and rebel (מרה). The thematic correspondence between the appeal in vv. 16-20 and the complaint in vv. 2-4 implies that through hearing and not rebelling Israel will know and understand. This implication is strengthened by the link between the land being 'devoured' (אכל) by the enemy as a consequence of lack of knowledge and rebellion in v. 7 (cf. v. 20) and 'eating' (אכל) the fruits of the land—the one the result of lack of knowledge and rebellion, and the other of hearing and not rebelling in v. 19. The appeal in vv. 19-20 therefore holds out the possibility of a transformation of the motif from 'not hear–not know' to 'hear–know'.

2. *Isaiah 5.8-24*

This passage contains a series of woe sayings. They appear to be

---

1.   פשע is collocated with מרה in Lam. 3.42, and with לא שמע in Isa. 48.8 and Jer. 3.13 (cf. also Ezek. 2.3-5).

2.   Cf. (with עזב) עזבם את־תורתי // לא־שמעו בקולי, Jer. 9.12.

arranged in a concentric pattern, though the symmetry is offset by the elaboration of the woe sayings in the first half of the pattern:

>   a. social evils (vv. 8-10)
>   b. drunkenness (vv. 11-17)
>   c. sin and iniquity (v. 18-19)
>   d. perversity (v. 20)
>   c'. wise in own eyes (v. 21)
>   b'. drunkenness (v. 22), together with
>   a'. social evils (v. 23-24)[1]

In vv. 12b-13a Israel's condition is once again described as lack of knowledge (בלי־דעת), though now it is rooted in the people's failure to see (לא הביט // לא ראה) the activity of Yahweh (פעל יהוה // מעשה ידיו). The context (vv. 11-12a) suggests that this failure arises from the mindless pursuit of drunkenness and revelry.

According to v. 19, Israel contend that the fault lies not in their failure to see but in Yahweh's failure to act—let Yahweh speed his work (מעשה) and carry out his plan, and they would see and know (ראה // ידע). These words adumbrate a transformation in the motif from 'not see–not know' (vv. 12-13) to 'see–know' as perceived from Israel's point of view. The prophet, however, takes a different point of view. The participle האמרים 'who say' (v. 19) is syntactically dependent on הוי 'woe' in v. 18. Thereby not only is Israel condemned for speaking such words, but the words are equated with iniquity (עון) and sin (חטאה, v. 18). Furthermore, the next saying highlights the perversity of Israel, who have inverted good and evil, light and darkness, the sweet and the bitter (v. 20). It too is introduced by הוי האמרים, which suggests it is a 'commentary' on Israel's words in v. 19. It might be noted that this comment on Israel's perversity lies at the centre of the concentric pattern. Consequently, the transformation adumbrated by Israel in v. 19 simply serves to reinforce their failure to see and know (vv. 12-13). At the same time, it also serves to intensify this failure. It arises not merely from a mindless pursuit of drunkenness and revelry, but from a deep-seated perversity which will not see what can be plainly seen.

---

1. This theme is sustained in the woe saying in 10.1-4, which probably originally formed part of the series.

There is thus a close connection between 1.2-20 and 5.8-24 centred on the relation between hearing/seeing and knowing/understanding. This correspondence is reinforced by a number of verbal and thematic links between the passages. The following key words are repeated: ידע (1.3; 5.13 [דעת]); עמי (1.3; 5.13); הוי (e.g. 1.4; 5.8); [חטאה] חטא // עון (1.4; 5.18; cf. 1.18); נאץ (1.4; 5.24); תורה (1.10; 5.24), קדוש ישראל (1.4; 5.19, 24), הרע // היטב (1.16-17 [cf. מרעים, v. 4]; 5.20 [טוב // רע].[1] The passages, therefore, are complementary expressions of the negative/negative form of the motif, giving an assessment of Israel's sinfulness against the Holy One of Israel with respect to hearing the words of Yahweh (1.2-20) and seeing the work of Yahweh (5.8-24).

3. *Isaiah 22.8b-14*

In this passage, the self-reliant policies pursued by Judah during the Assyrian crisis are condemned. Set against an oracle dealing with the Assyrian invasion and the rape of Judah (vv. 1-8a), in vv. 8b-11 a contrast is drawn between what Judah's response was and what it ought to have been: they 'looked' (ראה // הביט) to their weapons, fortifications and water supply, and did not 'look' (לא הביט // לא ראה) to Yahweh who had brought it about (עשיה). In vv. 12-14 a further contrast is drawn between the mourning to which Yahweh had summoned the people and the drunkenness and revelry to which they had abandoned themselves.

These verses are very closely related to 5.8-24. Here too there is a failure to 'see' (לא הביט // לא ראה, 22.11; 5.12) Yahweh's activity (עשיה, 22.11; מעשה ידיו, 5.12). The association between this failure and drunkenness recalls their connection in 5.11-12. Both passages have banquet scenes in view, and vividly portray revelry and excess through pairs of words linked by *waw* (22.13; 5.12a). In addition, the description of Israel's offence as 'this iniquity' (העון הזה, 22.14) echoes the equation of Israel's perverse refusal to see Yahweh's work with iniquity (עון) in 5.18-19 (cf. also 1.4). Finally, ונגלה באזני יהוה צבאות in v. 14 recalls באזני יהוה צבאות in 5.9.[2] In the light of these connections with 5.8-24, lack of knowledge (cf. 5.12-13) may be assumed to be implicit in the failure to 'see'.

---

1. Of these key words, עון, נאץ, and קדוש ישראל do not recur in chs. 1–5, while the root ידע otherwise has a quite different sense (5.5).

2. This expression is found only in these two passages.

4. *Isaiah 30.8-17*

These verses are set within the context of a condemnation of Judah's policy of alliance with Egypt during the Assyrian crisis (vv. 1-7). As in 22.8b-14, a contrast is drawn (ולא, 22.11; 30.1) between what the people did and what they ought to have done: they courted Egypt instead of consulting Yahweh (vv. 1-2). But Egypt's help is futile and will redound to their shame (vv. 3-7).

The condemnation takes the form of a woe saying against 'rebellious sons' (בנים סוררים, v. 1). The theme of Israel's rebelliousness is then picked up and developed in vv. 8-14 as the reason for writing down the prophet's words as a witness (v. 8). Its expression in v. 9 closely echoes the language of 1.2-20: Israel are a 'rebellious people // lying sons' (בנים כחשים // עם מרי; cf. בנים משחיתים + עם, 1.4; מריתם, 1.20) who are 'unwilling to hear' (לא־אבו שמוע; cf. אם־תאבו ושמעתם, 1.19) the 'instruction' (תורה; cf. 1.10 [also 5.24]) of Yahweh.

In vv. 10-14 Israel's rebellion against Yahweh's torah is spelled out in terms of their opposition to their seers and prophets, commanding them not to communicate divine torah in word and vision but to prophesy falsehood (vv. 10-11). In particular, Israel have despised Yahweh's word ('this word') concerning reliance on Yahweh alone (cf. v. 15) and have relied on oppression and perverseness (v. 12), but they will pay the price for 'this iniquity' (העון הזה, vv. 13-14). Here again there are close echoes of 1.2-20, especially at the points where 1.2-20 is related to 5.8-24. Thus, the charge that Israel have 'despised (מאס) this word (דבר)' recalls 1.4 (נאץ // עזב) and 5.24 (נאץ + אמרה // תורה + מאס), while the prominence given to the epithet 'the Holy One of Israel', whose word they have rejected (30.11, 12; cf. v. 15), echoes the rejection of the [word of] the Holy One of Israel in 1.4 and 5.24 (cf. also 5.19). Further, the definition of Israel's rejection of Yahweh's word as העון הזה (v. 13) recalls עון in 1.4, and corresponds to the refusal to see Yahweh's work as עון in 5.18-19. The expression itself recurs again only in 22.14, where it similarly provides the basis for an announcement of judgment on Israel for their refusal to 'see'. The conclusion to the passage (vv. 15-17) returns to the theme of Israel's response in the face of the Assyrian threat. Israel have rejected Yahweh's call to trust and rely on him alone as a means of security, and have relied on military strength. These verses seem to expand on the divine instruction Israel were unwilling to hear in v. 9. This is suggested by the repetition between לא־אבו שמוע (v. 9) and לא

אביתם (v. 15). Significantly, it also presupposes Israel's rejection of
the grounds for the transformation of the motif adumbrated by Yahweh
in 1.19: אם־תאבו ושמעתם. Interestingly, therefore, the judgment
announced in v. 17 echoes 1.8 through the repetition of נותר כ in a
poetic image of solitariness.

Thus, 30.8-17 and 22.8b-14 are very closely related to 1.2-20 and
5.8-24 respectively. In them the motif is applied to the Assyrian crisis,
once again from the complementary viewpoints of a failure to hear
and a failure to see.

Within these passages, Israel's lack of knowledge/understanding is
rooted, explicitly or implicitly, in a failure to hear the word of Yahweh
and to see the work of Yahweh. Hence, 'not know/understand' is
implied by 'not hear/see', while conversely 'know/understand' is
implied by 'hear/see'. The transformation of 'not know/understand' to
'know/understand' is therefore possible only through the prior transformation of 'not hear/see' to 'hear/see'. In their very different ways,
both 1.2-20 and 5.8-24 raise the possibility of this transformation,
though it remains unrealized (cf. 30.9). The relation between hearing/
seeing and knowing/understanding upon which the negative–negative
form of the motif rests is therefore essentially empirical and didactic
in character. It is clear that this form has its place within the general
context of Israel's judgment.

B. *Hear/See—Not Know/Understand*

1. *Isaiah 6.1-13*
In v. 9 Isaiah is instructed to go and say to the people: 'Hear (שמע)
indeed, but do not understand (בין), and see (ראה) indeed, but do not
know (ידע)'. By way of explanation, he is told his prophetic task is to
dull the people's organs of perception: to make their hearts fat, their
ears heavy, and to coat their eyes. The purpose of this is to make the
people deaf, blind and ignorant so that they might not repent and be
healed (v. 10), thereby making judgment certain (vv. 11-13).

Whereas the formulation of the motif in v. 9 expresses the relation
'hear/see—not know/understand', v. 10 interprets this rather more
prosaically in terms of the dulling of the organs of perception to prevent seeing, hearing and understanding. Thus, for example, the failure

of the ears to hear in v. 10 is equivalent to the failure of hearing to bring understanding in v. 9.

The motif is set within the context of the vision of Isaiah in vv. 1-7, in which hearing and seeing likewise play a central role. Isaiah 'sees' (ראה) with his 'eyes' the divine king (vv. 1, 5), and 'hears' the proclamation of his divine glory and holiness (v. 3; cf. אשמע, v. 8). This results in Isaiah's awareness of his own sinfulness and the sinfulness of the people. However, his lips are touched by coals from off the altar and his iniquity is removed and his sin is forgiven. It therefore seems that the experience of Isaiah stands in part as a model of what is to be denied to the people through his preaching: Isaiah has 'seen' and 'heard'—and, by implication, he 'understands'; the people will also see and hear, but they will not understand.

2. *Isaiah 28.1-29*

This chapter can be divided into four main sections: vv. 1-8, 9-13, 14-22 and 23-29. The sections are linked together to form a rhetorical and kerygmatic unit. The first section, with its announcement of judgment in vv. 2-4, is closely bound with the announcement that the agreement with Sheol will be annulled in vv. 14-22 through repetition of the key words (שטפים...ישטפו/ ברד // מים. מים) (vv. 2, 17; cf. v. 15), and forms of the root רמס (vv. 3, 18). Verses 1-8 and 14-22 thus form a framework around vv. 9-13. Verses 9-13 are further linked with vv. 14-22 through the repetition of the expression העם הזה (vv. 11, 14) and הבין/ שמועה (vv. 9, 19), and with vv. 23-29 through the repetition of the key word יורה (vv. 9, 26), while vv. 14-22 are linked with vv. 23-29 through the repetition between מאת אדני יהוה צבאות (v. 22) and מעם יהוה צבאות (v. 29).

Verses 1-8 centre on the drunkenness of the leaders of the people: the rulers and their fading majesty and pride, together with the priests and prophets and their blurred vision (שגו בראה).

Verses 9-13 begin with the question of who can be taught the message (v. 9a). In the light of v. 12, this message concerns wherein the true source of safety and security lies. The meaning of vv. 9b-10 is obscured by the enigmatic and repeated צו לצו קו לקו זעיר שם. This may be an allusion to the teaching of the alphabet, in which case the reference may be to the people's ridiculing of the message as 'elementary' and beneath them.[1] However, in v. 13 the same expression has in view the unintelligible sounds of a foreign language (cf. 33.19). The allusion in vv. 9b-10 might therefore be to 'baby talk',[2] the sense being that the message appeared to be no more intelligible to the people than that. At all events, vv. 9-10 appear to imply the teaching of the message in clear terms, together with the failure of the people to understand it, and therefore to presuppose the form of the motif 'hear–not understand'.

Set against this, vv. 11-13 affirm that Israel will hear Yahweh speaking to them in what will indeed be an unintelligible language: no longer a word of security (v. 12), but a word of judgment spoken through the foreign tongue of the invader. A contrast is thereby drawn between Yahweh's word of appeal in the past, and Yahweh's word of judgment for the future. In the retrospect to the past (v. 12), the unintelligibility of Yahweh's word (i.e. 'hear–not understand', vv. 9-10) is explained in terms of Israel's unwillingness to hear it (i.e. 'not hear–not understand'). In the prospect for the future, 'hear–not understand' is then 're-deployed' in an intensified form through the shift in its context from appeal to the announcement of judgment: a hearing of Yahweh's word that leads to knowledge (vv. 9a, 12) will now be denied to Israel, to be replaced by a hearing that harbingers destruction. Verse 19 reinforces this by looking back to v. 9 and making the ironic comment that this is a message that Israel would understand (הבין שמועה; cf. יבין שמועה, v. 9), but that it would convey nothing but sheer terror.

This link between v. 9 and v. 19 suggests that vv. 14-22 serve as an elaboration of the judgment announced in vv. 11-13. It is significant, therefore, that whereas in vv. 9-11 the judgment was set against rejection of the true source of security (v. 12), here it is set against reliance on a false source of security, an agreement with Sheol—an allusion to Judah's alliance with Egypt. Verses 14-22 also link up with the theme of judgment in vv. 2-4, thereby providing a thematic connection between the three units. Through the 'strong one', like a storm of hail (ברד) and like a storm of overwhelming waters (מים...שטפים, v. 2), Yahweh will speak to Israel (v. 11) a message of sheer terror

---

1. Cf. O. Kaiser, *Isaiah 13–39: A Commentary* (London: SCM Press, 1974), pp. 244-46.

2. Cf. J. Lindblom, *Prophecy in Ancient Israel* (Oxford: Basil Blackwell, 1962), p. 201.

(v. 19), and the hail (ברד) and waters (מים) will overwhelm (ישטפו) and sweep away the people's false source of security and them with it (vv. 17b-19). Appropriately, therefore, corresponding to the foreign tongue of the invader through which Yahweh will now speak is the strange work that he will now perform (v. 21)

The chapter concludes with the parable about the farmer (vv. 23-29). It contains two appraisals, the first of which echoes v. 9 and the other v. 22, that is, the beginning and the end of the two central sections in the chapter respectively. The first appraisal (v. 26) observes that the farmer derives his agricultural skills from divine instruction (אלהיו יורנו). This echoes the question who can be taught (יורה) knowledge in v. 9. Israel's refusal to listen to divine instruction thus stands in marked contrast with the farmer, whose knowledge of agriculture demonstrates his acceptance of divine instruction. The first appraisal thus serves as a comment on the perversity of Israel in refusing to accept divine instruction along much the same lines as the parable of the ox and the ass in 1.2.

In the second appraisal (v. 29), the words 'also this comes from Yahweh of hosts' is generally taken to refer to the agricultural processes outlined in vv. 27-28, but that is to make it a weak restatement of v. 26 and to deprive it of much of its evident climactic force. The echo between מעם יהוה צבאות in v. 29 and מאת אדני יהוה צבאות in v. 22 suggests rather that גם־זאת looks back to the decree of utter destruction that the prophet has heard. Strange and foreign though Yahweh's work of judgment will be (v. 21), it is no less an expression of the marvellousness of his plan and the greatness of his wisdom than that reflected in the skills of the farmer—much as a perverse Israel might scoff (v. 22a).

The formulation of the motif in vv. 9-13 contains several expressions which recall the call and commission of Isaiah in 6.1-13. Thus, (a) את־מי...ואת־מי concerning the understanding of the message (v. 9) echoes את־מי...ומי concerning its delivery in 6.8; (b) יבין שמועה (v. 9) echoes שמעו שמוע ואל־תבינו in 6.9; (c) the designation of Israel as הזה העם (v. 11; cf. 6.9); (d) a contrast is perhaps also implied between the foreign 'lip' (שפה) of the invader through whom Yahweh will now speak to 'this people' (v. 11) and the cleansed 'lips' (שפתים) of the prophet (6.5, 7).

In addition, vv. 9-13 are juxtaposed to a passage (vv. 1-8) that stands in stark contrast to the context for Isaiah's commission in 6.1-7. Juxtaposed against the glory and exaltation of the divine king stand the fading majesty and pride of the drunkards of Ephraim (vv. 1-4); against the temple and earth filled with Yahweh's glory (מלא, a key word, 6.1, 3, 4), stand tables filled (מלא) with vomit and filth (v. 8); and against Isaiah who 'saw' (ראה, 6.1, 5) Yahweh, stand priests and prophets who err 'in seeing' (בראה). There are probably also echoes of 6.1-13 in the decree of destruction which the prophet has heard (שמעתי, v. 22; cf. אשמע, 6.8) and in the use of the verb כפר of the annulment of the people's agreement with Sheol upon which they falsely rely (v. 18 [cf. 'this iniquity', 30.13]; 6.7).

3. *Isaiah 29.9-16*

This passage is comprised of three main units: vv. 9-12, 13-14 and 15-16. Verses 9-12 centre on the inability of the prophets and seers to discern Yahweh's work. There is indeed a 'seeing' (חזות הכל, v. 11), but what is seen is like a sealed book to one who can read and an unsealed book to one who cannot read—it brings no knowledge or understanding. The explanation given for this is that Yahweh has blinded their eyes and poured out a spirit of deep sleep upon them. These verses thus likewise imply the motif in the form 'see–not understand'.

The next two units seem to be more closely related to one another than to vv. 9-12. In the first (vv. 13-14), judgment is pronounced on the wisdom of the wise. In the second, a woe saying against those who make plans without reference to Yahweh is elaborated by a parable of the potter and the clay. The units are linked together by repetition of the roots סתר (vv. 14, 15), and בין (vv. 14, 16). On the other hand, the position of vv. 13-16 following vv. 9-12 is closely paralleled by the movement in the preceding passage from reflection on hearing and understanding the message (28.9-13) to an announcement of judgment (28.14-22) and a concluding parable (28.23-29). This correspondence is reinforced by the repetition of עצה, מעשה and the root פלא as key words (vv. 14-16; cf. 28.21, 29). The three units are thus evidently held together by the same thematic associations which manifest themselves in 28.9-29. A further indication of this is the reference to Israel as העם הזה in 29.13, 14 (cf. 28.11, 14).

In vv. 13-16 a wisdom and understanding which disregard Yahweh's word (cf. מצות אנשים, v. 13) and his work (cf. v. 16) are condemned as the root both of the people's false worship and of their self-reliance in pursuit of their plans. The proverbial saying on the potter and the clay emphasizes the utter perversity and absurdity of this.

This passage also contains a number of close links with the formulation of the motif in 6.9-10: (a) the repetition in tandem of imperatives of different verbal forms of the roots תמה[1] and שׁעע (29.9a) recalls the collocation of the imperative and infinitive absolute of the verbs שׁמע and ראה in 6.9; (b) this link is reinforced by the use of the root שׁעע in 6.10; (c) the sequence 'be[2] drunk but not // totter but not' (ולא, v. 9b) recalls 'hear + but do not // see + but do not' (ואל) in 6.9, with a similar negation of normal expectations: hearing and seeing normally result in knowledge and understanding; drunkenness and unsteadiness are normally the result of drinking wine and beer; (d) ויעצם את־עיניכם (v. 10) echoes ועיניו השׁע in 6.10.

These three passages therefore likewise contain closely related expression of the motif in its positive–negative form. It is clear that the relation between the terms in this form is quite different from the empirical and didactic relation between them in the negative–negative form. The term 'not hear/see' has been transformed to 'hear/see'—a transformation already contemplated, as we have seen, in 1.19 and 5.19. On the other hand, according to the didactic relation between the terms, this necessarily implies a corresponding transformation from 'not know/understand' to 'know/understand', whereas this term has remained unchanged. The relation between the terms in the positive–negative form is essentially theological rather than didactic in character, insofar as it rests on Yahweh's declared intentions and actions. Like the negative–negative form, however, it too finds its place within the context of Israel's judgment.

The First Transformation

The first transformation therefore centres on the shift from 'not hear/see' in the 'A' form of the motif to 'hear/see' in the 'B' form without a corresponding transformation in 'not know/understand'. The relation between these forms of the motif must now be examined.

1. Cf. *BHS*.
2. Cf. *BHS*.

The passages which express the 'A' form fall into two closely related pairs, the one primarily focused on Israel's failure to hear (1.2-20; 30.8-17), and the other on their failure to see (5.8-24; 22.8b-14). There is also a parallel movement within each pair from that failure within the context of Israel's moral, social and religious life in general (1.2-20; 5.8-24), to its failure within the context of political life during the Assyrian crisis (22.8b-14; 30.8-17; cf. also 31.1-3). The passages which express the 'B' form reflect much the same pattern. Thus, 6.1-13 combines hearing and seeing, whereas 28.1-29 is primarily concerned with hearing and 29.9-16 with seeing. Similarly, in 6.1-13 the motif is connected in a general or programmatic way with Isaiah's prophetic ministry as a whole, whereas in 28.1-29 and 29.9-16 it is applied to the Assyrian crisis. Taking both forms together, therefore, it is clear that 6.1-13 occupies a central and pivotal position, since it is the only passage which explicitly correlates hearing and seeing, and since it forms the climax of the more comprehensive and programmatic formulations of the motif in the first section of the book. In the light of these considerations, the relation between the forms may be examined at two levels: (1) the relation between 6.1-13 and 1.2-20, 5.8-24 as forming a paradigm; (2) the relation between 28.1-29, 29.9-16 and 1.2-20 + 30.8-17, with 5.8-24 + 22.8b-14 as an application of this paradigm to the circumstances of the Assyrian crisis.

1. *The Paradigm*

I have already remarked that Isaiah's experience in 6.1-7 serves as a model of what is to be denied to the people through his preaching, namely a 'seeing' and 'hearing' which leads to knowledge and understanding (6.9-13). There are a number of verbal and thematic links between 6.1-13 and 1.2-20, 5.8-24 that serve to complement and enhance this paradigmatic aspect of the account by drawing a corresponding contrast between the prophet's experience and Israel's condition.

The setting of Isaiah's vision (ראה, 6.1, 5) of Yahweh in the temple already evokes a contrast with Israel's trampling of Yahweh's court when they come 'to see'[1] Yahweh's face (1.12). This is strengthened by the echo between מזבח (6.6) and זבחיכם (1.11), and by the use of the language of 'un/cleanness' (טמא, 6.5; זכה [hithp.], 1.16).

Most significant in this regard, however, are the closely related

---

1. Reading לְרָאוֹת for לֵרָאוֹת; cf. *BHS*.

themes of the sinfulness of Isaiah/Israel and the holiness of Yahweh in association with hearing/seeing, which are found in all three passages. In 1.2-20 and 5.8-24, Israel's sinfulness (עון // חטא, 1.4; חטאה // עון, 5.18) is manifested in their unwillingness to hear (שמע; cf. 1.19) the word and to see (ראה, 5.12, 19) the work of the Holy One (קדוש) of Israel (1.4; 5.19, 24); in 6.1-7 Isaiah sees (ראה) Yahweh and hears (cf. אשמע, v. 8) the proclamation of his holiness (קדוש), and his sin (עון // חטאה) is forgiven (כפר). Isaiah's explicit identification of himself with Israel as alike having 'unclean lips' (6.5), together with the echo between אוי לי (6.5) and the repeated הוי (1.4; 5.8; etc.), helps to bring into focus and to heighten the contrast which these thematic elements draw between a sinful but responsive prophet ('hear/see') and a sinful but unresponsive Israel ('not hear/see'). It is also reflected in the condemnation of Israel's refusal to 'look' (לא הביט // לא ראה) to Yahweh during the Assyrian crisis in 22.8b-14 through the summary statement that 'this iniquity' (העון הזה) would not be forgiven (כפר).

Isaiah's experience in 6.1-7 thus serves not only as a model of what will be denied to Israel through his preaching (6.9-13), but also as a model of the kind of responsiveness to Yahweh which Israel so singularly lacked (1.2-20; 5.8-24), and thereby serves to connect the 'B' form of the motif in 6.9-13 with the 'A' form in 1.2-20 and 5.8-24. These passages therefore serve as an exposition of the sinful condition of Israel upon which 6.9-13 is predicated. Appropriately, therefore, the announcement of judgment in 6.9-13 recalls and confirms the judgment announced in 1.2-20 and 5.8-24. The healing (רפא) denied to Israel in 6.10 looks back to the description of Israel's chastisement in terms of sickness and woundings in 1.5b-6 (cf. 30.26), while 6.11-12 picks up 1.7 through repetition of the key words ארץ, אדמה, ערים and שממה, and 5.9 through the repetition of מאין יושב בתים, and שמה.

In 1.2-20 and 5.8-24, Israel's condition is described from the complementary viewpoints of a failure to hear and a failure to see. At the same time, there are important differences of emphasis between the two passages. First, although both adumbrate the possibility that Israel might hear/see, in the first it is adumbrated by Yahweh by way of an appeal to Israel (1.19), and in the second by Israel by way of a challenge to Yahweh (5.19). In 1.2-20 it is therefore a genuine possibility, whereas in 5.8-24 it simply reinforces the depths of Israel's failure. Secondly, in 5.8-24 much greater emphasis is laid on Israel's perversity. The homely parable of the ox and ass (1.3) gives way to a

vivid characterization of the complete inversion of the moral order
(5.20). Thirdly, while in 1.2-20 judgment and reconciliation are presented as alternatives (vv. 19-20), in 5.8-24 judgment appears to be
irrevocable: Israel are heading for exile for lack of knowledge (5.13).

These shifts in emphasis between 1.2-20 and 5.8-24 reflect a certain
'hardening' in Israel's perverse attitude and a diminution in the potential of their responsiveness to Yahweh resulting in the inevitability of
judgment. The 'B' form of the motif in 6.1-13 takes this a step further. Through an increasingly stubborn and perverse attitude, Israel
have severed themselves from hearing and seeing. Yahweh will therefore sever Israel from the knowledge and understanding to which
hearing and seeing should lead, so that even the most attentive hearing
of Yahweh's word and careful seeing of Yahweh's work will not
result in knowledge and understanding. Hearing, no more than not
hearing, and seeing, no more than not seeing, are paths for Israel to
knowledge and understanding.

The transformation of 'not hear/see' to 'hear/see' in 6.1-13 is therefore predicated on the sinful condition of Israel's as described in 1.2-
20 and 5.8-24—on their perverse refusal to hear Yahweh's word and
to see Yahweh's work, nurtured by drunkenness and conceit (5.21)
and manifested in their moral, social and religious life. It consists
essentially in the exclusion of the possibility of the alternative transformation of the motif to 'hear/see–know/understand', thereby confirming the people in the blindness and ignorance of their own
perversion, and making judgment certain.

2. *The Application of the Paradigm to the Assyrian Crisis*

1. *Isaiah 28.1-29*

There are a number of close connections between 28.1-29 and the
passages which express the 'A' form of the motif. They can be
grouped under three headings:

(a) *Hearing.* לא אבוא שמוע in 28.12 is connected with אם־תאבו ושמעתם
in 1.19, לא־אבו שמוע in 30.9 and לא אביתם in 30.15. In the light of יורה
in 28.9, 26, what Israel have refused to hear is Yahweh's instruction
(cf. 28.12), as explicitly in 30.9 (תורה) and implicitly in 1.19 (cf. תורה,
1.10; 5.24). Further, its application to instruction on the true source
of security and rest (הניח, מנוחה, 28.12) is also reflected in 30.15 (נחת).
In both these passages the divine word of instruction (אמר, 28.12;

30.15) is contrasted with Israel's own words (אמרתם, 28.15; ותאמרו, 30.16) in which they affirm reliance on a false source of security. Finally, the parable of the farmer in 28.23-29 recalls the parable of the ox and the ass in 1.3. Both underline the unnatural perversity of Israel's refusal to hear Yahweh's instruction.

(b) *Seeing*. The description of the drunkenness of the rulers, priests and prophets in 28.1-8 complements the description of the drunkenness of Israel in 5.11-12, 22 and 22.13, with a repetition of the key words שכר // יין (28.1 [שכרי], 7). It too is introduced by הוי (28.1; 5.11, 22). In 28.7-8 drunkenness is associated with the prophets erring in 'seeing' (שגו בראה), while in 5.11-12 and 22.13 it is similarly associated with Israel's failure to see (לא ראה) Yahweh's work. This connection with Yahweh's work (פעל // מעשה, 5.12; מעשה // עצה, 5.19; עשיה // יצרה, 22.11) is picked up in 28.1-29 through the reference to Yahweh's work (עבדה // מעשה, 28.21) as a manifestation of his counsel (עצה, 28.29).

(c) *Judgment*. The reference to Isaiah's hearing (cf. 6.8) a decree of total judgment upon Israel in 28.22 recalls באזני in 22.14 (cf. 5.9), where it likewise concludes a condemnation of reliance on a false security. Further, the announcement that Israel's covenant with Death (מות) will be broken (כפר, 28.18) is an ironic echo of the statement that 'this iniquity will not be forgiven (כפר) until you die (עד־תמתון)' in 22.14. The expression בבקר...ביום ובלילה (28.19) recalls בבקר // בנשף in 5.11—the one emphasizing the relentlessness of Israel's pursuit of drunkenness and revelry, the other emphasizing the relentlessness of Yahweh's judgment.

The verbal and thematic links centred on 'hearing' connect 28.1-29 with 1.2-20 and 30.8-17. Here too Israel have been unwilling to hear Yahweh's instruction, specifically now on the true source of security, an unwillingness which is likewise shown to be quite perverse. Moreover, this is stated within the context of an appeal made to Israel in the past which has been rejected by them (v. 12). This presupposes that Israel had the opportunity to hear (cf. 1.19). At the same time, since that appeal is now past, it is clear that through their unresponsiveness Israel have demonstrated its futility and have deprived themselves of the opportunity to hear it (cf. 30.15). This seems to reflect much the same kind of 'hardening' in Israel's unresponsive condition found between the invitation to respond in 1.2-20 and the confirmation of Israel's total lack of response and the consequent inevitability of their judgment in 5.8-24. The 'B' form of the motif in 28.11, 13 likewise takes this a stage further in that Yahweh now removes from Israel the possibility of the knowledge and understanding of the true source of security to which hearing would have led, by henceforth speaking to them through the foreign tongue of the invader.

The correspondences centred on 'seeing' connect 28.1-29 with 5.8-24 and 22.8b-14, though it is now Israel's leaders who are expressly in view. We have already seen that the description of the drunken leaders of Israel, particularly of their priests and prophets who 'err in vision', stands in marked contrast with the description of Isaiah's vision of Yahweh in the temple (6.1-7). Equally, however, they are described in terms which identify them with the sinful condition of Israel as found in 5.11-12, 22 and 22.13. Hence, the contrast between a responsive prophet (6.1-7) and an unresponsive people (5.8-24) is now extended to embrace Israel's leaders in general and their priests and prophets in particular. In 30.9-11 Israel's unwillingness to hear Yahweh's word is elaborated in terms of their command to their seers and prophets not to see (לא ראה // לא חזה), but to prophesy false things. Accordingly, the drunken prophets who 'err in vision' (בראה, v. 7) stand together with a drunken people who do not 'see' (לא ראה) as their preferred spokesmen of prophetic 'vision', and in particular as the exponents of the agreement with Sheol (vv. 15, 18) upon which Israel and their political leaders have chosen to rely.

2. *Isaiah 29.9-16*

These verses are also closely related to passages in which the 'A' form of the motif is expressed.

(a) In 29.9-12 the language of drunkenness in 5.11-12, 22 and 22.13 is again picked up and applied to Israel's prophets and seers. In comparison with 28.7-8, however, it is now developed in two directions. First, the condition of 'drunkenness' results not simply in the prophets 'erring in seeing', but more deeply in their inability to understand what they can see (cf. חזות הכל, v. 11). Secondly, they are in this condition not because they have drunk wine and beer, but because Yahweh has shut their eyes and veiled their minds. These developments reflect the relation between Israel's failure to see because of drunkenness in 5.11-12 and their inability to see through Yahweh's sealing of their eyes and minds in 6.9-10. Yahweh's shutting of the eyes of the prophets and seers is thus similarly predicated on a drunken condition that had already diminished their ability to see (28.7-8).

(b) The condemnation of Israel's worship in 29.13 recalls its condemnation in 1.11-15. We have already noted that Israel's trampling of Yahweh's courts when they come 'to see' Yahweh's face in 1.11-15 stands in contrast with Isaiah's vision of Yahweh in the temple in 6.1-7. There are reminiscences of this contrast in the reference to the people's 'mouth' and 'lips' (שפתים // פה; cf. 6.7).

(c) The saying against the wisdom of the wise (חכמת חכמיו // בינת נבניו) in 29.14 recalls the woe saying against those who are wise (חכמים // נבנים) in their own eyes in 5.21.

(d) The 'woe' saying in 29.15 condemning Israel's pursuit of their plans (עצה // מעשה) is closely echoed in 30.1, where Israel's policy (לעשות עצה) of alliance with Egypt is a manifestation of rebellion and sinfulness against Yahweh. But whereas in 30.9-16 this is developed in terms of Israel's unwillingness to hear, looking back to 1.2-20, in 29.15-16 it is elaborated in terms of Israel's perversity, looking back to 5.8-24. Israel's pursuit of their own plans (עצה // מעשה), together with their assertion that Yahweh is blind (מי ראנו) and ignorant (מי יודענו) of their actions, goes together with their failure to see Yahweh's work (עצה, מעשה, 5.12, 19) and their consequent lack of knowledge (דעת, 5.13; cf. ידע // ראה, 5.19). Israel's words, 'who sees us' and 'who knows us', are the ultimate comment on their perverse turning of things upside down (cf. הפככם, v. 16, and 5.20): the rightful object (Yahweh) of the verbs 'see' and 'know' has been turned into the subject, and the rightful subject (Israel) has been turned into the object. The very language of response to Yahweh has been so twisted as to eliminate it altogether.

(e) In 29.16 the absurdity of Israel's perverse pursuit of their own plans and activities is emphasized through the saying about the potter and the clay. Israel's conduct is as absurd as a clay pot denying that it is the work of the potter (יצר // עשה). The point could be that Yahweh is the creator of Israel, and therefore Israel cannot hide anything from him. On the other hand, in 22.11 the same participles refer to Yahweh as the creator of events, events that Israel have in effect denied as being the work of Yahweh by pursuing their own course of action instead of looking (ראה) to Yahweh. The point of the saying may therefore be that Israel's perverse self-reliance is an absurd denial of and challenge to Yahweh's sovereignty in matters of עצה and מעשׂה.

In 28.1-29 and 29.9-16 the drunken prophets (literally and meta-phorically) are placed alongside an unresponsive and perverse people as equal partners to the failure of knowledge and understanding mani-fested through reliance on a false source of security (28.15; 29.15). In 28.1-29 Israel's unresponsiveness is described in terms recalling the expression of the 'A' form of the motif in 1.2-20 and 30.8-17, while in 29.9-16 Israel's perversity is described in terms which recall its expression in 5.8-24 and 22.8b-14. Further, in 28.1-29 the 'B' form is applied to Israel in terms of 'hearing', whereas in 29.9-16 it is then applied to the prophets in terms of 'seeing'. In these respects 28.1-29 and 29.9-16 stand together and complement one another as an applica-tion to the Assyrian crisis of the paradigm constituted by the relation between 6.1-13 and 1.2-20 and 5.8-24, first to the people themselves and then to their false prophets.

Taken together, therefore, the transformation of the motif in these passages is similarly predicated on Israel's perverse refusal to hear, together with the erroneous 'seeing' of prophets and seers—once again fuelled by conceit (29.14) and manifested in their religious life (29.13), but now most especially in their political life. Here too the transformation consists essentially in the severing of Israel and their false prophets from the possibility of knowledge and understanding to make judgment certain, now through Yahweh's 'blinding' of the prophets and his speaking to the people in an unintelligible language.

C. *Hear/See—Know/Understand*

This form of the motif finds more or less explicit expression in three passages:

(1) Isaiah 17.7-8: Israel will 'look' (שׁעה // ראה) to the Holy One of Israel and will no longer 'look' (לא שׁעה // לא ראה) to the altars and idols their hands have made.

(2) Isaiah 29.22-24: Israel will never again be put to shame. They will 'see' (ראה) the redemptive work of Yahweh's hand in their midst. They will then acknowledge Yahweh's holiness, the erring will gain understanding (בינה) and murmurers will learn what is taught.

(3) Isaiah 30.18-26: Yahweh will be gracious to his people. Their eyes will see (ראה) their teacher, and their ears will hear (שׁמע) his word which directs them along the right path. They will rid themselves

of their idols and Yahweh will bless their land with fertility. The light of the sun and moon will be increased in the day when Yahweh heals his people.

These expressions of the motif are also closely connected. The first two centre on 'seeing'. In 17.7-8 Israel 'look' (ראה // שעה) to Yahweh as their Maker (עשהו) and not to the work of its their hands (מעשה ידיו), while in 29.22-24 Israel 'see' (ראה) the work of Yahweh's hands (מעשה ידי). Further, in 29.22-24 the redemptive context (cf. פדה, v. 22) of Israel's 'seeing' is now made explicit, and its consequences for the attainment of knowledge and understanding are spelled out. The third passage (30.18-26) brings together 'seeing' and 'hearing', but 'seeing' now has its object Yahweh as מורה 'teacher', so that its emphasis falls on hearing Yahweh's teaching. This picks up and develops the reference to the acceptance of teaching (ילמדו־לקח) in 29.24. Its redemptive context is also further elaborated, both in the more immediate and emotive terms of divine response to the people's lament (vv. 18-19) and in terms of the attendant transformation of nature (vv. 23-26).

The attainment of knowledge and understanding expressed or implied in these passages is the result of looking to Yahweh, seeing his work and hearing his words. Hence, as in the 'A' form of the motif connected with Israel's judgment, the relation between the terms in the positive–positive form is also empirical and didactic in character. This form, however, belongs rather within the context of Israel's salvation.

The Second Transformation

The didactic character of the 'C' form of the motif in 17.7-8, 29.22-24 and 30.18-26 suggests that it is a transformation of the 'A' form in 1.2-20 + 30.8-17 and 5.8-24 + 22.8b-14 and that it is bound up with the larger transformation from judgment to salvation.

1. Isaiah 17.7-8

In their structure and language, these verses run closely parallel to 22.8b-14. They have in common: (a) an introductory 'in that day' (ביום ההוא, 17.7; 22.8b); (b) a contrast between 'looking' to X and 'not looking' to Y (ראה [לא] // שעה [לא], 17.7-8; הביט [לא] // [לא], 22.8b, 11b); (c) looking/not looking to Yahweh as a 'maker' (עשה, v. 7 [of Israel]; 22.11 [of events]), set against what Israel themselves

have 'made' (מעשה ידיו, v. 8; עשיתם, 22.11); (d) the themes of depen-
dence on military strength (22.8b-14) and idolatry (17.7-8) are closely
connected as complementary expressions of Israel's self-reliance (cf. ·
2.7-8). These correspondences help to underline the critical difference
between the two passages, namely the inversion between military
strength/idols and Yahweh as the object of 'looking', and between
Yahweh and military strength/idols as the object of 'not looking'.
Hence, the 'C' form of the motif in 17.7-8 is expressly formulated as a
reversal of the 'A' form in 22.8b-14.

2. *Isaiah 29.22-24*

These verses are closely linked with 5.8-24. Most notably, 'when they
see the work of my hands' (בראתו מעשה ידי, v. 23)[1] stands in direct
contrast with Israel's failure to see (לא ראה) the work of Yahweh's
hand (מעשה ידיו) in 5.12 (cf. 5.19). A corresponding contrast is also
drawn with regard to the holiness of Yahweh. Thus, in concert with
the recurrence of the epithet the Holy One of Israel/Jacob (5.19, 24;
29.23), in 5.16 Yahweh demonstrates his holiness (האל הקדוש נקדש)
through his judgment of a people who have failed to see the work of
his hand; having seen the work of his hand in their redemption, in
29.23 the people will acknowledge Yahweh's holiness (יקדישו...והקדישו).
Further, the gaining of understanding by those who 'err in spirit' (תעי
רוח) in v. 24 evokes a contrast with the drunken priests and prophets
and their errant 'vision' in 28.7 (תעו מן־השכר // שגו בראה) and thereby,
more remotely, with the failure of a drunken people to see (ראה) in
5.11-12. On the other hand, the word רוגנים in v. 24 is related to
Israel's unwillingness to hear.[2] These verses therefore stand primarily
and most explicitly as a reversal of the 'A' form of the motif as
expressed in 5.8-24, though in more oblique terms a reversal of the
'A' form in 1.2-20 + 30.8-17 is also implied.

3. *Isaiah 30.18-26*

The emphasis on hearing Yahweh's word connects these verses most
closely with the expression of the motif in 1.2-20 and 30.8-17. In
30.9-11 Israel were unwilling to hear Yahweh's 'teaching' (תורה; cf.
1.10, 5.24), and commanded their prophets to prophesy false words so
as to turn them from the right way (דרך) and to 'make cease from

1.　Omitting ילדיו as a gloss; cf. *BHS*.
2.　Cf. Deut. 1.26-27 (with לא אבה // מרה); Ps. 106.25 (לא שמע //).

their faces/before them' the Holy One of Israel. This is more or less directly picked up and reversed through the formulation of the motif in 30.20-21: Israel's eyes will see their 'teacher' (מורה) and they will hear a word (behind them!) guiding them along the right way (דרך). Moreover, its introduction as a response to a lament (vv. 18-19) is reminiscent of 1.15. There Yahweh declares that he will shut his eyes and not listen (איני שמע) to Israel; but now Yahweh will hear (שמע) and answer them. Possibly the expression 'no longer hide himself' (לא־יכנף עוד, v. 20) has 1.15 partly in view (cf. also 8.17). The occasion for Israel's responsiveness to Yahweh's teaching, and for the renunciation of idolatry and the transformation of nature, is also described in terms which recall the judgment brought about by their failure to hear in 1.2-20 and 30.8-17; it is the day when Yahweh 'binds up' (חבש; cf. לא חבש, 1.6) the 'shattering' (שבר; cf. 30.14) of his people, and heals (רפא; cf. 6.10) the bruising caused by his blow (מכה; cf. 1.6).

In 17.7-8, ביום ההוא serves to define the context of the reversal as the judgment described in vv. 4-5. Here the emphasis on the decimation of the people and the solitariness of those who remain (נשאר...כ) echoes 1.8 (נותרה...כ), and 30.17 (נותרתם...כ). In 30.18-26 the same connection is equally reflected in its position immediately following v. 17. Hence, the contexts of 17.7-8 and 30.18-26, as well as the conclusion of the latter (v. 26), serve to connect the transformation of the motif with the judgment brought about by Israel's failure to hear in 1.2-20 and 30.8-17. Although 29.22-24 follows another promise of salvation, v. 22 likewise sets the reversal against Israel's judgment through a reference to their earlier shame (יבוש יעקב). This may well be an echo of the consequences of Israel's unresponsiveness to Yahweh by seeking alliance with Egypt in 30.3-5 (בשת, vv. 3, 5; הביש,[1] v. 5).

The expressions of the 'C' form of the motif in these passages therefore stand together almost as a point by point reversal of Israel's unresponsiveness as set out by the various expressions of the 'A' motif, with 17.7-8 reversing 22.8b-14, 29.22-24 reversing 5.8-24, and 30.18-26 reversing 1.2-20 and especially 30.8-17. The transformation is primarily predicated on the realization of the judgment

1. Reading the *qere*.

visited upon Israel in all its severity as the consequence of their failure to see and to hear, together with the change in Israel's attitude that this brings about and to which Yahweh responds (30.18-19).

D. *Not Hear/See—Know/Understand*

Although this form of the motif is not clearly articulated, it may be seen to be presupposed by a number of passages. The passages which fall into this category are as follows:

(1) Isaiah 29.17-21. An increase in fertility (v. 17), together with the judgment of the wicked (vv. 20-21), will create conditions in which the deaf will hear (שמע) and the blind will see (ראה), and the humble and poor will rejoice in the Holy One of Israel (vv. 18-19).

(2) Isaiah 32.1-8. Under the just rule of a future king and royal princes (vv. 1-2), the eyes of those who see (ראים) will not be coated,[1] and the ears of those who hear (שמעים) will hearken (v. 3), the rash will discern knowledge and the stammerer will speak clearly, while fools will no longer be called honourable (vv. 4-8).

(3) Isaiah 33.17-24. Israel will see (ראה // חזה) the divine king and the land in all its extent and will not see (לא ראה) a people whose obscure speech they cannot understand (אין בינה, vv. 17-19). Their eyes will also see (ראה) Jerusalem, whose foundations will be forever secure (vv. 20-21), for Yahweh is their king and will save them (v. 22). At that time, none will be sick and the iniquity of the people will be forgiven (v. 24).

(4) Isaiah 35.5-6. The transformation of the desert into a fruitful garden land (vv. 1-2, 6b-7) and the coming of Yahweh in vengeance to deliver his people (vv. 3-4) will lead to the eyes of the blind and the ears of the deaf being opened, the lame jumping and the dumb singing for joy (vv. 5-6a), and to the return of the people to Zion (vv. 8-10).

A negative–positive polarity is most clearly expressed through the contrast 'not see–see' in 33.17-24. The statement that Israel will 'not see' the invader speaking in an unintelligible language (עם עמקי שפה מלשמוע נלעג לשון אין בינה, v. 19) seems clearly intended to reverse the statement in 28.11 that Yahweh will speak to Israel a message of

1. Cf. *BHS*.

judgment through the unintelligible speech (בלעגי שפה ובלשון אחרת) of the invader, which presupposed the contrast 'hear–not understand'. Further, here Israel's 'seeing' is less a matter of responsiveness to Yahweh than of their understanding and appropriation of the salvation and security brought about by Yahweh—an understanding fostered by reflection (לבך יהגה, v. 18) on what they can no longer see. In relation to 28.1-29, therefore, 'not see–see' in these verses appears to be equivalent to 'not see–understand'.

In 6.9-10, the failure of hearing and seeing to lead to knowledge and understanding (v. 9) was interpreted as the failure of ears to hear and of eyes to see through a condition equating with deafness and blindness (v. 10). It is, of course, not surprising that the deaf and blind are unable to hear and see (v. 10), but it is anomalous that hearing and seeing should not result in knowledge and understanding (v. 9). Hence, though the statement in 29.18 that the deaf will hear and blind eyes see recalls the imagery of 6.10 (cf. also 29.10), its collocation of contradictory terms directly evokes the anomaly of 6.9. In relation to 6.9-10, therefore, the underlying form in this passage is likewise equivalent to 'not hear/see–know/understand'.

The description of the rash and stammerers in 32.4 and of the lame and dumb in 35.6 have the same anomalous character as the blind seeing and the deaf hearing in 29.18. Indeed, this formulation would have fitted well into both these passages. However, in 32.3 and 35.5 the anomaly between the performance (hear/see) of what one is incapable of performing (deaf/blind) has been resolved in terms of the removal of the disability that the deaf hearing and the blind seeing implies—35.5 stressing its removal and 32.3 stressing that it will never again afflict the people. In 32.3 the disability is referred to in terms that recall the 'B' form of the motif in 6.1-13 and 29.9-16 (לא תשעינה עיני ראים, v. 3; cf. עיני השע, 6.10; השתעשעו ושעו, 29.9).

The close relation between the three passages dealing with Israel's 'blindness' is further strengthened by a number of other links. Thus, 29.17-21 and 32.1-8 share a concern for the plight of the poor at the hands of their oppressors, especially through the perversion of justice. This is reinforced by the repetition of ענוים // אביונים and of און, and by the echo between בדבר and באמרי־שקר used of false accusation or evidence (29.19-21; 32.6-7). Similarly, ch. 35 is connected both with 29.17-21 and 32.1-8 through the repetitions לבנון // כרמל (v. 2; 29.17), שמחה (v. 10; 29.19), גיל (vv. 1-2; 29.19); נמהרי־לב (v. 4;

32.4), the root תעה in connection with 'fool(s)' (אוילים, v. 8; 32.6
[נבל]), and through the echo between נחלים בערבה // במדבר מים (v. 6)
and פלני מים בציון (32.2).

All four passages presuppose the removal of a debilitating circum-
stance or condition—the presence of the invader in the land, or the
people's deafness and blindness. The foreign invader is clearly removed
as the result of Yahweh's saving activity (cf. 33.22). That Israel's
condition of blindness and deafness is also removed through Yahweh's
saving action is implied by the use of שׁמע in 32.3 (cf. 6.9-10; 29.9-10)
and by the close association between the motif and the transformation
of the natural order in 35.1-7 and 29.17-18. Hence, the relation
between 'hear/see' and 'know/understand' underlying these passages is
theological rather than didactic in character. In this respect it con-
forms to 'B' form of the motif. Like the 'C' motif, however, it
belongs within the context of Israel's salvation.

The Third Transformation

Once again, the theological character of the relation between the terms
in the 'D' form of the motif in 29.17-21, 32.1-8, 33.17-24 and 35.5-6
suggests that it is a transformation of the 'B' form in 6.1-13, 28.1-29
and 29.9-16, and that once again it forms part of the larger transformation from judgment to salvation. The parallels that have just
been observed between these forms of the motif serve to confirm this,
in particular the reversal of the motif in 6.9-10 (cf. 29.9-11) through
the removal of Israel's deafness and blindness, and in 28.9-13 through
the removal of the foreign invader from the land.

Alongside and reinforcing these reversals, there are a number of
verbal and thematic elements in these passages that reflect the predi-
cation of the 'B' form of the motif on the 'A' form, both as a paradigm
(6.1-13) and as an application of this paradigm to the Assyrian crisis
(28.1-29; 29.9-16).

A. *Reversal of the Paradigm*

(1) The statement in 33.17 that Israel's eyes will see (חזה // ראה) the
king echoes Isaiah's vision (ראה) of the divine king in 6.1-7. Just as
Isaiah's vision led to the forgiveness (כפר) of his iniquity (עון), so too
Israel's iniquity (עון) will now be forgiven (נשׂא, v. 24). This reference
to Israel's iniquity, however, also directly recalls the statements of the

people's sinfulness (עון) in 1.4 and 5.18. Similarly, the parallel expression בל־יאמר...חליתי in v. 24 recalls the affliction (חלי) of Israel in 1.5-6 as a consequence of their iniquity, together with the healing (רפא) denied to Israel in 6.10. Verses 17 and 24 therefore form something of a thematic *inclusio*, together evoking the earlier contrast between a sinful and unresponsive people (1.2-20; 5.8-24) and a sinful but responsive prophet (6.1-7), but as one which will no longer exist. Thereby Isaiah's vision also becomes the model of what Israel will no longer lack and what will therefore no longer be denied to them.

(2) This paradigmatic aspect of Isaiah's vision in relation to Israel's salvation is further reflected in the description of the way to Zion (35.8) as a 'way of holiness' (קדוש) along which none who are unclean (טמא) will pass.[1] As we have seen, Isaiah's confession of his own and Israel's uncleanness (טמא) in 6.5 in response to the declaration of Yahweh's holiness (קדוש, 6.3) serves to reinforce the contrast between the prophet who sees and hears and is cleansed from his sin, and the people who refuse to see and hear the word and work of the Holy (קדוש) One of Israel (1.4; 5.19, 24), and who remain unclean (cf. 1.16). This contrast too will exist no longer.

(3) A reversal of Israel's sinful condition as manifested in their religious life is implied through the description of Zion in 33.20 as the city of 'our appointed feasts' (מועדנו). This recalls the condemnation of Israel's worship in 1.11-15 (cf. מועדיכם, v. 14).[2]

(4) Similarly, a reversal in the sinful character of Israel's social life is implied through the annihilation of those who pervert justice in 29.21 (cf. 33.7). This echoes the condemnation of the perversion of justice in 5.23 (cf. 1.17) through the repetition of צדיק and the echo between מחטיאי אדם (29.21) and מצדיקי רשע (5.23).

B. *Reversal of its Application to the Assyrian Crisis*

(1) The expectation of a king and princes who would rule justly (32.1-8) stands in contrast to the condemnation of Israel's rulers in 28.1-4, 14-22. This contrast is already anticipated by 28.5, which momentarily looks forward to the time when Yahweh would be a 'spirit of justice' to those responsible for discharging it. As against the present

---

1. Within chs. 1–39 the root טמא is otherwise found only in 30.22, where it is used of Israel defiling their idols.

2. Within chs. 1–39 the word is found only in 14.13, referring to the divine assembly.

rulers who falsely claimed to have a protective shelter (סתר) from the
destructive storm waters (ברד // מים, 28.17; cf. זרם ברד, v. 2), the
future king and princes will be a shelter from the storm (סתר זרם),
and will be like life-giving waters (מים, v. 2). Hence the reversal of
the motif in 32.3 goes together with a reversal in the corrupt character of Israel's leaders, and a reversal in the prospects for the security
of the people.

(2) The reversal in the prospects for Zion's security is also set
alongside the reversal of the motif in 33.17-24 in terms which recall
the fate of Zion under Israel's rulers in 28.17b-18. Thus, in 33.21
Zion's security is described through the metaphorical expression that
no galley ship (צי // אני־שיט) would pass over (הלך // עבר) its broad
rivers, which contrasts with the 'overwhelming whip' (שוט שוטף) that
would pass over (עבר) the nation in judgment, and that would sweep
away their false refuge (28.15, 17b-18).

(3) The characterization of the wicked fool in 32.6-8 reflects the
dual concern of vv. 1-2 with the establishment of social justice and of
national security under the new rulers. The first of these themes is
dealt with in vv. 7-8 (cf. above) and the second in v. 6. Here the
expressions 'do what is ungodly' (לעשות חנף) and 'speak error (תועה)
concerning Yahweh' echo the implementation of the plan (לעשות עצה)
of alliance with Egypt without reference to God (30.1), together with
the drunken priests and prophets (תעו מן־השכר) who 'err in vision' (שגו
בראה, 28.7), and who were spokesmen for the alliance. That the fools
will be recognized for what they are implies that they will be punished
accordingly. Similarly, although primarily concerned with the perversion of justice, the parallel reference in 29.20 to the annihilation of
scoffers (כלה לץ) recalls the description of Israel's rulers as אנשי לצון
in 28.14 and the corresponding threat אל־תתלוצצו...כי־כלה in 28.22.
Taken together, these passages imply in their different ways that those
who promote such political courses of action as those pursued by
Israel's rulers and encouraged by their priests and prophets will be
rooted out. Thus not only is the way in 35.8 a 'holy way' which the
unclean will not pass over, but it is also one in which fools will not
err (יתעו).

(4) Finally, as against the abandonment of the people to the revelry
(ששון ושמחה) of their drunken feasts instead of the lament to which
Yahweh had been summoning them through the Assyrian threat
(22.12-13), those who pass over to Zion will do so with 'gladness and

joy' (ושמחה ישיגו, 35.9),[1] fear and sighing having passed away.

With the exception of 29.17-21, these reversals are set within the context of Yahweh's vindication of Zion through his judgment on the foreign nation(s). Thus, 32.1-8 follows an oracle of doom upon the Assyrians (31.8-9); 33.17-24 centres on the absence of the invader from the land, and falls within the general context of Yahweh's salvation of Zion through the destruction of the destroyer, while ch. 35 follows an oracle of doom against the nations in general and Edom in particular (ch. 34), described as the day of Yahweh's vengeance (נקם, v. 8) for the cause of Zion. This connection is reinforced by the reference to Yahweh coming with vengeance (נקם) in 35.4, which forms the immediate context for the removal of the people's blindness and deafness in v. 5. In 29.17-21 the transformation of Lebanon provides the occasion for the removal of Israel's disabilities. In the light of the withering of Lebanon in 33.9, however, this too may presuppose Yahweh's vindication of Zion.

These expressions of the 'D' form of the motif therefore stand together not only as a reversal of the 'B' form, but also as a reversal of the sinful condition of Israel and its political and religious leadership through which Israel's failure to hear and see was manifested and encouraged.

The 'D' and the 'C' forms of the motif therefore view Israel's responsiveness to Yahweh from two different, but largely complementary, perspectives. As a transformation of the 'A' form with its didactic character, the passages which express the 'C' form appropriately centre on the change in Israel's attitude which results from the extremity of the judgment and which leads the people to turn to Yahweh and to accept instruction. In these passages the emphasis falls on the *fact* of Israel's responsiveness, with the motif forming the main subject matter of the passage.[2] By contrast, as a transformation of the 'B' form with its theological character and its sealing of Israel's judgment, the passages which express the 'D' form appropriately centre on the change in the conditions which had in part manifested and in part encouraged Israel's failure to hear and see, together with

---

1. These are the only two occurrences of the phrase in chs. 1–39.
2. Even in 30.18-26, where its redemptive context is most elaborated, the motif itself is detailed at some length.

the consequences of these changes for the future prospects of Zion. In these passages the motif invariably appears as one among a variety of thematic elements that describe the transformation of Zion and its inhabitants, with the emphasis now falling on the *miracle* of the transformation of which Israel's responsiveness is part.

Conclusion

This examination of the motif took as its starting-point the assumption that the various forms of the motif in Isaiah 1–39 together formed an integrated structure centred on the set of four possible relations when positive and negative values are given to the terms hearing/seeing and knowing/understanding. The rhetorical and thematic interconnections that have been observed between passages which express the same form of the motif, and between passages which express different forms of the motif, serve to realize this structure and to specify the relations and the transformations between the different forms of the motif. Thus:

1. The forms fall into two contrasting pairs, one concerned with Israel's lack of knowledge within the context of judgment (A, B), and the other concerned with Israel's attainment of knowledge within the context of salvation (C, D).
2. Within the first pair, a didactic form of the motif (A) presents Israel's lack of knowledge as the consequence of their perverse failure to hear (1.2-20; 30.8-17) and to see (5.8-24; 22.8b-14), a failure manifested in the people's moral, social and religious life (1.2-20; 5.8-24) as well as in their political life during the period of the Assyrian crisis (22.8b-14; 30.8-17).
3. Predicated on this failure and its manifestations, this didactic form is transformed into a theological form (B) whereby, in accordance with the divine purpose of securing Israel's judgment, hearing and seeing will now no longer result in knowledge. This transformation is likewise expressed at a more programmatic level (6.1-13) and in relation to the Assyrian crisis (28.1-29; 29.9-16).
4. Within the second pair, Israel's lack of responsiveness (A) is transformed through a corresponding didactic form (C) with respect both to their failure to hear (30.18-26) and to their

failure to see (17.7-8; 29.22-24), thereby resulting in the attainment of understanding.

5.   Israel's inability to attain knowledge and understanding through hearing and seeing (B) is likewise transformed by means of a corresponding theological form (D) whereby, in accordance now with the divine purpose for Israel's salvation, the disabilities which had prevented knowledge and sealed Israel's judgment are removed, and the sinful condition of Israel and its political and religious leadership upon which these disabilities were predicated is reversed (29.17-21; 32.1-8; 33.17-24; 35.5-6).

ON *ûmᵉśôś* IN ISAIAH 8.6*

Marvin A. Sweeney

ABSTRACT

Based on a discussion of its grammatical problems, its textual witnesses and its relationship to Isa. 66.10-14, this paper argues that *ûmᵉśôś* in Isa. 8.6 must not be emended. When read in the context of the sexual imagery of Isa. 8.5-8, *ûmᵉśôś* expresses Judah's willingness to submit to the Syro-Ephraimitic coalition. It also establishes a link between Proto- and Trito-Isaiah.

I

The appearance of the Hebrew term *ûmᵉśôś* in Isa. 8.6 has long constituted a difficult exegetical crux. In its present form, the term is a combination of a conjunctive *waw* with the construct form of the *mem*-preformative noun *māśôś*, which means 'exultation' or 'rejoicing'. Unfortunately, a noun makes little sense in the present context in that the following clause, *'et-rᵉṣîn ûben-rᵉmalyāhû*, 'Rezin and the son of Remaliah', begins with the direct object particle *'et-*, which normally requires an antecedent verb. The fact that *māśôś* appears in its construct form only complicates the issue, since a genitive noun does not appear after *ûmᵉśôś*. Consequently, a verbal form parallel to *mā'as hā'ām hazzeh*, 'this people has rejected', would best fit this passage. Because of the problems posed by the verse in its present form, *ûmᵉśôś* is frequently understood as a verbal noun and *'et-* as the preposition 'with' so that the verse literally means 'and rejoicing with Rezin and the son of Remaliah' (cf. Irvine 1990: 185). But this

*   This is a slightly revised version of a paper read at the Southeastern Regional Meeting of the Society of Biblical Literature, Atlanta, March 15–17, 1991. I would like to thank the Yad Hanadiv/Barecha Foundation which provided the funds for my 1989–90 sabbatical at the Hebrew University of Jerusalem where the research for this paper was completed.

rendering is awkward and continues to provoke attempts to explain or emend the unusual form of the verse.

On the other hand, prior attempts to resolve the problem by explaining the grammatical form of *ûm^eśôś* as a verbal noun or by emending the passage have hardly proved satisfactory. After surveying these attempts and the readings of the ancient versions, this paper will propose a new solution to the problem based on the results of recent research concerning the emergence of the final form of the book of Isaiah in the late fifth century. It will argue that Isa. 8.6 originally contained the reading *ûm^eśôś 'et-*, on the basis of the interpretation of the passage presupposed in Isa. 66.10-14, which employs similar vocabulary and themes to describe the rejoicing of Jerusalem and the inflowing glory of the nations following the defeat of YHWH's enemies.

II

An attempt to interpret *ûm^eśôś* as a verbal noun appears as early as the late thirteenth/early fourteenth century in the commentary of R. David Kimhi. Commenting on the phrase *ûm^eśôś 'et-r^eşîn*, he says that 'they (i.e. many in Judah and Jerusalem) will be exulting and rejoicing with them (i.e. Rezin and ben Remaliah) if they will be ruling in Jerusalem' (Finkelstein 1926: 55). He further states that *m^eśôś* is in the construct state with *'et-*, but he does not explain how *'et-* is to be understood. Kimhi was followed by W. Gesenius, who argues that *m^eśôś* is a verbal noun used poetically as a finite verb (1821: 332). Gesenius claims that the verb *śûś* stands here with the accusative as in Isa. 35.1. He further says that *m^eśôś* is in the construct state because of the following preposition and cites *k^eśimhat baqqāşîr* in Isa. 9.2 as a supporting example (1821: 333). But this interpretation must be rejected. Although the verb *śûś* is commonly followed by the preposition *'al* (Deut. 28.63; 30.9; Isa. 62.5; Jer. 32.41; Zeph. 3.17; Ps. 119.162) or *b^e* (Isa. 61.10; 65.19; Pss. 19.6; 35.9; 40.17; 68.4; 70.5; 119.14; Job 39.21), it never appears with the direct object preposition *'ēt*. The only other example of a construct form followed by a direct object pronoun appears in Jer. 33.22, *m^eśār^etê 'ōtî*, 'those who minister to me', but this reading is problematic and frequently is emended (cf. *BHS* note; Rudolph 1968: 218; Holladay 1989: 227).

Gesenius' Hebrew Grammar attempts a different approach by identifying this phrase as an example of the use of the construct state before the preposition '*ēt*, 'with' (1983: §130a), but such a construction does not appear elsewhere in the Hebrew Bible. Barthélemy *et al.* (1986: 50) attempt to revive this understanding by pointing to the use of the same root with the preposition '*ēt*, 'with', in Isa. 66.10. Unfortunately, the phrase reads, *śîśû 'ittāh māśôś*, 'exult with her (in) exultation'. This indicates the use of the preposition following the verbal form, but it also indicates that a nominal construction would be unusual. Furthermore, the use of the direct object preposition '*ēt* in parallel statements in Isa. 8.6a and twice in Isa. 8.7a suggests that '*ēt* should not be understood as 'with' in Isa. 8.6b, but as the direct object marker.

The most commonly accepted solution to this problem is to emend the text from *ûm^{e}śôś* to *ûmāsôś* (cf. Procksch 1930: 131, 133; Wildberger 1972: 321; Clements 1980: 96; Kaiser 1983: 183). This proposal was originally made by Hitzig (1833: 98-99), who notes the difficulties pertaining to the phrase *ûm^{e}śôś* '*ēt* and argues that a scribal misreading of *śin* for *samek* resulted in the change of *ûm^{e}śôś* to *ûm^{e}sôs*, 'and dissolving'. This emendation presupposes the appearance of the term *kimsôs* in Isa. 10.18 and combines a conjunctive *waw* with the infinitive absolute form of the verb *mss*, 'to dissolve, melt'. Hitzig argues that the accusative '*ēt* appears in place of the expected *mipp^{e}nê*, 'because of', and cites the use of '*rṣ* in Job 31.34 as an example of this implicit use of an accusative construction. In the present context, the phrase is interpreted as a reference to the people's 'dissolving' or 'melting' in fear of Rezin and the son of Remaliah as in the RSV translation, 'Because this people have refused the waters of Shiloah that flow gently and melt in fear before Rezin and the son of Remaliah'.

Bredenkamp (1887: 49) likewise emends *ûm^{e}śôś* to *ûm^{e}sôs*, but maintains that the infinitive absolute form functions in an adverbial sense (e.g. 'and gently') that modifies 'the waters that flow slowly (and gently)'. He argues that '*ēt* means '*coram, praesente*', indicating that 'this people rejected the waters...in the face of (i.e. because of) Rezin and ben Remaliah'. Giesebrecht (1888: 225-29) follows Bredenkamp's infinitive absolute rendering but retains the consonantal text as *ûmāsôs* (i.e. 'the waters that flow slowly and exultantly'). He consequently deletes the last four words of v. 6b as a gloss. Finally, Duhm (1892; cf. 1914: 57) combines the solutions of Hitzig and Bredenkamp by emending *ûm^{e}śôś* to the perfect verbal form *māsas* and arguing that '*ēt* entered the text in place of the original *min* as a result of the scribal error that produced *ûmᵉśôś* (cf. Marti 1900: 84).[1]

But the emendation of *ûmᵉśôś* to various forms of *mss* also presents problems (Fullerton 1924: 265-67). Chief among them is that it does not properly account for the following *'ēt*. The verb *māsôs* in the sense of 'despair' commonly requires the cause of despair to be introduced by *millipnê* (Ps. 97.5), *mippᵉnê* (Josh. 5.1; Mic. 1.4; Ps. 68.3) or *min* (Isa. 34.3). Attempts to emend *'et-* to *mippᵉnê* or *millipnê* (Marti 1900: 84), *min* (Duhm 1914: 57) or *miśś'ēt* (Budde 1926: 65-67; Wildberger 1972: 321) lack a firm textual basis and must be rejected. Likewise, Hitzig's and Bredenkamp's attempts to render *'et-* in this sense are somewhat forced. Furthermore, the suggestion that *ûmāsôs* can be understood in an adverbial sense parallel to *lᵉ'aṭ* and that the clause *'et-rᵉṣîn ûben-rᵉmalyāhû* is a gloss (Giesebrecht 1888: 227-29; cf. *BHS* note; Procksch 1930: 131, 133; Clements 1980: 96) is also unsatisfactory for a number of reasons. These include the grammatical difficulties of reading the infinitive *ûmāsôs* in an adverbial sense and the unlikely hypothesis that the glossator would have equated the waters of Shiloah with Rezin and the son of Remaliah (Fullerton 1924: 267-68). Likewise, Fullerton's suggestion to reject all of v. 6b as a gloss does not satisfactorily account for the supposed glossator's choice of the peculiar form *ûmᵉśôś* or even the emended *ûmāsôs* (Fullerton 1924: 269-70).

Finally, Schroeder's attempt to claim that *ûmᵉśôś* is a gloss on *rᵉṣîn* merely avoids the issue (Schroeder 1912: 301-302) and results in a statement that condemns the people for rejecting Rezin and the son of Remaliah, which makes little sense in view of Isaiah's condemnation of these rulers (Isa. 7.1-9; cf. 17.1-6). Likewise, Klein's explanation that the grammatical difficulties of this verse represent Isaiah's poetic license sidesteps the problem, despite his attractive interpretation of the verse in relation to v. 7 and his cogent observations about the parallel of *mā'as 'ēt* and *ûmᵉśôś 'ēt* (Klein 1980).

---

1. Cf. Lindblom (1958: 44), who emends *ûmᵉśôś* to *ûmāsôs* and renders *'ēt* as the preposition 'with', so that the passage refers to 'this people' which 'dissolves together with Rezin and the son of Remaliah'. Although Lindblom's suggestion accounts for *'ēt*, the emendation of *ûmᵉśôś* to *ûmāsôs* presents problems in that textual evidence for the emendation is entirely lacking. For an analysis of the textual versions, see below.

III

Any attempt to resolve the problems posed by Isa. 8.6 must take account of the ancient textual versions of this passage. A survey of these texts indicates that there is no support for an emendation of *ûm^{e}śôś* to *ûmāsôs* or any other expression based on the root *mss*. Nor is there evidence for the deletion of v. 6b as a gloss. It does indicate, however, that each version employs a verbal form in place of *ûm^{e}śôś*. The fact that each verb is based on the Hebrew root *śwś/śyś* and that the verbal forms vary among the translations suggests that each version presupposes the reading *ûm^{e}śôś* and attempts to render it in a verbal sense.

The text of 1QIsa^a reads Isa. 8.6 as *y'n ky' m's h'm hzh 't my hšwlh hhwlkym l'wṭ wmśyś 't rṣyn w't bn (rm)l(y)h* (Trever 1972: 28-29), 'Because this people has rejected the waters of the one who sends (i.e. YHWH) which run gently and causes Rezin and the son of Remaliah to rejoice'. Although the original editors of this manuscript read *wmśwś* (Burrows, Trever and Brownlee 1950: pl. vii), a closer examination of the photograph indicates that the correct reading is *wmśyś*, a hiphil masculine singular participle based on the verb root *śwś*, 'to exult, rejoice', combined with conjunctive *waw*.[1] The use of the hiphil form of this verb accords well with the following *'ēt*. In the present context, it refers to the people's rejection of the waters of Shiloah (or in accordance with 1QIsa^a, *haššôlēaḥ*, 'the one who sends', i.e YHWH) as the cause for Rezin's and the son of Remaliah's rejoicing. Nevertheless, this reading does not appear to reflect the 'original' text of Isa. 8.6 but the Qumran scribe's attempt to interpret the passage. The introduction of the extra direct object particle *w't* before *bn (rm)l(y)h* (cf. MT: *ûben-r^{e}malyāhû*) suggests the scribe's attempt to support the verbal rendering of an original *wmśwś* as *wmśyś*. That the scribe was willing to take liberties with this text is evident from the rendering of *'ēt mê haššilōaḥ*, 'the waters of Shiloah', as *'t my hšwlh*, 'the waters of the one who sends'. This is a reference to YHWH who elsewhere in Isaiah

---

1.   This is indicated by the sharply angled hook shape of the letter in question, similar to the *yod*'s of *my*, *hhwlkym*, and *rṣyn* from the same line in the manuscript. Like these *yod*'s, the letter is much shorter than the *waw* that appears at the beginning of the word as well as those of *hšwlh*, *hhwlkym*, *l'wṭ*, and *w't* (cf. Barthélemy *et al.* 1986: 49).

is portrayed as the one who sends 'a word' against Jacob (Isa. 9.7) and
sends Assyria against Israel (Isa. 10.6).

Targum Jonathan reads *hᵉlap degaṣ 'amā' hadên bᵉmalkûtā' dᵉbêt
dawîd dimdabᵉrā' lᵉhôn bināh kᵉmê śilôḥā' dᵉnāgᵉdîn bināh wᵉ'itrᵉ'î'û
birṣîn ûbar rᵉmalyâ* (Sperber 1962: 16), 'Because this people loathed
the kingdom of the house of David which led them gently like the
waters of Shiloah which flow gently and preferred Rezin and the son
of Remaliah'. Again, the choice of the verb *wᵉ'itrᵉ'î'û*, 'and they preferred', demonstrates that *ûmᵉśôś* stands behind this text. The Aramaic
verb *r'y* means 'to desire, take delight in'. In its present ithpeal perfect form, it means 'and they delighted in' or 'and they chose', which
demonstrates the translator's attempt to render the disputed expression
as a verbal form in reference to the people's preference of Rezin and
the son of Remaliah over the Davidic dynasty.

The LXX reads *dia to mē boulesthai ton laon touton to hudōr tou
silōam to poreuomenon hēsuchei alla boulesthai echein ton Raassōn kai
ton huion Romeliou basilea eph' humōn* (Ziegler 1967: 150), 'Because
this people did not want the water of Siloam which goes gently but
wanted to have Rezin and the son of Remaliah as king over you'. The
use of the expression *boulesthai echein...basilea eph' humōn*, 'wanted
to have...as king over you', corresponds to a verbal understanding of
ûmᵉśôś, but the translator's understanding of the conjugation is
ambiguous. It could be hiphil in that the people's choice of Rezin and
the son of Remaliah as their rulers would certainly cause Rezin and
the son of Remaliah to rejoice. After all, their attack against Judah
during the Syro-Ephraimitic War was designed to gain them control
of the Davidic throne, insofar as it was an attempt to remove the
ruling Davidic monarch and replace him with a certain ben Tabeel
(Isa. 7.1-6). On the other hand, the Greek expression may reflect an
understanding of *ûmᵉśôś* as 'delight in' or 'choose' as represented by
Targum Jonathan. Unfortunately, the use of the infinitive *boulesthai*
gives no indication of the conjugation of the verbs in the Hebrew
Vorlage, but the use of *mē boulesthai/boulesthai*, 'did not want/
wanted', indicates the translator's attempt to associate *māʾas* and
ûmᵉśôś as parallel verbal forms that were related by assonance. The
appearance of *eph' humōn*, 'over you', merely reflects the translator's
attempt to harmonize the third-person pronouns referring to the
people in the Hebrew text of vv. 6-8 with the second-person pronoun
applied to Emmanuel at the end of v. 8.

The Vulgate reads *pro eo quod abiecit populus iste aquas Siloae quae vadunt cum silentio et adsumpsit magis Rasin et filium Romeliae* (Weber 1975: 1104), 'in view of the fact that this people left the waters of Shiloah which run silently and stood by Resin and the son of Remaliah instead'. Like LXX, the use of *adsumpsit magis*, 'stood by... instead', indicates the translator's attempt to render a verbal expression based on *ûm^{e}śôś*, but it gives no clue as to how the translator would have conceived the conjugation of this expression.

Finally, the Peshitta reads *'l d'šlyw 'm' hn' my' dšylwḥ' drdyn bšly' wḥdyw brṣn wbbr rwmly'* (Brock 1987: 14), 'Because this people rejected the waters of Shiloah which run securely and have rejoiced in Rezin and the son of Remaliah'. The use of *wḥdyw* indicates an attempt to render the disputed expression as a verbal statement, but the use of the peal perfect form of the verb instead of the aphal participle indicates that the translator had *ûm^{e}śôś* in the *Vorlage*.

IV

The preceding surveys of prior scholarship on Isa. 8.6 and the ancient textual versions establish two basic points. First, the presence of *ûm^{e}śôś* in this verse presents difficult grammatical and syntactical problems that prior attempts to explain the form or to emend it have failed to resolve. Secondly, the ancient textual versions uniformly presuppose the term *ûm^{e}śôś*, but render it as a verbal expression based on the root *śwś/śyś* from which *ûm^{e}śôś* is derived. Obviously, these points indicate the need to present a new solution for the problem of the appearance of *ûm^{e}śôś* in Isa. 8.6. Furthermore, they demonstrate that any proposed solution must explain the presence of *ûm^{e}śôś* in the present form of the verse.

The versions point to a potential solution by positing a hiphil form of the verb *śwś/śyś*. This is especially clear in 1QIsa^a, which reads *ûm^{e}śîś*, and Targum Jonathan and Peshitta which employ readings that would best be rendered in Hebrew by the *waw*-consecutive hiphil imperfect *wayyāśîśû* (cf. LXX and Vulgate). Nevertheless, although each of these readings offers certain advantages, neither is entirely satisfactory.

The reading *ûm^{e}śôś* takes *hā'ām hazzeh*, 'this people', from the beginning of the verse as its subject and provides a parallel based on assonance for the initial verb *m's*, 'reject'. It also forms an appropriate antecedent for the following direct object particle and provides a syntactical parallel with v. 7, which employs the participial form *mā'^{a}leh*, 'raises up', as the antecedent for two object clauses introduced by *'ēt*. But the participial form of *ûmēśiś* presents a problem in that it is an unlikely syntactical parallel for the perfect verb *mā'as*, which introduces the verse. Rather, the participial form of *ûmēśiś* in 1QIsa^a appears to be derived from the following *mā'^{a}leh* in v. 7 and the preceding *hahōl^{e}kîm* in v. 6a.

The readings *w^e'itr^e'î'û* in Targum Jonathan and *wḥdyw* in the Peshitta both appear to presuppose the *waw*-consecutive hiphil imperfect plural form *wayyāśiśû*, although the verb does not appear to be in the *Vorlage* of either version. Such a form would provide an appropriate antecedent for the direct object particle in v. 6b, but the change in number conflicts with the singular formation of the verb *mā'as* in v. 6a and its grammatically singular subject *hā'ām*. The problem could be solved by positing the singular form *wayyāśiś* for Isa. 8.6, but the form *yāśiś* appears elsewhere in the Hebrew Bible only in the qal conjugation (Deut. 28.63; Isa. 62.5; Zeph. 3.17; Ps. 19.6; Job 39.21). The 3ms imperfect hiphil form of *śwś/śyś* is identical to the 3ms imperfect qal form, but the hiphil form of the verb is attested only in Rabbinic and Qumran Hebrew, and there only occasionally (cf. Jastrow 1967: 1542-43). Consequently, *wayyāśiś* would be the only hiphil form of the verb in the entire Hebrew Bible. Although such a solution is not impossible, the absence of other hiphil forms of *śwś/śyś* undermines its credibility.

This means that there is no secure alternative to the reading *ûm^{e}śôś* in Isa. 8.6. But a solution to the problem may appear in relation to recent research concerning the emergence of the final form of the book of Isaiah, especially insofar as many texts in Trito-Isaiah appear to develop themes and readings that are present in First or Second Isaiah (Odeberg 1931: 62-74, 94; Lack 1973; Childs 1979; Brueggemann 1984; Rendtorff 1984; Rendtorff 1989; Beuken 1986; Beuken 1989; Sweeney 1988; Vermeylen 1989; Steck 1989; cf. Clements 1982; Clements 1985). Isa. 66.10-14 is particularly significant in this regard in that it contains several important lexical and thematic associations with Isa. 8.6-8. Isa. 66.10-11 calls for rejoicing with the restored Jerusalem, here portrayed as a mother with suckling infants at her breast. Verses 12-14 convey YHWH's promise to extend the 'glory of the nations' (*k^{e}bôd gôyim*; cf. *w^e'et-kol-k^{e}bôdô* in Isa. 8.7) over her 'like a river of peace and like an overflowing stream' (*kᵉnāhār šālôm ûkᵉnahal šôṭēp*; cf. Isa. 8.8 on *šāṭap*). It would appear that the author of Isa. 66.10-14 intended to present this text as the ultimate fulfilment for YHWH's pledge to inundate the people with the 'river' (*nāhār*) of the king of Assyria 'and all his glory' (*wᵉ'et-kol-kᵉbôdô*) in Isa. 8.6-8. Not only does Isa. 66.10-14 present a thematic and lexical correspondence to Isa. 8.6-8, it also has a bearing on the reading *ûmᵉśôś* in Isa. 8.6. Isa. 66.10bα reads *śîśû 'ittāh māśôś*, 'rejoice with her (in) exultation'. This reading is especially significant for understanding *ûmᵉśôś* in Isa. 8.6. Not only does Isa. 66.10b contain the noun *māśôś*, but it also includes the phrase *śîśû 'ittāh*, 'rejoice with her'. This phrase represents the only text in the Hebrew Bible in which the verb *śwś/śyś* takes *'ēt*, 'with', indicating an indirect object. The reading is all the more remarkable in that the preceding phrase in v. 10a, *śimhû 'et-yᵉrûšālayim wᵉgîlû bāh*, 'rejoice with Jerusalem and celebrate with her', likewise contains the only instance in the Hebrew Bible in which the qal form of the verb *śmh* is followed by *'ēt*. Inasmuch as Isa. 66.10-14 appears to be derived from Isa. 8.6-8, this indicates that the author of Isa. 66.10-14 read *ûmᵉśôś* in Isa. 8.6. It further indicates that this author understood *ûmᵉśôś 'et-rᵉṣîn ûben-rᵉmalyāhû* to mean, 'and rejoicing with Rezin and ben Remaliah', in that *māśôś* is associated with the unusual forms *śîśû 'ēt* and *śimhû 'ēt* in Isa. 66.10, thereby clarifying the meaning of *ûmᵉśôś 'ēt* in Isa. 8.6.

The reading may appear awkward, but it must stand. The reason for its awkward nature becomes clear, however, when it is considered in relation to the sexual imagery that stands behind both Isa. 66.10-14 and Isa. 8.6-8. Isa. 66.7-9 presents the imagery of Zion's giving birth to children prior to the commands to rejoice with Jerusalem in Isa. 66.10-14. Isa. 8.6-8, on the other hand, ends with a reference to the Assyrian king's 'stretching out his wings' (*wᵉhāyâ muṭṭôt kᵉnāpāyw*, 'and the extending of his wings'), thereby filling the land of Emmanuel (i.e. Judah) with the overflowing waters of the great and mighty river mentioned in vv. 7-8. The spreading of wings or skirts frequently serves as an idiomatic reference to marriage or sexual relations (Ezek. 16.8; Ruth 3.9; cf. Deut. 23.1; 27.20), as does the imagery of flowing waters (Song 4.15; Prov. 5.15-20; 9.13-18). Although the sexual imagery is not explicit until v. 8, it is clear that in rejecting the waters of Shiloah, Judah opens itself to another lover, or rapist as the case may

be, in the form of the Assyrian king.¹ Certainly, this associates
Isa. 8.5-8 with Isa. 8.1-4, where Isaiah reports his sexual relations
with the prophetess that resulted in the birth of Maher-Shalal-Hash-
Baz.² In this respect, the awkward nature of the reading of ûm^eśôś 'ēt
in Isa. 8.6 becomes significant. Although *māśôś* usually refers to
general rejoicing, its appearance in the context of Jerusalem's giving
birth in Isa. 66.10 and the rejoicing of a bridegroom over his bride in
Isa. 62.5 indicates that the term can be used in reference to marriage.
Like the general imagery of water in Isa. 8.6-7, the lexical meaning of
māśôś in v. 6 is non-specific, but the awkward nature of the reading
disrupts the syntax of vv. 6-7 and calls attention to itself. Inasmuch as
the term *māśôś* and the imagery of waters suggests the possibility of
sexual connotations, the term conveys a *double entendre* that is only
realized in v. 8 when the extended skirts of the Assyrian monarch fill
the land. In this respect, the awkward phrasing of ûm^eśôś 'et-r^esîn

1. Scholars frequently argue that 'this people' in v. 6a refers to the northern
kingdom of Israel in that they rejected the Davidic dynasty by following Rezin and
Pekah (e.g. Rignell 1957: 41-42). But there are several reasons for maintaining that
'this people' refers to Judah: (1) the northern kingdom had rejected the house of
David long before their decision to follow Rezin and Pekah; (2) the reference to
Emmanuel in v. 8 indicates that Judah is threatened in this passage; and (3) the
'waters of Shiloah' are frequently taken as a reference to the Davidic dynasty (so
Kimḥi and Targum Jonathan) or as a symbol of YHWH's guarantee of security to
Jerusalem. Note that Isa. 7.3 locates Isaiah's encounter with Ahaz at 'the end of the
conduit of the upper pool on the highway to the Fuller's Field' (RSV). Inasmuch as
Ahaz appears to be inspecting his water system in anticipation of a siege by Israel and
Aram, Isaiah's reference to the people's rejection of 'the waters of Shiloah' suggests
their lack of confidence in the city's defenses. The fact that Ahaz eventually
summoned Assyrian assistance in the Syro-Ephraimitic War (2 Kgs 16.7-9) indicates
that he likewise lacked confidence in the city's ability to resist a siege. Insofar as the
Syro-Ephraimitic coalition would be concerned to augment their forces by bringing
Judah into its camp against the Assyrians, their attack would be designed to remove
Ahaz and convince the Judaean population to join the coalition rather than destroy the
country. Isa. 8.6 suggests that such a strategy was working. Cf. Irvine (1990: 189-
91), who relates the imagery of 'the waters of Shiloah' to the role that the Gihon
spring plays in guaranteeing the security of the Davidic dynasty.

2. It also has implications for understanding *qešer*, 'conspiracy', in Isa. 8.12
and the general concern with the people's need to fear YHWH in Isa. 8.11-15. The
root of *qešer* literally means 'to bind, join', which may suggest a further sexual
double entendre insofar as the people had rejected YHWH's promises of security in
favor of an alliance with the Syro-Ephraimitic coalition.

ûben-rᵉmalyāhû is a deliberate attempt to prepare the unsuspecting reader for the sexual metaphor of v. 8.

Just as the book of Isaiah as a whole sees the Assyrian invasions and later the Babylonian captivity as divine punishments that precede the restoration of the people, so also the associated sexual and river imagery of Isa. 8.6-7 and 66.10-14 present parallel but contrasting descriptions of the circumstances that led to the punishment and the results of the restoration. In conclusion, it should be noted that inasmuch as Isa. 66.10-14 appears as part of the climax of the book of Isaiah, it corresponds to the imagery at the beginning of the book (Isa. 2.2-4) of the nations 'flowing' (*wᵉnāhᵃrû*, Isa. 2.2) to Zion to receive YHWH's Torah. By basing the description of rejoicing in Isa. 66.10-14 on the language and imagery of Isa. 8.6-8, the author of Isa. 66.10-14 presents evidence that *ûmᵉśôś* appears in the text of Isa. 8.6 in the time of Trito-Isaiah, generally ascribed to the fifth century, and establishes a major link in the overall structure of the final form of the book.

BIBLIOGRAPHY

Barthélemy, D., *et al.*
    1986   *Critique textuelle de l'ancien testament*. II. *Isaïe, Jérémie, Lamentations* (Freiburg: Editions Universitaires; Göttingen: Vandenhoeck & Ruprecht).
Beuken, W.A.M.
    1986   'Isa. 56.9–57.13—An Example of the Isaianic Legacy of Trito-Isaiah', in J.W. Van Henten, *et al.* (eds.), *Tradition and Re-Interpretation in Jewish and Early Christian Literature: Essays in Honour of Jürgen C.H. Lebram* (Leiden: Brill): 48-64.
Beuken, W.A.M.
    1989   'Servant and Herald of Good Tidings: Isaiah 61 as an Interpretation of Isaiah 40–55', in Vermeylen 1989a: 411-42.
Bredenkamp, C.J.
    1887   *Der Prophet Jesaia* (Erlangen: Deichert).
Brueggemann, W.
    1984   'Unity and Dynamic in the Isaiah Tradition', *JSOT* 29: 89-107.
Brock, S. (ed.)
    1987   *The Old Testament in Syriac according to the Peshiṭta Version. Part III/1. Isaiah* (Leiden: Brill).
Budde, K.
    1926   'Jes 8, 6b', *ZAW* 44: 65-67.
Burrows, M., J.C. Trever and W.H. Brownlee
    1950   *The Dead Sea Scrolls of St Mark's Monastery*. I. *The Isaiah Manuscript and the Habakkuk Commentary* (New Haven: American Schools of Oriental Research).

Childs, B.S.

1979   *Introduction to the Old Testament as Scripture* (Philadelphia: Fortress Press).

Clements, R.E.

1980   *Isaiah 1–39* (NCB; Grand Rapids: Eerdmans; London: Marshall, Morgan & Scott).

1982   'The Unity of the Book of Isaiah', *Int* 36: 117-29.

1985   'Beyond Tradition History: Deutero-Isaianic Development of First Isaiah's Themes', *JSOT* 31: 95-113.

Duhm, B.

1914   *Das Buch Jesaia* (Göttingen: Vandenhoeck & Ruprecht, 3rd edn).

Finkelstein, L. (ed.)

1926   *The Commentary of David Kimḥi on Isaiah* (Columbia University Oriental Series, 19; New York: Columbia University).

Fullerton, K.

1924   'The Interpretation of Isaiah 8, 5-10', *JBL* 43: 253-89.

Gesenius, W.

1821   *Philologisch-kritischer und historiker Commentar über den Jesaia* (Leipzig: F.C.W. Vogel).

Gesenius, W., E. Kautzsch and A.E. Cowley

1983   *Gesenius' Hebrew Grammar* (Oxford: Clarendon Press; 2nd English edn).

Giesebrecht, F.

1888   'Die Immanuelweissagung', *TSK* 61: 217-64.

Hitzig, F.

1833   *Der Prophet Jesaja* (Heidelberg: C.F. Winter).

Holladay, W.L.

1989   *Jeremiah, II* (Hermeneia; Minneapolis: Fortress Press).

Irvine, S.

1990   *Isaiah, Ahaz, and the Syro-Ephraimitic Crisis* (SBLDS, 123; Atlanta: Scholars Press).

Jastrow, M.

1967   *A Dictionary of the Targumim, the Talmud Babli and Yerushalmi, and the Midrashic Literature* (Brooklyn: P. Shalom).

Kaiser, O.

1983   *Isaiah 1–12: A Commentary* (trans. J. Bowden; Philadelphia: Westminster Press, 2nd edn).

Klein, H.

1980   'Freude an Rezin', *VT* 30: 229-34.

Lack, R.

1973   *La Symbolique du livre d'Isaïe: Essai sur l'image littéraire comme élément de structuration* (AnBib, 59; Rome: Biblical Institute Press).

Lindblom, J.

1958   *A Study on the Immanuel Section in Isaiah: Isa. vii,1–ix, 6* (Lund: Gleerup).

Marti, K.

1900   *Das Buch Jesaja* (Tübingen: Mohr).

Odeberg, H.
1931   *Trito-Isaiah (Isaiah 56–66): A Literary and Linguistic Analysis* (UUÅ, Theologi, 1; Uppsala: Almqvist & Wiksell).
Rendtorff, R.
1984   'Zur Komposition des Buches Jesaja', *VT* 34: 295-320.
1989   'Jesaja 6 im Rahmen der Komposition des Jesajabuches', in Vermeylen 1989a: 73-82.
Rignell, L.C.
1957   'Das Orakel "Maher-salal Has-bas". Jesaja 8', *ST* 10: 40-52.
Rudolph, W.
1968   *Jeremia* (HAT, 12; Tübingen: Mohr [Paul Siebeck], 3rd edn).
Schroeder, O.
1912   '*umeśoś* eine Glosse zu raṣon', *ZAW* 32: 301-302.
Sperber, A.
1962   *The Bible in Aramaic. III. The Latter Prophets according to Targum Jonathan* (Leiden: Brill).
Steck, O.H.
1989   'Trito-Jesaja im Jesajabuch', in Vermeylen 1989a: 361-406.
Sweeney, M.A.
1988   *Isaiah 1–4 and the Post-Exilic Understanding of the Isaianic Tradition* (BZAW, 171; Berlin: de Gruyter).
Trever, J.C.
1972   *Scrolls from Qumran Cave I: The Great Isaiah Scroll; The Order of the Community; The Pesher to Habakkuk* (Jerusalem: The Albright Institute of Archaeological Research and the Shrine of the Book).
Vermeylen, J.
1989   'L'unité du livre d'Isaïe', in Vermeylen 1989a: 11-53.
Vermeylen, J. (ed.)
1989a   *The Book of Isaiah/Le Livre d'Isaïe: Les oracles et leurs relectures. Unité et complexité de l'ouvrage* (BETL, 81; Leuven: University Press and Uitgeverij Peeters).
Weber, R. (ed.)
1975   *Biblia Sacra iuxta Vulgatum Versionem* (Stuttgart: Württembergische Bibelanstalt).
Wildberger, H.
1972   *Jesaja 1–12* (Neukirchen–Vluyn: Neukirchener Verlag).
Ziegler, J. (ed.)
1967   *Septuaginta: Vetus Testamentum Graecum Auctoritate Academiae Litterarum Gottingensis Editum. XIV. Isaias* (Göttingen: Vandenhoeck & Ruprecht).

OF LIONS AND BIRDS: A NOTE ON ISAIAH 31.4-5

Michael L. Barré

ABSTRACT

Isa. 31.4-5 is a problematic text: it is difficult to decide whether it is an oracle of doom or salvation with regard to Jerusalem. The lion simile appears to be negative, the birds simile positive. There is some evidence to indicate that the passage is a unity and thus that the two similes belong together. In their original intent both are negative, a fact obscured by the standard mistranslation of *yāgēn... 'al* in v. 5 as 'protect'. But by the addition of four words at the end of v. 5 later editors have given a positive cast to the oracle as a whole.

In his commentary on Isaiah R.E. Clements makes the observation that Isa. 31.4-5 has 'occasioned not a little difficulty to commentators'.[1] This oracle consists of two similes: one relating to a lion (v. 4) and the other to birds (v. 5). The main point of controversy has to do with whether the oracle is positive or negative vis-à-vis Zion. At first glance, at least, the first simile (v. 4) strikes one as negative, while the second (v. 5) gives every indication of being positive. Another disputed issue is that of interpolation: to what extent have these verses undergone editorial expansion?

In this paper I shall argue that the correct understanding of the earliest form of this passage has been hampered both by the failure to recognize the OT parallels to the 'lion...birds' imagery in the oracle, and by the erroneous interpretation of one word by virtually all translations and commentators up to the present. Once these things are recognized, the harmony between the similes (in the original text) becomes evident, and determining the editorial additions to the passage becomes a simple matter.

It is obvious that at least in v. 5b and the subsequent verses the tone becomes more positive, in contrast to the oracle in vv. 1-3. For this

---

1. R.E. Clements, *Isaiah 1–39* (NCB; Grand Rapids: Eerdmans, 1980), p. 256.

reason some who take v. 4 in a negative sense understand v. 5 as a later addition.[1]

But a strong case can be made for the unity of the two similes. First, there is the repetition of the preposition '*al* between the two; the poet is evidently playing on its ambiguity.[2] Another bit of evidence is the distribution of the formulaic pair 'Zion' // 'Jerusalem' between them.[3] This pair is found 44 times in the MT, most frequently in this sequence.[4] Over a third of the occurrences (16×) are in the Book of Isaiah, more than in any other OT book.

More significantly, the terms '(wild) beasts' and 'birds' occur together about 35 times in the MT ('lion'... 'birds' would appear to be a variation on this *topos*).[5] In 16 of these occurrences the image is neutral.[6] But in the majority of cases (19×) it appears in a *negative* context, concerned with human bodies (usually of God's people) given to the birds and beasts as prey.[7] A number of these 19 passages show similarities to Isa. 31.4-5. Like the two similes in Isa. 31.4-5, five of them have the preposition '*al* with the prey upon whom the animals act (2 Sam. 21.10; Isa. 18.6; Jer. 12.9; Ezek. 31.13; 32.4). Three (2 Sam. 21.10; Deut. 28.26; Jer. 7.33) mention the attempt to chase off or frighten away the predators. One of the most enlightening passages

---

1. So B.S. Childs, *Isaiah and the Assyrian Crisis* (SBT, 2/3; London: SCM Press, 1967), p. 59. His position seems somewhat inconsistent, however. He states, '[v. 5] could hardly be an independent oracle which was only latter attached', but on the same page goes on to remark, 'v. 5 is of younger origin than v. 4' (*ibid.*).

2. See J.C. Exum, 'Of Broken Pots, Fluttering Birds, and Visions in the Night: Extended Simile and Poetic Technique in Isaiah', *CBQ* 43 (1981), p. 338.

3. Occasionally 'Mount Zion' replaces 'Zion' in the pair, as in our passage: 2 Kgs 19.31; Isa. 10.12, 32; 24.23; 37.32; Joel 3.5 [Eng. 2.32]; 4.17 [Eng. 3.17].

4. 'Zion... Jerusalem': 2 Kgs 19.21; Isa. 2.3; 4.3, 4; 10.12, 32; 24.23; 30.19; 31.9; 33.20; 37.22; 40.9; 41.27; 52.1; 64.9 [Eng. 10]; Jer. 26.18; 51.35; Joel 3.5 [Eng. 2.32]; 4.16, 17 [Eng. 3.16, 17]; Amos 1.2; Mic. 3.10, 12; 4.2, 8; Zeph. 3.14; Zech. 1.17; 8.3; 9.9; Pss. 51.20 [Eng. 18]; 102.22 [Eng. 21]; 128.5; 135.21; Lam. 1.17; 2.10; 'Jerusalem... Zion': 2 Kgs 19.31; Ps. 147.12; Isa. 37.32; 52.2; Zech. 1.14; Lam. 2.13.

5. Lions and birds are mentioned together in the following passages: 2 Sam. 1.23; Isa. 38.13-14; Jer. 12.8-9; Amos 3.4-5; Job 28.7-8; 38.39-41.

6. 1 Kgs 5.13 [Eng. 4.33]; Jer. 9.9 [Eng. 10]; 12.4; Ezek. 17.23 [LXX]; 31.6, 13; 38.20; Hos. 2.18; 4.3; Ps. 148.10; Job 12.7; 35.11; Dan. 2.38; 4.12, 14, 21 [Eng. 9, 11, 18].

7. Deut. 28.26; 1 Sam. 17.44, 46; 2 Sam. 21.10; Isa. 18.6 [2×]; Jer. 7.33; 12.9; 15.3; 16.4; 19.7; 34.20; Ezek. 29.5; 31.13; 32.4; 39.4, 17; Ps. 79.2.

in this connection is 2 Sam. 21.10. David took the two sons of Rizpah, Saul's concubine, and had them hanged on a mountain. She stationed herself there to guard her sons' bodies from the predations of wild animals and 'did not allow the *birds* of the air to light upon them by day or the *beasts* of the field by night'.

These last three texts provide the setting from which to explain the detail about the shepherds in the lion simile. Like Rizpah, they are attempting to scare the wild beast away from his prey. But when the lion roars over (*'al*) his victim, no one can distract him from consuming it. By the use of simile the poet is saying that Yahweh cannot be distracted or dissuaded from his fateful purpose by the actions of human beings. The image does not portray the lion as 'protecting' his kill.[1] Nor is the identity of the shepherds significant here. They serve merely to flesh out the expression in Deut. 28.26 and Jer. 7.33: 'And there shall be no one [able] to drive them [the birds and beasts] away'.[2] Clearly, the lion simile is negative.[3] The point of the simile as a whole is that Yahweh will come down to fight against (*'al*) Mount Zion. Here the preposition bears two meanings, each connected to a preceding verb: (1) it completes the meaning of *yēṛēd*, 'he will come down'; (2) it completes the meaning of *liṣbō'*, 'to fight, war'; outside this passage *ṣb' 'al* always means 'to fight *against*' (Num. 31.7; Isa. 29.7, 8; Zech. 14.12).

But if the lion and the birds similes are connected, how does one explain the fact that the former is negative and the latter is positive vis-à-vis Zion? The question is, is v. 5 really positive? More than one commentator has observed that 'flying birds' is hardly a transparent figure of protection.[4] As originally written, this simile is also negative. This has been obscured by the mistranslation of the expression *yāgēn*

---

1. So, for example, O. Kaiser, *Isaiah 13–39: A Commentary* (OTL; Philadelphia: Westminster Press, 1974), p. 316; H. Wildberger, *Jesaja 28–39* (BKAT, 10/3; Neukirchen–Vluyn: Neukirchener Verlag, 1982), pp. 1240-42; G. Fohrer, *Das Buch Jesaja* (3 vols.; Zürich: Zwingli Verlag, 2nd edn, 1974), pp. 120-21; A. Schoors, *Jesaja* (Roermond: Romen & Zonen, 1972), pp. 188-89; R. Fey, *Amos und Jesaja* (WMANT, 12; Neukirchen–Vluyn: Neukirchener Verlag, 1963), pp. 134-36.

2. Cf. Isa. 5.29-30 in a similar context.

3. See Childs, *Isaiah and the Assyrian Crisis*, pp. 58-59: 'The evidence points conclusively to taking v. 4 as a threat against Jerusalem'.

4. E.g. Kaiser, *Isaiah 13–39*, p. 317; Exum, 'Broken Pots', p. 338. Kaiser (*ibid.*) cites as a parallel to the protective interpretation of the flying birds image Deut. 32.11, but the verb in this case is *rḥp*, not *'wp*.

... *'al* in v. 5. Now Hebrew lexica give only one meaning for *gnn 'al*, namely, 'to protect'. However, the same verb also occurs in the Aramaic dialects. In Syriac (where it is attested in the aphel) it has at least three meanings: (1) 'to protect' (with *'al*), (2) 'to descend, come to rest upon' (with *'al*), and (3) 'to rest upon, reside in' (with *b^e*- or *'al*).[1] If the verb is multivalent in another West Semitic language, it is possible that the semantic field of its Hebrew cognate may not be restricted to one meaning.

Given *yēred*... *'al* in the lion simile, the meaning of *yāgēn*... *'al* in Isa. 31.5 is evident. It means 'to (descend and) light upon'. The idiom resembles *nwḥ* and *škn* with *'al*, which can likewise denote 'to light upon'.[2] *nwḥ 'al* can also have a hostile sense, as in 2 Sam. 17.12 and 21.10. The latter passage, as we have seen, tells how Rizpah would not let the birds 'light on' [*lānûaḥ 'al-*] the corpses of her sons. Far from being an image of protection, then, the 'flying birds' simile evokes the picture of carrion birds swooping down and lighting upon their prey. Although Yahweh is elsewhere likened to a marauding lion,[3] only here is he presented in the bold and gruesome image of a predatory bird.[4]

In light of the foregoing considerations, the earliest form of the oracle may be translated as follows:

> Thus says Yahweh my God:
> As a lion or a young lion
> roars over his prey—
> (And) when a band of shepherds
> is called out against him
> He is not afraid of their sound
> nor daunted by their noise—
> So will Yahweh of Hosts come down
> upon Mount Zion to fight against it and its hill.
> Like flying birds (of prey),
> so will Yahweh of Hosts (descend and) light upon Jerusalem.

1. R.P. Smith, *A Compendious Syriac Dictionary* (Oxford: Clarendon Press, 1903), p. 73.

2. *nwḥ*: 2 Sam. 21.10; *škn*: Ezek. 31.13; 32.4.

3. Isa. 38.13; Jer. 25.38; 49.19; 50.44; Hos. 5.14; 11.10; 13.7, 8; Job 10.16; Lam. 3.10.

4. In this connection we might recall that in the OT Yahweh is occasionally pictured as winged, like certain deities of the ancient Near East, although such language may be merely figurative (Exod. 19.4; Deut. 32.11 [a simile]; Pss. 17.8; 36.8 [Eng. 7]; 57.2 [Eng. 1]; 61.5 [Eng. 4]; 63.8 [Eng. 7]; 91.4; Ruth 2.12). But in these cases the image is always positive.

The last four words of v. 5 (*gānôn wᵉhiṣṣîl pāsōaḥ wᵉhimlîṭ*) are an editorial addition. One of the meanings of *gnn* is 'protect', as we have seen. By repeating this verb and associating it with three words that mean 'deliver' or the like, the editors have reinterpreted *yāgēn*... *'al* so that it might be read in a positive light.[1] Their efforts have been eminently successful, since until now no one has questioned the positive meaning of the verb. Thus only the end of v. 5 shows editorial activity, which B.S. Childs aptly terms 'a corrective commentary'.[2] One is reminded of Babylonian *ṣâtu*-commentaries on literary works, in which the word excerpted for comment is followed by one or more synonyms.[3]

Oddly enough, then, both schools of thought about Isa. 31.4-5 turn out to be correct to one extent or another. In its *original* form, as I have attempted to demonstrate, the two similes within the oracle are *negative* and constitute a prophecy of doom against Jerusalem. However, in the *present* or canonical form (i.e. the MT), the oracle as a whole—including the lion simile—is meant to be read in a *positive* light. This no doubt presents a problem for the modern translator: should these verses be rendered so as to reflect their original intent or according to their 'corrected' meaning? Undoubtedly both stages of the history of this passage should somehow be represented in translation.

1. One sees this process elsewhere in the prophetic books—for example, in Amos 9. Verse 7 marks the end of a clearly negative oracle ('Behold, the eyes of Yahweh God are upon the sinful kingdom // And I will destroy it from the surface of the ground'). There can be little doubt that the next line (v. 8) is a prosaic, editorial addition that seeks to undo this negative judgment: 'Except that I will not utterly destroy the house of Jacob'.

2. *Isaiah and the Assyrian Crisis*, p. 59. However, he applies this label to the entirety of v. 5.

3. See E. Leichty, *The Omen Series Šumma Izbu* (Texts from Cuneiform Sources, 4; Locust Valley, NY: J.J. Augustin, 1970), pp. 22-23. 'Commentaries' of this type are generally lexical in nature, giving synonyms for rare, poetic terms. In the case of verbs, the infinitive form is usually given (as in Isa. 31.5), regardless of the verbal form in the text (see W.G. Lambert, *Babylonian Wisdom Literature* [Oxford: Clarendon Press, 1960], pp. 32-54, 70-88). Were it not for the *waw* before *hiṣṣîl*, v. 5b might be interpreted as a lexical comment on the infrequent verb *gnn* (8× in the MT) which would be similar to what is found in the Babylonian commentaries ('*gānôn* [here means] "to deliver", "skip over", "rescue"'), which later became incorporated into the text. However, the poetic balance of v. 5b—qal inf. + *wᵉ* + hiphil inf. // qal inf. + *wᵉ* + hiphil inf.—may suggest rather that the four words were a deliberate insertion from the beginning.

THE CONSTRUCTION OF THE SUBJECT AND THE SYMBOLIC ORDER: A READING OF THE LAST THREE SUFFERING SERVANT SONGS*

Francis Landy

ABSTRACT

After a brief section setting the so-called servant songs in the context of Jewish–Christian dialogue, the bulk of this article consists of a close reading of Isa. 49.1-6 and 50.4-9, with a summary foray into Isa. 53. The focus is on the different ways the subject is constructed in these poems, the disjunction between extreme symbolization and disintegration, the impossibility of attaining any quiddity in the swirl of conflicting personae and explicative paradigms. Between the polarities of utter negation and theophanous vindication, between unbearable pain and unflinching resistance, the subject tries different strategies for achieving coherence and an adequate relationship with the maternal/paternal symbolic order. By the last poem, all we are left with is insistent contradiction and the sense of tragedy, as, with pity and fear, we watch the subject going to his death on our behalf, and beyond death.

1. *The Suffering Servant Songs in Jewish–Christian Dialogue*

Let us begin with David Clines's study of Isaiah 53, *I, He, We, and They*.[1] The great virtue of Clines's work is that it moves us away from 'the poem as problem' to 'the poem as language event', an event in which 'the silence becomes painful, almost unbearable',[2] in which there is a complete absence of action, dialogue, or even, strangely for Isaiah, affective language.[3] It is an event, an experience, of a world

---

*   Lecture given at the 22nd Jewish–Christian Bible Week in Bendorf, Germany, 25th July, 1990. I am grateful to my audience and their comments, to a very stimulating study circle, and to my colleague, E. Ben-Zvi, for invaluable discussion.

1.   *I, He, We, and They. A Literary Approach to Isaiah 53* (JSOTSup, 1; Sheffield: JSOT Press, 1976), p. 59.

2.   L. Alonso Schökel, 'Isaiah', in R. Alter and F. Kermode (eds.), *The Literary Guide to the Bible* (Cambridge, MA: Harvard University Press, 1987), p. 180.

3.   *I, He, We, and They*, pp. 44-46.

that is 'topsy-turvy',[1] yet recognizably our own, that fascinates us, as the 'they' of the text interprets us, insofar as we identify with the servant, and reproaches us for 'our easy activisms', from a silence that is simply 'the silence of suffering',[2] that is nevertheless the service of God.

My problem with the text, however, is not simply that I am involved in the event, but that I experience a visceral recoil from the notion of vicarious suffering, or simple fright. The silence, passivity and emotional vacuity that Clines finds in the text corresponds to critical paralysis. Repression of that which dies with each person, as well as self-preservation, separation from that person—the complex of survivor guilt, reparation, anaesthesia. Our text is, centrally, mourning; the mourning seeks its comfort (the great theme of Second Isaiah), is framed by it, yet discontinous with it.

German and anglophone scholarship sharply divide over the so-called servant songs, as they do over everything else. German scholarship tends to isolate the servant songs from the rest of Deutero-Isaiah, to see them as a separate collection, to ascribe them to the circle of Trito-Isaiah, to see in them the influences of Jeremiah and Ezekiel, and to determine text-critically the growth of the text, rather as a dendrologist determines the age of a tree. In 49.1-6, R.P. Merendino, for example, traces the transformation of a poem originally about Cyrus to one about the servant and then about Israel.[3] In English scholarship, in contrast, we encounter increasing scepticism about the very existence of the servant songs, a refusal to isolate them from their Deutero-Isaianic context and the Isaianic tradition as a whole, and an awareness—at least in a recent article by John Sawyer—of the sexism that has focused on the servant rather than on his complement, the daughter of Zion.[4]

But this is overshadowed by the deeper problem, the Jewish–

---

1. *I, He, We, and They*, p. 61.

2. *I, He, We, and They*, p. 65, for both these expressions.

3. 'Jes 49 1-6: Ein Gottesknechtslied?', *ZAW* 92 (1980), pp. 236-48.

4. J.F.A. Sawyer, 'Daughter of Zion and Servant of the Lord in Isaiah: A Comparison', *JSOT* 44 (1989), pp. 89-107. Cf. also R.E. Clements, 'Beyond Tradition-History: Deutero-Isaianic Development of First Isaiah's Themes', *JSOT* 31 (1985), pp. 95-113. For a contrary view, however, cf. C. Stuhlmueller, 'Deutero-Isaiah: Major Transitions in the Prophet's Theology and in Contemporary Scholarship', *CBQ* 42 (1980), pp. 1-29.

Christian one. Isaiah 53 has been a witness to the truth of the Gospel, and a snare and a thorn to Jews. The Jewish response has been tacit decanonization; Isaiah 53 is not recited in the synagogue among the readings from the prophets, there are no Midrashim about Isaiah 53. Only with the development of sequential commentaries in the Middle Ages were Jews forced to confront the problem of Isaiah 53; this was exacerbated by the frequency of disputation and the intellectual and emotional crisis in the wake of the Crusades and the challenge of philosophy. For many commentators, such as Rashi and Ibn Ezra, the servant is Israel; for the latter, this is linked with Judah Halevi's idea that Israel is the heart of the world, and suffers for its diseases.[1]

Now the problem is not the equivocal survival of the christological interpretation in modern Christian commentaries, but that it is very hard to read Isaiah 53 except through the lens of its history of interpretation and its traumatic consequences: the vindication of the New, and the theodicy of substitutionary atonement. How can we innocently read Isaiah 53 as Christians and Jews, without or across the appalling memories of dialogue as persecution? How can we come to terms with the notion of vicarious suffering? Perhaps I, as a biblical critic, can avoid this history. But I would do so only in the face of my responsibility as a person and as a Jew.

But there is a deeper problem still: that the text resists interpretation, that one is left with a sense of incomprehensibility that cannot be accommodated in our respective theologies. The text cuts through its history; every attempt to identify the servant, to use Isaiah 53 in interfaith polemics, falsifies the experience of the text as something present in and beyond our faiths, traditions and languages. Clines compares its silence to Abraham's journey to Mt Moriah;[2] it is the same journey.

2. *Isaiah 49.1-6*

How did we get there? God called me from my mother's womb, reciting my name (49.1). There in the womb something was speaking, language was forming; it was not me speaking, but it gives me my name and destiny; I come to be in hearing that name and hearing that

1. For a recent treatment of mediaeval Jewish interpretation of Isa. 53, see J.E. Rembaum, 'The Development of a Jewish Exegetical Tradition regarding Isaiah 53', *HTR* 75 (1982), pp. 289-311.
2. *I, He, We, and They*, p. 46.

voice. Perhaps it is a ghostly father in the womb, summoning me to the world and to my death; so a Lacanian might say; but it does not sound like that. For the voice is a stranger to the matrix, and yet it sounds deeper, even more innate.

The phrase הזכיר שמי, 'made mention of my name', comes from the language of sacrifice, and refers to the invocation of YHWH that accompanies the offering. The imagery is reversed; YHWH comes down into the womb, and invokes my name there.[1] Is he worshipping, celebrating my existence? or is the place of my coming-to-be that of YHWH's sacrifice?

And he made me, and my mouth in which he and I speak the words that remember this precipitation of self from language, the words that fructify the earth and last for ever (40.8; 55.10-11), and that are also those of the prophecy of redemption and consolation. But my mouth is 'like a sharp sword' (v. 2), an instrument of death; its language is ambiguous, human and divine, vital and fatal, expressive and mysterious. Thus the sharp, discriminatory sword is hidden in God's hand; the polished, bright arrow is concealed in his quiver.[2] God's calling me and my language into existence in the womb is then also an undoing, a creation of death. Not only am I invoked by YHWH, but I embody the transformation of death into life that is of the essence of sacrifice.

Something else encloses me: YHWH's hand, his quiver. The womb is displaced, perpetuated, by YHWH's shadow, on the trajectory through life; this is combined, however, with the imminence of violent ejection. Phallic, militaristic imagery replaces maternal address; language turns to warfare, which releases the subject from the divine enfolding.[3] Between the two sets of images there seems to be no continuity.

1. R.P. Merendino ('Jes. 49 1-6', p. 243), finds it inconceivable that such a restrained (*zurückhaltender*) prophet as Deutero-Isaiah should use such language about himself, and therefore attributes the reference to Cyrus. Quite apart from the question of Deutero-Isaiah's restraint, one wonders whether it would be rendered less outrageous with reference to a foreign king.

2. Both adjectives have their linguistic correlates; חדה, 'sharp', is paradigmatically linked to חידה, 'riddle'; ברור, 'polished', is likewise used of speech (e.g. Zeph. 3.9).

3. There is a clear parallel in the Aqhat legend, in which Anat encloses her agent Yatpan, transformed into an eagle, in her pouch in order to murder Aqhat. For text, translation and commentary, see most recently B. Margalit, *The Ugaritic Poem of Aqht* (Berlin: de Gruyter, 1989), pp. 129, 156, 340.

Then there is another transformation. God says, 'You are my servant, Israel, in whom I will be glorified' (v. 3). The servant in the divine grasp becomes the container of God. The womb imagery is inverted. And as YHWH entered the womb to invoke his name, so he enters the prophet and radiates from him.

The prophet is identified with Israel. Much has been made of this as evidence of early interpretation. But in fact it is a commonplace—the prophet speaks for Israel, just as he speaks for God.[1] From the pre-natal commission to its fulfilment in the flight of the arrow from God, we come to a third phase: the brilliant deadliness of the arrow as theophany.

The prophet is identified with Israel, as servant of God, emissary, transmitter of divine glory. But he has failed, he says, precisely in his relation to Israel. ואני אמרתי לריק יגעתי לתהו והבל כחי כליתי, 'And I said: I have exhausted myself for nothing; for chaos and illusion I have consumed my strength' (v. 4). Instead of theophany we have תהו, 'chaos', interposed between the prophet and his mission, and corresponding to it psychic and physical prostration—a familiar prophetic as well as shamanistic motif. The threshold of despair and death over which one passes is an initiation into new life; it has its correlates in the blindness and deafness of the servant and Israel in 42.7, 18-20 and 43.8.[2] But here it is upstaged by a new commission: to be a light to the nations. The transition between the failed task of reclaiming Israel and this ultimate horizon is equivalent to the double origin and the passage from death to life in the first verses. God speaks, invokes, in the mother's womb; in v. 5 he forms me there, to restore the integrity of Mother Israel; but his speech goes beyond that. I see myself reflected in his eyes, his language and values; his fortitude (עזי)—or YHWH as fortitude—relieves my failed strength. But this is facile, a cliché; 'It is too easy to be a servant...' (v. 6). The maternal enclosure of history, so nostalgically repeated in vv. 5 and 6, to return those who have

---

1. See especially the argument of P. Wilcox and D. Paton-Williams, 'The Servant Songs in Deutero-Isaiah', *JSOT* 42 (1988), esp. pp. 88-92. A very full and sensitive account of this ambiguity in relation to Jeremiah is to be found in T. Polk, *The Prophetic Persona: Jeremiah and the Language of the Self* (JSOTSup, 32; Sheffield: JSOT Press, 1984).

2. R.E. Clements ('Beyond Tradition History', pp. 101-104) argues that Deutero-Isaiah here develops a theme notably present in First Isaiah (e.g. 6.9-10; 29.18).

been preserved[1] of Israel to their origins, is superseded by this other voice, that makes him a light to the nations. Structurally, the enclosure is reversed; the outer ring, formed by the address to the 'islands' and 'peoples afar' in v. 1 and the task of bringing salvation to the ends of the earth in v. 6, envelopes the ingathering of Israel and the immanence of YHWH in the womb, and at the centre, negating YHWH's presence, the prophet's emptiness and failure.[2]

Is this the answer to the prophet's plea for justice and recognition of his labour in v. 4? To add to his troubles? Or is YHWH also the plaintiff, his failure and weariness corresponding to that of the prophet?[3] Is the prophet's complaint against the people, as 50.6-9 would suggest, or against YHWH, who set him on this thankless venture? Is God's unfairness then compounded, the complaint unanswered? But in some strange way it does seem to be a response—not only suggesting the absolute value YHWH places on the prophet, but some connection between success and failure, some sense that the prophet's exhaustion and despair are necessary for the further mission. This is typical of any liminal stage, of any endeavour that takes us beyond the known circle.

What is it to be a light to the nations? Light brings us back to creation, as well as to Abraham's brief to bring blessing to the families of the earth (Gen. 12.3); through parallelism, it is equivalent here to ישועה, 'salvation', and thus consummation; geographical extension is thereby correlated with historical totality. But it also focuses our attention on the person as theophany, as God's salvation and light.[4]

---

1. Whybray proposes a derivation from נצר, 'shoot', reading נצירי (K) or נצורי (Q) as נִצְרֵי, 'offshoots, descendants', on the grounds of the improbability of the meaning 'preserved' (*Isaiah 40–66*, p. 139). The latter, as well as being more common, would also be less bland; נצירי/נצורי as 'preserved' is not only more emotive than 'descendants', but also perhaps lends support to the *ketib* of לו יאסף in v. 5 as לא

יאסף, 'that has not been gathered up', i.e. perished.

2. The contrast is strengthened by alliteration between the strategically important words רחוק, 'afar', on the periphery of the passage (v.1), and ריק, 'emptiness', at its centre (v. 4). ריק lacks the central consonant of רחוק; it is, as it were, emptied at the centre of those distances.

3. Cf. H.J. Hermisson, 'Der Lohn des Knecht', in J. Jeremias and L. Perlitt (eds.), *Die Botschaft und die Boten* (Neukirchen–Vluyn: Neukirchener Verlag, 1981), p. 276. For YHWH's exhaustion, cf. 43.24.

4. There is a certain ambiguity here: is the light the salvation itself, and are the

The sharpness of the individual is juxtaposed with extreme symbolization. This is the source of the fascination and the difficulty of these
passages; I am called in the womb as myself, in a language that is not
mine; but that which names, fashions, offers itself up in my invocation, transmits itself and finds its home in me, is both my very self and
other than me. On the one hand, the so-called Suffering Servant Songs
offered a romantic biblical scholarship[1] the possibility of reality; the
actual individual talking for himself in his *haeccitas*; a biographical
delusion that could be translated in terms of a realist novel.[2] On the
other hand, this person, when probed, disappeared in theological
abstractions and formulaic language; his sufferings, for example,
shaped according to the psalms of lament. This, however, is the central problem: the wish to identify myself with the symbolic order,
flesh with word, to house and be contained by God—and our diver-
gence, the collapse inwards when the effort fails.

3. *Isaiah 50.4-9*

God speaks; morning by morning I listen, my ear opened, awakened
by God, the tongue given by God (50.4-5). My speech and that which
I hear is divine language; I teach and learn repetitively, as one learns
the tools and canonical texts of a culture. The imagery of the origina-
ting speech and international luminary is transposed to the everyday;
God speaks with the dawn, the coming to be of the day coinciding
with the light and consciousness. Yet if education is conservative, an

parallel clauses thus equivalent, or is it that which *brings* salvation, the second clause
thus being consequent to the first? If the former, then the prophet as light embodies
salvation; if the latter, then the illumination is teleological, to be understood in terms
of justice or whatever. It is not clear whether there is a necessary distinction between
the two possibilities. Illumination = prophet might be experienced as salvation and
provide a vision of ethical or political truth. The problem is complicated by the
coupling of להיות in 'to be for me a servant' and 'to be my salvation'. These could
either be equivalent (i.e. prophet is salvation) or להיות ישועתי could simply mean 'that
my salvation should be...'

1. It is noteworthy that the hypothesis of a collection of servant songs developed
in the heyday of late German romanticism, with B. Duhm's commentary, *Das Buch
Jesaia* (Göttingen: Vandenhoeck & Ruprecht, 1892).

2. I am grateful for an observation by G. Josipovici, in the question period after
the lecture, contrasting the identification mandated by the realist novel with the
empathy whose precondition is distance.

induction into the old symbolic order, this speech is novel, heralding the new age. Its symbolic language is thus in a sense anti-symbolic, that which overturns old symbols or even all symbols.

I suffer, quite traditionally, for my sedition: my back lacerated, my beard torn...I become a victim, my body a symbol for the rejection of God, the coercion of the powers that be. Sacrifice is then inverted; instead of God invoking my name in the womb, in me God's speech is repressed. As in 49.1-6, the ordeal is in the central position. But whereas there it resulted in exhaustion and failure, here my face is transformed into flint, obdurate and unflinching (50.7). Moreover, this is because 'my lord YHWH helps me' (50.7, 9); תהו, 'chaos', is replaced by divine infusion. The paradoxes and the duplex structure[1] of 49.1-6—with its juxtaposition of death and life, divine immanence and alienation, crisis as dissolution of the brilliant weapon and its reforging as immaterial light—these are not so much reversed as negated. The flint masks over or is without relation to the experience of emptiness; petrification as symbol for the prophet/God's passive resistance activates a prophetic agenda different from that of the power of word, light and arrow; the continuity of divine speech and aid in persecution occludes the narrative intensity, even absurdity, of the former passage. Is there any contiguity between the two interpretations? Or simply disjunction in the prophet's self-construction? Is there continuity between the ways in which we accommodate intolerable experience—pain, exposure, humiliation—and the experience itself? Then the biographical quest meets the resistance of the body to meaning, and correspondingly a crisis arises in the transition from its kinesis to the symbolic structure of the stable, formed, understood self.

The phrase יעזר לי, 'He helps/will help me', is ambiguous. Is God's help present or future? It seems to be both; the help is trust that he *will* help, taking vengeance on the prophet's enemies (50.9, 11). There is a hiatus then between help as confidence and the absence of help as rescue. In this indeterminacy the smoothness of the passage founders. We do not know whether the prophet's assurance will be justified. This openness affects in turn the closure of the embryonic myth of

---

1. Isa. 49.1-3 is recapitulated in vv. 5-6; thus the summons in the womb is recollected in v. 5, the appointment as servant in v. 6, the mission to/as Israel in vv. 5-6, and God's manifestation in the servant, 'in you I will be glorified' (v. 3), in v. 6. Cf. Merendino, 'Jes. 49.1-6', p. 238, and Hermisson, 'Der Lohn des Knechts', p. 273, who speaks of it as a 'Reprise'.

creation in 49.1-6. In the תהו of the prophet YHWH forms, names light. But we do not know what this light means, how it will spread, and in what way the prophet embodies it.

This light is 'my justice' (51.4; cf. 42.1), parallelistically equivalent to my תורה (51.4), the words that I hear day by day and presumably comprising Deutero-Isaiah. But it is this justice that is left in question by the indeterminacy of יעזר לי, 'helps/will help me'. In 50.8, the litigant, בעל משפטי, is dared to appear; in 49.4, as we have seen, this judgment is referred to YHWH. There a certain ambiguity surrounds the complaint, directed at YHWH as well as the people; this is compounded—to anticipate—by the assumption that the persecution comes from YHWH (53.4). A community persecutes a dissident in the name of social and sacred order. If the dissident is a prophet, persecution may become part of his or her calling, a proof of authenticity. It is an essential component of the prophet's self-construction. Then the judgment both stands against the community that rejects the word of YHWH, and raises the question of the complicity of YHWH (and prophet?) in the ordeal.

What can one say about the personality of the prophet/servant? He is blind and deaf, according to 42.19; he walks in darkness (50.10), while his persecutors use the light of their own torches—and will be burnt by them (50.11). Yet he is to free others from blindness, darkness and imprisonment, as the light to the nations (42.7); he is to restore the devastated estates to their owners (49.8), as part of his expanded mission, to raise up the earth (להקים ארץ) as well as Israel (להקים את שבטי יעקב). In each case this is what it is to be a ברית עם, 'a covenant of people' (42.6; 49.8), the intermediary between humanity and God. Yet he is concealed by God's hand (49.2; 51.16), the sharp sword and polished arrow as yet veiled. In 51.16, he is obscured by the shadow of God's hand 'to plant heavens and to found earth' (לנטע שמים וליסד ארץ),[1] just as God stretches forth (נוטה) the heavens and founds the earth (51.13), a clear echo of the imagery of creation in 49.6. Yet the context is the destruction of creation in 51.6, in which God's salvation, spread by the prophetic divine light in 49.6, continues

---

1. The metaphor 'to plant', which Whybray finds unusual and consequently emends to לנטות, 'to stretch' (*Isaiah 40–66*, p. 162), clearly echoes and amplifies Jeremiah's commission to the nations in Jer. 1.10 (cf. also 18.7-9). A further connection is formed between Jer. 1.5 (10), in which Jeremiah is appointed as a prophet to the nations, and Isa. 49.6.

forever. Destruction and recreation, theophany and concealment, blindness and brilliance, are thus paired; the contraries converge on the last and most famous of the 'Servant' passages, Isaiah 53.

4. *Isaiah 52.13–53.12*

Isaiah 53 evokes pre-eminently the tragic dimension of the Bible: an audience, spectators, watch with pity and fear someone going on their behalf to death and beyond death. We see the collapse of his hopes for vindication, for justice; having rested his case with YHWH (49.4), and having triumphed prospectively over his opponents, he is now 'taken away from justice' (53.8). No one can speak with or for his generation (53.8), except ironically this silence and death; thereby he intercedes for the sinners (53.12). We watch with horror, or at least fascination, combined with guilt, since he dies[1] for our sins; the mystery is in part that of death—that which we feel when anyone dies—in part it is the release of socially legitimated violence, the complicity of a crowd at an execution,[2] and hence the confrontation with our own murderousness; but it is also that of growing identification, from the non-recognition of the first verses—we did not think of him (v. 3), he had no image—to concentrated if mistaken thought about him as the object of God's wrath, to a sympathy at first metaphorical, displaced onto conventionally pathetic sheep, and finally focused by the insistent evocation of his נפש, his soul or psyche (vv. 10, 11, 12). We thus identify with him and murder him. But even more insidiously, the mystery is formulated through paradox, the condensation and reversal of the imagery of the whole prophecy. Terror and violence are absurd, since human beings are mortal—'Where is the violence of the destroyer?' (51.13). Only the servant will not die, nor descend to the pit (שׁחת) (51.14).[3] Yet here he dies, and incarnates the pit: משׁחת מאישׁ מראהו 'his

---

1. I am not concerned at this point with the question of what really happened, whether the servant was actually executed, or whether he merely had a close encounter. What is important is the symbolic enactment of this death.

2. B. Levine ('René Girard on Job: The Question of the Scapegoat', *Semeia* 33 [1985], pp. 125-33) argues that, even more than Job, the servant in Isa. 53 is a classic scapegoat, though the text differs from most instances in that the scapegoat is rescued and recognized as such.

3. It is ambiguous whether the subject is representative of Israel, as most commentators suppose, or has a particular reference to the prophet; this is compounded by the ambiguous identity of the prophet, as individual and as symbol for Israel. In

visage more waste, more pit-like than any person' (52.14).[1] He was to bring habitation to the desolate lands (להנחיל נחלות שממות); but he himself is desolate, the desolation cast on him by others: כאשר שממו עליך רבים (52.14). His word and salvation were to outlast heaven and earth, but he does not speak. Kings and princes were to bow down before him; they were to nurture Israel (49.23), with whom he is ambigously identified—the maternal imagery transferred from God, Sarah and the womb in which the prophet was called, to the nations. Kings, in 52.15, are astonished, speechless, because of seeing something beyond the narratives of the world, understanding something beyond articulation. What this is we cannot say; but between it and the suppression of sedition embodied in the servant/prophet there is an inexplicable breach.

Three further points. The servant, as well as planting heaven and earth, is to say to Zion עמי אתה, 'You are my people', a clear reference to Hos. 2.25. Like the servant, Zion has been rendered desolate, and subjected to judgment, because of the sins of her children (50.1-3); as Sawyer has shown, the passages concerning Zion and the servant correspond to each other throughout these chapters. In 52.7, the herald, an obvious projection or persona of the prophet himself, comes to Jerusalem announcing its deliverance, to bring about the reunion of God and Zion.[2] There follows immediately ch. 53, with the servant's isolation, shame, passage through death, and apotheosis. Are these

51.12-16 the ambiguity is especially evident in the paralleling of the addressee of vv. 12-13, which seems to be general, with that of v. 16, which is more specifically the prophet, as shown by correlations with Jeremiah's commission (Jer. 1.9-10) and the metaphor of being covered with God's hand in 49.2. The subject of v. 14 mediates between the two addressees. There is, however, a contrast between אנוש, 'man, humanity' (v. 12), who does die, and the subject of v. 14, who does not. This, without closing the ambiguity, makes identification with the prophet more pointed—his immortality will be augmented by his function of co-creator in v. 16. For the modelling of the servant passages in Deutero-Isaiah as commission oracles, see O.H. Steck, 'Aspekte des Gottesknechts in Deuterojesajas "Ebed-Jahwe-Liedern"', *ZAW* 96 (1984), pp. 372-90, and 'Aspekte des Gottesknechts in Jes. 52, 13–53, 12', *ZAW* 97 (1985), pp. 36-58.

1. I adopt here the usual emendation of the MT מִשְׁחַת to מָשְׁחַת. A. Brenner has made the attractive suggestion that מִשְׁחַת is a play on משח, 'to anoint'.

2. For the parallelism between the herald, מבשר, in 52.7, and Zion as herald, מבשרת, in 40.9 is noted by Sawyer, 'Daughter of Zion and Servant of the Lord', p. 103.

simply ironically contrasted, or is the servant's ordeal in some way equivalent to the romance? Are the mystically vindicated servant beyond death and the joyful mother Zion, whose children return to her womb, metaphors for each other, or the same?

Secondly, there is the obtrusive overlapping of contradictory terms. That which is not thought is thought; that which is not heard (52.15) is our incredible hearing (53.1); that which is seen (52.15) is the servant/ prophet who has no appearance (53.2). In 53.1 the arm of YHWH is revealed presumably to the kings who 'see' in the previous verse, but also over the servant, who is crushed by it. But the arm of YHWH has once crushed Rahab and tortured the sea-dragon (51.9); it is summoned to awake—to torment its servant. The same verb (מחלל/מחוללת) is used for the agony of serpent and servant 'for our sins' (53.5). But it is also used for the birthpangs of Sarah (51.2). Chaos (תהו) and creation, death and birth, serpent and mother, are thus superimposed on each other.

Thirdly, what is the point of view of God in the poem? God called me in the womb, invoking my name, in an evocation of sacrifice, the voice coming from beyond the womb, yet entering it, becoming part of it. The symbolic order on its own strange trajectory. Now God strikes me (הפניע) that I may intercede (יפניע). I am a substitute—for the many or for God? In 53.10, God sets him as an אשם, a trespass offering, for the desecration of sancta. Is this an אשם given by God for the violation of the womb, for the invasion of death into life? What is important, however, is the effect: the servant sees and knows, beyond life and death. Like God, he is high and uplifted (52.13; cf. 6.1). But there is also a transformation in the womb image. God finds him, sees him, growing like a root in a dry land—presumably a comment on the world and Israel—and he is a יונק, a suckling, suckling in the dryness, but also on God, that voice, vision, beyond the womb...

RADICAL IMAGES OF YAHWEH IN ISAIAH 63

John F.A. Sawyer

ABSTRACT

The use of the Hebrew words *ḥāmûṣ* (cf. *ḥōmeṣ* 'vinegar') and *ṣō'eb* (used elsewhere only of prostitutes, prisoners and gypsies) suggests a description of Yahweh as a tired, bloodstained warrior returning from battle, in dirty clothes, not 'crimsoned garments' (RSV), and 'stooping' wearily, not 'marching' triumphantly (RSV). This remarkable image, which is developed further in vv. 5 and 9, is often removed by textual emendation, but fits quite well into its context in Isaiah where images of Yahweh also include a woman in labour (42.14), an apologetic husband (54.7-8) and a midwife (66.9).

There is a widespread assumption that images are in some way inferior to abstract ideas and concepts.[1] In a recent discussion of images in Biblical poetry, Luis Alonso Schökel argues against this view: 'when we are dealing with poets', he says, 'what comes before the image is not the concept, but the formless experience'.[2] A phrase like 'the hand of God', for example, does not mean the same thing as an abstraction like 'the power of God'. Of course we can analyse the meaning of images by reference to concepts, but the imagery comes first. In a passage like Isa. 63.1-6, the imagery has first to be taken seriously and examined in its own right as reflecting the author's experience and relating to our own. Only then are we getting near to the meaning of the text.

There are theologians and philosophers who are taking images seriously too. For Sallie McFague, images and metaphors are as important in their own right as theological concepts and doctrines. In her *Metaphorical Theology*, for example, she shows how influential the

---

1. This is the revised version of a paper read at the IOSOT Congress in Leuven in August, 1989.

2. *A Manual of Hebrew Poetics* (Subsidia Biblica, 11; Rome: Pontifical Biblical Institute, 1988), pp. 100-101.

traditional model of 'God as Father' has been in Christian theology, almost to the point of idolatry, and how closely bound up it is with the experience of the community or institution that developed it.[1] Such an image has to be scrutinized very carefully, and even treated with a certain scepticism, not least because it may not have the same relevance in every age.

The search for new metaphors or models that might reflect the experiences of the modern world better does not restrict itself to the Bible. Some theologians find the biblical text so irredeemably irrelevant or patriarchal that they look elsewhere for authority. Others, like Sallie McFague and Phyllis Trible,[2] seek to find traces of a less irrelevant or less patriarchal religion within scripture. It is then a matter of selection and interpretation—'Searching for Lost Coins', to use the title of a book by another recent theologian,[3] within scripture and within tradition. McFague starts her discussion of one new model, her best known one, namely, that of 'God as friend', by quoting scriptural authority for it: Isa. 41.18, Hos. 2.23, Jn 15.13 and so on.[4] Passages in which the image of 'God as mother' clearly occurs receive a new emphasis in today's world for similar reasons.[5]

Against this background I want to look again at Isa. 63.1-6, where unexpected words and images, implying something quite extraordinary, are apparently applied to Yahweh. Before we remove them as scribal errors or resort to other methods of weakening their effect (which is what is done in the majority of commentaries and, without comment,

---

1. *Metaphorical Theology: Models of God in Religious Language* (Philadelphia: Fortress Press, 1982), pp. 145-92.

2. Cf. M. Daly, *Beyond God the Father* (Boston: Beacon Press, 1973); P. Trible, *God and the Rhetoric of Sexuality* (Philadelphia: Fortress Press, 1978); *idem*, *Texts of Terror: Literary Feminist Readings of Biblical Narratives* (Philadelphia: Fortress Press, 1984); cf. R.R. Ruether, *Sexism and God-Talk* (London: SCM Press, 1983); L.M. Russell (ed.), *Feminist Interpretation of the Bible* (Oxford: Blackwell, 1985); D.F. Middleton, 'Feminist Interpretation', in R.J. Coggins and J.L. Houlden (eds.), *Dictionary of Biblical Interpretation* (London: SCM Press, 1990), pp. 231-34.

3. A. Loades, *Searching for Lost Coins: Explorations in Christianity and Feminism* (London: SPCK, 1988).

4. *Metaphorical Theology*, pp. 177-78.

5. E.g. Deut. 32.18; Ps. 131.2; Isa. 31.5; 42.14; 46.3-4; 49.15; 66.13. Cf. Trible, *God and the Rhetoric of Sexuality*, pp. 21ff.; McFague, *Metaphorical Theology*, pp. 169ff.; Ruether, *Sexism and God-Talk*, pp. 54-56.

in some of our English versions),[1] we should look very closely at the text as it stands to see whether, like the feminine images in some other passages, these are images that have been suppressed or underplayed for identifiable theological reasons. Textual emendation, even when it is supported by the evidence of the ancient versions, is not always the correct solution. The dictum *difficilior lectio potior est* is often proved correct, and sometimes it is easy to see why the 'difficult' reading or interpretation has been bypassed.

I

Verse 1. The passage begins with a question: 'Who is this?' Many commentators assume that this is a rhetorical question, like 'Who is this coming up from the wilderness?' in the Song of Songs (8.5), or 'Who is the king of glory?' in Psalm 24.[2] The speaker knows perfectly well who the approaching person is and the question is just a figure of speech designed to heighten the effect of the welcome he receives. But this interpretation assumes that the passage describes a normal encounter between two people, conversing with each other in everyday speech. This seems to me to be quite unjustified. In the first place, no encounter between a human being and Yahweh is normal. The very least we would expect here is a question, not a rhetorical question but a genuine one—the speaker does not recognize Yahweh at first.

Secondly, there is a question in v. 2 as well, which is a genuine question asking for information: 'Why the red stains on your clothes?' Surely this is another indication that the first question is a real one too, not merely a rhetorical one. Both questions reflect the actual emotions of someone confronted by an extraordinary sight, like Moses confronted by the burning bush (Exod. 3.3) or Gideon by the angel of the Lord sitting under the oak at Ophrah (Judg. 6.11-24), or Daniel

1. E.g. RSV; B. Duhm, *Das Buch Jesaia* (Göttingen: Vandenhoeck & Ruprecht, 3rd edn, 1914), pp. 433-34; G.H. Box, *The Book of Isaiah* (London: Pitman, 1908), p. 327; R.J. Jones, 'Isaiah 56–66', in *Peake's Commentary on the Bible* (Edinburgh: Nelson 1962), p. 533; J.L. McKenzie, *Second Isaiah* (AB; New York: Doubleday, 1967), pp. 186-87; C. Westermann, *Isaiah 40–66* (OTL; London: SCM Press, 1969), p. 380; C. Stuehlmueller, 'Isaiah 40–66', in *Jerome Biblical Commentary* (London: Geoffrey Chapman, 1969), p. 384; R.N. Whybray, *Isaiah 40–66* (NCB; London: Oliphants, 1975), pp. 253-54.

2. Alonso Schökel describes them as 'questions which pretend ignorance' (*Manual of Hebrew Poetics*, p. 152). Cf. Westermann, *Isaiah 40–66*, pp. 380-81.

by the vision of four great beasts and the Ancient of Days (Dan. 7.15-16). His first reaction is to ask, 'Who can this extraordinary looking person be?', and then, when the figure introduces himself as Yahweh, 'In that case', he asks, 'why do you look like somebody who has just come from working in a winepress?'

Much depends, of course, on the meaning of the rest of the question in v. 1. It consists of a description of the approaching figure in two exactly parallel clauses introduced by the demonstrative *zeh*: Who is (A) this person coming from Edom... and (B) this person glorious in his apparel...? Each clause is divided into two halves, and it seems to me that it is the semantic opposition between these two halves that gives us the clue to what the description means. In both clauses the first half draws on traditional language and imagery and is easy to understand in the context of an anthropomorphic description of Yahweh. He comes from Edom, as in the Song of Deborah (Judg. 5.4) and elsewhere (Deut. 33.2; Hab. 3.3), and he is 'clothed with majesty' as in Ps. 104.1 (*hôd weḥādār lābaštā*).

The other half of each clause, in contrast, is extremely unexpected and unconventional, and has the effect of confusing and perhaps frightening the speaker. If this is the longed-for return of Yahweh to Zion, referred to in 40.10 ('Behold the Lord God comes with might'), 52.8 ('for eye to eye they see the return of the Lord to Zion') and elsewhere, then it is not at all what was expected. Can this be Yahweh, or is it someone else? Like Yahweh, he is coming, as of old, from the direction of Edom, and, like Yahweh, he is 'clothed with majesty'. But he is also *ḥamûṣ begādîm* and *ṣō'eh*. Whatever these words mean, as applied to Yahweh, they must surely refer to some un-Yahweh-like features of the description in order to explain the speaker's bewildered questions—at first, Who can this be, and then, if it is Yahweh, Why does he look like this?

A widespread interpretation of the verse involves translating *ḥamûṣ begādîm* as 'in crimsoned garments' (RSV) or the like, perhaps suggesting colours fit for a king, and emending the second participle to *ṣō'ēd* 'marching' (RSV).[1] The first problem with this interpretation is

---

1. E.g. Symmachus, Vulgate, RSV; R. Lowth, *Isaiah: A New Translation* (London, 1779); T.K. Cheyne, *The Prophecies of Isaiah*, II (London, 1881), p. 100; Box, *Isaiah*, p. 327; G.A. Smith, *The Book of Isaiah XL–LXVI* (London, 1910), p. 443; McKenzie, *Second Isaiah*, p. 187; Westermann, *Isaiah 40–66*, p. 380.

that it completely removes the point of the speaker's two questions. If there is nothing odd about Yahweh's appearance, as he marches majestically back from Edom, dressed like a king in glorious crimson garments, there is nothing to explain the speaker's apparent bewilderment. The other problem concerns the precise meaning of the two Hebrew words $ḥ^a mûṣ$ and $ṣō'eh$.

Verse 2 implies that $ḥ^a mûṣ$ means something like 'red, stained with red wine', for the same $b^e gādîm$ that are described as $ḥ^a mûṣ$ in v. 1 are described in v. 2 as 'red and looking as though they had been in a wine-press'. BDB suggests that Syriac *'ethamaṣ* ('to blush, be ashamed') might provide a possible etymology, but it is not a very convincing one. In a context where it is associated with the terms *gat* 'wine vat', *pûrâ* 'wine-press', *dārak* 'to tread grapes' and *šākar* 'to get drunk', the ordinary everyday Hebrew word *ḥōmeṣ* 'vinegar' surely provides a much better explanation. There is also probably a wordplay in the choice of the Edomite place-name *boṣrâ*, in preference to the conventional Paran or Se'ir as parallel to Edom in v. 1, playing on its association with *bōṣēr* 'grape-picker', *bāṣîr* 'vintage' and so on.[1] So should we not translate $ḥ^a mûṣ$ 'winestained', if that is what is meant, however incongruous an image of Yahweh it conjures up?

The first thing to say about the other word, $ṣō'eh$, is that, whatever it means, it too is incongruous in a description of Yahweh. Apart from this passage it occurs three times in the Hebrew Bible, twice in the context of imprisonment and oppression (Isa. 51.14; Jer. 48.12), and once of a prostitute (Jer. 2.20). It has become customary in modern times, mainly for etymological reasons, to take it in the sense of 'stooping, cowed, unresisting': the prisoner is 'bowed down' (RSV; cf. NEB 'he that cowers'), and the prostitute 'sprawls in promiscuous vice' (NEB). With that background it surely cannot mean in Isaiah 63, as some have suggested, 'with his head bent back proudly' or the like.[2] In Jewish tradition, followed by the King James Version, the verb is usually glossed as $l^e ṭalṭel$ 'to wander from place to place' like gypsies or travellers with no fixed abode.[3] Again it surely cannot mean

---

1. Cf. Alonso Schökel, *Manual of Hebrew Poetics*, p. 30.
2. E.g. Gesenius, Delitzsch: see Cheyne, *The Prophecies of Isaiah*, p. 100; P.-E. Bonnard, *Le Second Isaïe* (Paris: Gabalda, 1972), p. 436.
3. E.g. Kimḥi, Ibn Ezra, J. Skinner, *Isaiah XL–LXVI* (Cambridge: Cambridge University Press, 1902), p. 195 ('travelling'): cf. A. Even-Shoshan, *Hammillon hehadaš* (Jerusalem: Kiryat Sefer, 1980), V, p. 2249.

'marching' or 'striding' (RSV). Whether we take the sense of 'stooping' or the traditional Jewish one of 'wandering from place to place', the term, like $h^a m\hat{u}s$, conjures up a picture of Yahweh acting out of character. He is wearing the majestic royal garments that befit him— but they look as if they are stained with wine; his great strength, as of the Lord of heaven and earth, is evident ($b^e r\bar{o}b\ k\bar{o}h\hat{o}$)[1]—but he looks lost and weary. That explains the speaker's bewilderment. Who can this ambiguous figure be?

Yahweh's answer is usually understood to be an announcement of victory and salvation, taking $s^e d\bar{a}q\hat{a}$ in the sense of 'victory, vindication' (RSV): 'It is I, who announce that right has won the day, I who am strong to save' (NEB). This follows logically from the removal of all the dirt and weariness from the description of Yahweh in the preceding question, and it is then a quite conventional picture of Yahweh returning to Zion bringing news of victory. But if we retain the ambiguity of the description and the bewilderment of the questioner, then the answer might have a different nuance. The first part also addresses the speaker's doubts: 'It is I. I am speaking $bis^e d\bar{a}q\hat{a}$ 'in righteousness = truthfully' (JB 'with integrity'; cf. 45.23; 48.1). The sense would then be: '(Do not be put off by appearances.) Believe me, it is I, Yahweh, mighty to save.'

II

Verse 2. The speaker's second question needs little further comment, except to re-emphasize the striking incongruity of the imagery. According to this verse Yahweh looks like a $d\bar{o}r\bar{e}k\ b^e gat$ 'a treader of grapes'. The image of God trampling on his enemies (including 'the virgin daughter of Zion', Lam. 1.15; cf. Isa. 63.3; Rev. 19.15) occurs elsewhere, but here he actually looks like 'a treader of grapes', that is to say, like someone who has been working in a wine-press, tired, sweaty, his clothes stained with the juice of the grapes.

Most of the verbs in the next section (vv. 3-6), after the first one, $d\bar{a}rakt\hat{i}$ 'I have trodden', appear to be modal (imperfects with w^e), corresponding to the implied modality in v. 1, 'Who could this be?', and suggesting perhaps the extraordinary, almost unreal nature of the scene described: 'trampling on them myself... my clothes spattered

---

1. Cf. Whybray, *Isaiah 40–66*, p. 254 ('victory'); Bonnard, *Le Second Isaïe*, p. 436 ('justice').

with their lifeblood... I was panic-stricken...'[1] Jewish tradition and KJV consistently translate them as futures. The unconventional imagery of this passage may well be reflected in what seems to be a quite consistent and deliberate choice of verb forms. They are difficult, if not impossible, to translate, but that is no reason to emend them all to simple narrative past tenses with *waw* consecutive, as *BHS* and others recommend.[2] Surely it must be significant that the only normal past tenses in the text as it stands describe the successful completion of the task, in traditional theological language (*ûšᵉnat gᵉ'ûlay bā'â* 'the year when my people are redeemed had come' and *wattōša' lî zᵉrō'î* 'Then my own arm saved me...'), while the other, less conventional verbs are consistently modal.

Yahweh's answer explains why he is looking so weary and bedraggled. There was no one to help him. He had to do the whole job by himself. This is repeated four times, twice in the first line (*lᵉbaddî* and *'ên-'îš 'ittî*) and twice in v. 5, where once again we find radical anthropomorphism. The idea that the one God, creator of heaven and earth, acts alone and needs no one to help him is a familiar one, especially in Isaiah 40–66. But this is different: here Yahweh is described as wanting help, indeed looking round desperately for help. The verb *hištōmēm* is used of someone 'crushed to the ground' by his enemies and 'made to sit in darkness like those long dead' (Ps. 143.3-4) and of a man sick with terror (Dan. 8.17, 27). It is applied to Yahweh twice: here, and in a similar context in 59.16. Unlike *ḥᵃmûṣ* and *ṣō'eh* in v. 1, its meaning is well known. It differs from the other intransitive stems of the root *šāmam* (qal and niphal) only in being restricted to personal subjects. While the qal and niphal forms are applied to the devastation and desolation of lands and cities as well, the hithpolel form is used only of human beings and Yahweh, of psychological or emotional devastation, as it were, not physical.

The extreme anthropomorphism implied by the application of this verb to God has once again been hard for commentators and translators to accept. One way of avoiding it is to reduce the force of the

---

1. Cf. A.B. Davidson, *Hebrew Syntax* (Edinburgh: T. & T. Clark, 1894), pp. 90-95; J.F.A. Sawyer, *A Modern Introduction to Biblical Hebrew* (London: Routledge & Kegan Paul, 1976), pp. 86-89.
2. E.g. Duhm, *Jesaia*, p. 434; Box, *Isaiah*, p. 327; McKenzie, *Second Isaiah*, p. 186; Bonnard, *Le Second Isaïe*, p. 434; Whybray, *Isaiah 40–66*, p. 254. Skinner tries to understand MT as it stands (*Isaiah XL–LXVI*, p. 196).

word by rendering it as 'wondered' (59.16 AV, RSV; 63.5 AV),
suggesting mild surprise, or 'amazed, aghast' (63.5 NEB). Jerome goes
farther in this anti-anthropomorphic direction with *quaesivi* 'asked,
inquired'. As well as weakening the effect, this introduces a new and
quite irrelevant anthropomorphism, namely the idea that God did not
have the wisdom to realize that he had no allies in his fight against
evil. Others introduce the notion of moral outrage: '(Yahweh) was
outraged (NEB) or appalled (RSV) that no one intervened' (59.16).[1]
But this moral dimension in the word *hištōmēm* seems on the face of
it unlikely. Surely in this context we need to understand it in its ordinary sense of shock and horror, as of someone panic-stricken and
aware both of the enormity of the task to be done and of the fact that
there is no one in the world to help him do it. In the second half of the
book of Isaiah, where images of Yahweh include those of a woman in
labour, gasping and panting (42.14), and of a midwife assisting at the
birth of a baby (66.9), not to mention that of Yahweh wandering
wearily back from work, his clothes looking as if they are stained
with the juice of grapes, we have no justification for playing down the
anthropomorphism expressed by this verb, or any of the other radical
images in this passage.

Another important point that has to be made about Yahweh's speech
is that the same ambiguity or vacillation which was identified in vv. 1
and 2 runs through this also. Alongside those striking glimpses of
God's stained garments, his loneliness and his horror, we find conventional references to his wrath, his day of vengeance and the saving
power of his arm. In one verse he is the subject of both *hištōmēm* 'to
be horrified' and *hôšîaʿ* 'to save', just as in v. 1 he is both 'coming
forth from Edom', as in days of old, and 'wearily stooping', both
'glorious in his apparel' and 'in blood-stained clothes'. He suffers, and
at the same time inflicts suffering.

There is also vacillation between the image of the weary labourer
returning from the winepress and the bloodstained warrior returning
from the scene of carnage on the day of judgment. The figure is that
of a bloodstained warrior, but the red stains on his clothes make him
look like someone who has been working in a wine-press; and this
leads to a comparison between a bloody battle in which he crushes his
enemies and the trampling of grapes in a winepress.[2] But the sense is

1. Cf. Cheyne, *The Prophecies of Isaiah*, p. 101.
2. Cf. Joel 4.13 (English 3.13); Lam. 1.15. Westermann sees an allusion here

clear throughout. The poet portrays Yahweh not as a triumphant gloating warrior, swaggering back from battle, unmoved by the enormity of what he has had to do, but as tired and bloodstained, barely recognizable, as someone who knows what it is to suffer.

One final point about this remarkable passage concerns its relationship to the passages immediately preceding and following it. The phrase *š^{e}nat g^e'ûlay* 'the year of my redeemed ones' in v. 4 (RSV footnote) picks up the reference to 'the redeemed of Yahweh' in the picture of redemption at the end of the previous chapter (62.11-12). Redemption, especially in these chapters, involves the ruthless crushing of the forces of injustice. The 'victory' or 'salvation' at the climax of the picture in v. 5 is made possible by Yahweh's wrath ('my wrath upheld me')—anger, that is, at the injustice done to his people. It was that anger that gave him strength to fight against the oppressor, and spurred him on to crush and humiliate them so mercilessly.

Those called 'redeemed of Yahweh' feature just as prominently in the following passage, which contains some other important points of continuity as well. It is a hymn in praise of Yahweh's love for his people: 'I will tell of Yahweh's loving actions (*h^{a}sādîm*)... all that he has done for them in his deep love...' Four words for 'love' are used, including *rah^{a}mîm*, a term of special significance in these chapters (e.g. 49.13-14). *hôšîa'* 'to save' and *gā'al* 'to redeem' both reappear. But most extraordinary, almost as though intended as a comment on the immediately preceding passage we have been considering, is the phrase *b^{e}kol-ṣārātām lō' ṣār* in v. 9: 'in all their affliction, he was afflicted' (KJV, RSV). As one would expect, most commentators cannot take this and emend the text: e.g. 'in all their troubles. It was no envoy...' (NEB).[1] Kimhi makes sense of the Hebrew text as it stands and glosses it with the sentence *wattiqṣar napšô ba'^{a}mal yiśrā'ēl* 'he [God] could not endure the suffering of Israel' (of course, he adds, *w^{e}hakkōl derek māšāl* 'everything is by way of allegory'). I see no reason why we too should not try to understand the text as it stands,

to the Babylonian myth of the battle between Marduk and Tiamat (*Isaiah 40–66*, pp. 382-83), and in a Ugaritic parallel the goddess Anat returns home from battle covered in blood.

1. Cf. LXX, Old Latin; Skinner, *Isaiah XL–LXVI*, p. 200; Westermann, *Isaiah 40–66*, p. 385; Whybray, *Isaiah 40–66*, p. 257; Bonnard, *Le Second Isaïe*, p. 443.

especially since, as we have seen, there seems to be a surprising consistency in the language and imagery used here.[1]

III

To go back to Alonso Schökel's comment on images with which we began, we might ask the question, What kind of 'formless experience' preceded the extraordinary imagery of this passage? If we place it alongside a number of similar passages in Isaiah 40–66, it is not hard to recognize behind the poet's images an experience of his God Yahweh that is consistent and convincing. Possibly in his own suffering, or in that of the community where he lives, the poet has encountered the human face of Yahweh in a peculiarly intimate way. Perhaps the term that best sums up his experience of Yahweh is $rah^a m\hat{i}m$, with its earthy associations with a mother's physiological closeness to the baby in her womb (cf. 49.14-15; 46.3-4).[2] This experience inspired the images he uses: the mother going through the pains of childbirth for him (42.14), the remorseful husband swearing almost on bended knee never to lose his temper again (54.7-10), the midwife attending the birth of a baby (66.9),[3] and the bloodstained soldier, returning from fighting his battle (63.1-6), alone, weary, unrecognized. The common theme in all these images is the deep, close, comforting involvement of Yahweh in the struggle for justice and freedom in the world: 'the year of my redeemed ones has come' (63.6).

As we have seen, not every one has been able to relate to some of these radical images, and elaborate means have been sought to remove them or reduce their effectiveness. But in view of other radical innovations in these chapters, notably the new emphasis on explicit monotheism and the analysis of vicarious suffering in Isaiah 53, it is hard to deny that they are there in the Hebrew text, as Jewish traditionalists like Kimḥi, as well as the KJV and others, have acknowledged, and it is a sign of the times that modern commentators have begun to take such things seriously again.

1. Cf. Smith, *Isaiah XL–LXVI*, p. 450; I.W. Slotki, *Isaiah* (London: Soncino Press, 1949), p. 307.

2. Cf. Trible, *God and the Rhetoric of Sexuality*, pp. 31-59; Ruether, *Sexism and God-Talk*, p. 56; McFague, *Metaphorical Theology*, pp. 169-70.

3. J.F.A. Sawyer, 'The Daughter of Zion and the Servant of the Lord in Isaiah: A Comparison', *JSOT* 44 (1989), pp. 89-107.

What are the implications of this for 'metaphorical theology'? The earliest interpretation of the passage in Christian tradition comes in Revelation, where it is Christ who is 'clad in a robe dipped in blood' and who will 'tread the wine-press of the fury of the wrath of God the Almighty' (Rev. 19.13-15). It was later also related to the crucifixion. There is, for example, in Christian art the famous scene derived from Augustine, in which the great wooden frame of a wine-press is modified to represent a cross, and, instead of grape-juice, it is the blood of Christ that flows out into a chalice beneath.[1] Both of these interpretations explain the extraordinary ambiguity of the passage by reference to the person of Christ, both divine and human, both glorious, powerful and life-giving on the one hand, and suffering, tortured, weary, on the other. They also voice the problem posed by a model of God that has been hard for commentators to accept.

But, as Calvin pointed out, the passage is actually about Yahweh, not Jesus, and thus must provide scriptural authority for a model of God rather different from the traditional ones.[2] To end as we began with McFague's 'metaphorical theology' and her notion of 'God as friend', such an image shifts the emphasis from transcendence and once-for-all salvation in a father/child mode, as she says, to a continuing adult relationship marked by sacrifice, suffering and solidarity with others: 'God is the friend who makes sacrifices on our behalf... co-operates with gifts of power, perseverance and insight... and when we fall... forgives us'.[3] In Genesis, words containing the root 'ṣb are used both of the 'pain' and 'toil' of Eve and Adam, and of the pain that Yahweh felt in his heart when he saw the evil that was being done on the earth he had created.[4] Isa. 63.10 is another example. For those who have eyes to see, the Hebrew Bible contains many 'proof-texts' for such alternative models of God. Isa. 63.1-6 is surely one of the most poignant.

1. Cf. L. Lee, G. Seddon and F. Stephen (eds.), *Stained Glass* (London: Mitchell Beazley, 1976), p. 140.

2. G.A. Smith, quoting Calvin, finds here a description of 'the passion, the agony, the unshared and unaided effort which the Divine Saviour passes through for his people' (*Isaiah XL–LXVI*, p. 433). Cf. Skinner, *Isaiah XL–LXVI*, p. 194; Slotki, *Isaiah*, p. 307; J.F.A. Sawyer, *Isaiah*, II (Philadelphia: Westminster Press, Edinburgh: St Andrews Press, 1986), pp. 195-96.

3. McFague, *Metaphorical Theology*, p. 186.

4. Cf. C. Westermann, *Genesis* (Philadelphia: Fortress Press, 1984), I, pp. 410-11.

Part II

EZEKIEL

EZEKIEL 16: ABANDONED CHILD,
BRIDE ADORNED OR UNFAITHFUL WIFE?[*]

M.G. Swanepoel

ABSTRACT

Ezekiel 16.1-63 uses different metaphors in bringing its message home. For instance it uses the shocking metaphor of immorality in order to eliminate the false confidence in human merit. We find Yahweh in this text as a outraged and exasperated lover. The pendulum swings in Ezekiel 16, metaphorically, from an abandoned child of suspect parentage (judgment) to ceremonies of fetching the bride (restoration); from a wedding (restoration) to a prostitute who pays her lovers (judgment); and from the disgraceful conduct of her daughters (judgment) to a new everlasting covenant (restoration). This is a mirror image from life with a meaning for life. Opposites meet in this text. Here is magnificent mercy, regardless of filth and vileness; and then the love of Yahweh in spite of the evil of human beings. The purpose: A new understanding and appreciation of Yahweh.

1. *Introduction*

Surely one of the most gripping units in the book of Ezekiel is ch. 16. Yet scholars like Gowan (1985: 65) are of the opinion that this important part of the book of Ezekiel cannot stand on its own but can only be discussed in connection with other texts. The message of Ezekiel 16 is also described as 'shocking' or 'unacceptable' (Gowan 1985: 66). Here we see the Lord in his love mortified by an abandoned child to whom he had shown compassion. Therefore Lemke (1984: 176) justifiably remarks on Ezekiel 16: 'All the rot and vileness of the nation had to be exposed mercilessly; all the false confidence in human merit, all the facile claims on God's mercy had to be undercut radically once and for all'.

---

[*]   This article is a translation of an Afrikaans article that appeared in *Skrif en Kerk* 11 (1990): 80-102.

This section has also led to widely differing interpretations. Lang (1981: 137) quotes some of these views. He quotes Koch, who says, 'In all of world literature, there is hardly a document that portrays the history of its own people in such a negative and guilt-stricken light'. And Jaspers refers to 'sexual metaphors in Ezekiel 16 and 23 which occur with schizophrenia' (Lang 1981: 62).

Greenberg (1983: 299) however gives an interesting view: 'By extending the metaphor in time, Ezekiel provided the adulterous wife of Hosea and Jeremiah with a biography'. It is very clear that Ezekiel 16 makes use of metaphors like that of the unfaithful wife to say something to the Jerusalem of his own time as well as to the children of God today. The content of the metaphor has far-reaching consequences for the relationship between the Lord and his children. Lemke (1984: 176) speaks of Yahweh as the 'outraged and exasperated lover, rather than a tender and forgiving parent...' when he thinks of Ezekiel 16.

Ezek. 16.1-63 forms a neat, well-defined unit. It begins in 16.1 with the conventional *Wortereignis*-formula which introduces most of the prophecies in the book of Ezekiel. The appropriate conclusion of the unit comes at the end of 16.63 with the conventional *Gottesspruch*-formula. Ezek. 16.1-63 is in addition the longest prophecy in the book of Ezekiel (Greenberg 1983: 292).

2. *Text-Critical Notes*

The aim of this investigation is to establish the theology of Ezekiel 16. In order to achieve this a thorough study of the Hebrew Masoretic text (*BHS*) is necessary. Some text-critical observations are important in this case:

16.6b-b. The original LXX and the Syriac translation, together with a few other manuscripts, leave this part out because of the possibility of dittography. In my opinion the MT reading should be retained because the repetition emphasizes the idea.

16.7 c-c. The reading of the text-critical note is בעת עדים or בעדים. This may be translated, 'in the time of menstruation'. It makes better sense in the context if the MT, where בעדי עדיים may be translated as 'finest ornaments', is followed.

16.15b-b. The MT reading is לו־יהי (it was for him). According to Fuhs (1984: 83), 'the end of the verse in H is incomprehensible'. The LXX throws no light on the matter. Zimmerli (1979: 325) points out that 'this undoubted secondary element in the text is interpreted by Halevy (Toy) as לו יהי לו (whoever he may be)'. Here perhaps we should say that we do not know. Fuhs (1984: 83) is of the opinion that perhaps it should be left untranslated. The MT reading is therefore retained for want of a better alternative.

16.23b-b. According to the text-critical note this section is wanting in the LXX, namely אוי אוי לך (woe, woe to you). It does not make much difference to the meaning, and so the MT can readily be retained.

16.24a. The text-critical note points out that many other manuscripts vocalize גַב and then translate it as 'platform' or 'artificially constructed hill', according to Wevers (1969: 99). The MT vocalizes as גֵב (dam, hollow or bed). It looks as if the text-critical note makes more sense in the context. I therefore agree with Wevers.

16.29b. The text-critical note indicates that the LXX does not include this word. It may perhaps have been added. The MT reading is כנען (land of commerce). I agree with Wevers (1969: 99) that Canaan here has the possible meaning of 'trader' and is used as an adjective. There is therefore no reason to deviate from the MT.

16.53a. According to the text-critical note the reading is ושבתי (if I change). The MT reading is וְשָׁבְתִי (captivity of). The latter does not make sense in the context. The text-critical change is therefore preferable.

16.57a. The note proposes ערותך (your nakedness) instead of רעתך (your wickedness). The note makes better sense in the context.

16.57c. The MT reading is ארם (Aram/Syria). The text-critical note is אדם (Edom), on the basis of the Syriac translation of the LXX and many other manuscripts. The Edom-motif appears in Ezek. 25.12 and 36.5. The Aramaeans are also not shown elsewhere as enemies of Jerusalem (Greenberg 1983: 290). The LXX is not however a good external criterion for accepting the note. I stand, therefore, by the MT.

16.61. The LXX (Latin translation) of the reading of papyrus 967 is in Hebrew בקחתי (I take). The text-critical amendment is preferable to the MT, because Yahweh is the subject and nobody else.

3. *The Structure*

When we study the structure of Ezekiel 16 we find some interesting phenomena. The structural analysis of ch. 16 is therefore of cardinal importance for the understanding of the pericope.

As has already been said, Ezek. 16.1 begins with the conventional *Wortereignis*-formula which we find 45 times in the book of Ezekiel (cf. von Rabenau 1955–56: 681). The fact that the word of Yahweh comes to his prophet is in very truth an event. This event is of decisive importance for the whole of the rest of the pericope. It can justifiably be accepted that 16.1 is the matrix in which everything that follows is embedded.

The *waw*-consecutive and imperfect tense in 16.1 is followed by direct speech in 36.2, where the prophet is addressed as בן-אדם (son of man), and is instructed to act as an intermediary between Yahweh and Jerusalem.

3.1. *From Abandoned Child to Beauty Queen*

It is very clear that (16.3-14) forms sub-pericope A. The sub-pericope begins with the messanger's formula in 16.3 and ends with the *Gottesspruch*-formula at the end of 16.14. The dominant role played by the first-person subject, Yahweh, is striking. Yahweh is in control of every event enacted in this sub-pericope. Jerusalem's father was an Amorite and her mother a Hittite, according to v. 3. In 16.4, 5 the treatment of the newborn baby is discussed (Greenberg 1983: 274). McKeating states unequivocally that Ezekiel has a preference for 'metaphors involving filth, dirt and loathsome matter'.

The alternation of first-person verbs with second-person verbs shows the caring activities and personal relationship which develop between Yahweh and the abandoned child. The *Stichwort* דם (blood) is used in close relation with חיה (life) in 16.7. Wevers (1969: 96) rightly observes that Ezekiel cleverly plays on the term 'blood'. A new metaphor is used in 16.7, namely that of רבבה (plant of the field), with the aim of placing the emphasis on life, vitality and growth. It is clear that the foundling child thrives under Yahweh's loving care.

It is therefore not strange that Yahweh's care and tender compassion result, in 16.8, in a ברית (bond) with the now young and nubile girl (Greenberg 1983: 276). Here we find the covenant formula (Greenberg 1983: 278), and Zimmerli (1979: 340) is therefore correct in his opinion that this mention of a betrothal is based on Yahweh's initiative. 'On her own she had no status for marriage. Then the second wonder occurred'. The cleansing of menstrual blood (דם) links back to v. 7 and forward to v. 22 (Greenberg 1983: 278).

Yahweh's abundant mercy is depicted further when he clothes (כנפי)

the girl to cover her nakedness (cf. Gen. 3). Wevers (1969: 96) shows
that the covering of nakedness is a symbol of marriage. The girl now
belongs to Yahweh (Greenberg 1983: 277). This process of adorning
and beautifying (16.9, 10) leads the girl to a bridal crown (Wevers
1969: 96), and in 16.12 she is seen as a princess (Greenberg 1983:
278). The profusion of clothes and gifts is probably evidence of
Egyptian influence, according to Fuhs (1984: 82). This girl is breath-
takingly beautiful (ותיפי במאד מאד) and it is understandable that she
goes out (ויצא) among the nations and wins fame for her 'Lover' (בהדרי)
(16.14). The nations (בגוים) is a term that has a political meaning. The
Gottesspruch-formula in 16.14 places the seal on the fact that Yahweh
is the subject of every love affair. Sub-pericope A (16.3-14) can
correctly be described in the phrase: *From abandoned child to beauty
queen*.

3.2. *Unfaithful*

Sub-pericope B begins with a *waw*-adversative in 16.15. This is also
the beginning of a succession of second-person singular verbs in the
imperfect in which the reckless misdeeds of Jerusalem are emphasized.
The frequent appearance of the root זני (fornication) is noticeable
throughout the sub-pericope, so that one can say that זני is the con-
tinous theme of this sub-pericope. Indeed this root appears in 16.15
(2×), 16, 17, 20, 21, 25, 26, 28 (2×), 29, 30, 31, 33 (2×) and 34 (2×).
Ezek. 16.34 concludes this pericope. The dissolute misdeeds have been
recorded. Two opposing הפך phrases form an *inclusio* in v. 34. The
two main verbs form a chiasmus (cf. Greenberg 1983: 293). This can
be regarded as a summary of the foregoing.

The sins of Israel are piled up high in sub-pericope B. Wevers
(1969: 98) shows convincingly that ותקחי (you took) appears in vv. 16,
17, 18 and 20, as well as נתתי in v. 19. In this way the emphasis is
placed on the idea that the gifts that Yahweh gave are now misused:
v. 16: the clothes are used for idolatry (sacred prostitution, according
to Greenberg 1983: 280); *v. 17*: the misuse of cultic objects: gold and
silver; *v. 19*: the misuse of food; *vv. 20-22*: the sacrifice of children
(newborn children are the result of fornication). It is therefore clear
that the gift has superseded the Given (Zimmerli: 1979: 343). In v. 22
there is a reference back to v. 6 with the repetition of the same phrase
מתבוססת בדמך (floundering in your blood). The object of this is to
accentuate the contrast between what Yahweh has done in A (vv. 3-14)

and what Jerusalem is doing now in B (vv. 15-34).

The lament in v. 23 is strengthened by the *Gottesspruch*-formula which is a reminder that it is Yahweh speaking. Notwithstanding this fact, there is an emphasis on the increase of fornication (ותרבי את־תזנותך), strengthened by the frequentative piel of פשׂק in v. 25 (Greenberg 1983: 282). From vv. 23 to 29 a number of political lovers are named: the Egyptians (v. 26), the Philistines (v. 27), the Assyrians (v. 28) and the Chaldaeans/Babylonians in v. 29 (cf. Greenberg 1983: 282). Each is representative of a specific political period in Israel's history. The shocking image of immorality is used to express Yahweh's aversion to the fact that in his love for Jerusalem he has been forsaken. Verses 23 to 29 in fact say that every era in Israel's history has been characterized by infidelity and disobedience.

We are not even spared the greatest shock. The shocking fact is that 'you do not receive a fee, you give it' (v. 34). Maarsingh is surely referring, among others, to this section when he says of the book Ezekiel, that there are parts that chill one to the bone (Le Roux: 1987: 190). That you pay your men instead of them paying you is surely the summit of immorality. In v. 32 the wife is described as adulterous and unfaithful (piel of נאף). It must however be remembered that Zimmerli (1979: 343) is probably correct in asserting that the fornication on the high places points rather to the metaphor than the deed itself. The book of Ezekiel wishes to express in this way Israel's shocking departure from Yahweh. The fornication is a metaphor for Israel's search for political security apart from Yahweh.

3.3. *Judgment*

Sub-pericope C (16.35-43) is introduced with the messenger formula (v. 35) and an inferential לכן in 16.36. This לכן is, according to Fishbane (1984: 148), 'a legal nexus between the sins and the divine decision to punish them'. As a result of the great number of זני verbs, Jerusalem is now called זונה (whore). She has done it so often that it has became almost a proper name. The messenger formula (16.36) indicates that Yahweh is still in control of this moral crisis. Verse 36 refers again to זני and relates it to v. 21 (the child murder). The punishment (לכן) in v. 37 consists in bringing the former lovers together, and 'then I will strip you naked before them so that they can see your whole body naked'. Nakedness is a constant theme in this sub-pericope. The nakedness (ערותך) that is revealed is a symbol of the loss of Yahweh's protection (Wevers 1969: 96). Fishbane (1984: 138) rightly says, 'She will be stripped naked before her lovers (thus reversing the robing motif of her youth)'. Yahweh is in full control of the punishment (vv. 36-38)—notice the large number of first-person verbs. Yahweh gathers the erstwhile lovers (v. 37). He judges (ושפטתיך) the adulterers and the shedders of blood. The end (דם) is like the beginning (דם) in v. 6 (Greenberg 1983: 286). In v. 39 he hands over the bad woman to the lovers. The punishment fits the revolting deeds of the unfaithful wife. God himself sends her to a violent death (Greenberg 1983: 294) in which the adulterous wife is stoned (vv. 40-41).

Yahweh remains in control of the action of this judgment, but it is important to note the fact that it is the erstwhile lovers who gather (קהל) against the woman and stone her (ורגמו) and burn her (v. 41). Of Yahweh it is said only that he will put an end to the fornication (והשבתיך מזונה). Within this judgment there is yet salvation. For Yahweh the ending of the fornication is more important than the violence of the punishment. All that happens is that Yahweh gives the lovers the opportunity to show themselves in their true colours. And now they do not spare their erstwhile darling. No, they are responsible for her return to the time when she lay defenceless and floundering in her own blood (v. 6) (Fishbane 1984: 138). It must happen in order to place Yahweh's gifts once again in the right perspective. The *Gottesspruch*-formula in 16.43 ratifies Yahweh's fury and anger, deserted by Jerusalem in his unbounded love.

3.4. *Like Mother, Like Daughter?*
Sub-pericope D begins with the exclamatic הנה in 16.44. It is followed by a משל (proverb), 'Like mother, like daughter', or 'She is a chip off the old block'. Verse 45 harks back to v. 3 with its reference to the mother as a Hittite and the father as an Amorite.

The influence of Jerusalem reaches further. Zimmerli (1979: 350) rightly refers to the second-person singular feminine suffix which suddenly changes to the plural. Thus the unity of the whole pericope is maintained by means of cross references. The same tune (message) is played throughout in another key (metaphor). In v. 46 there is a reference to a specific tradition about Samaria and Sodom. Jerusalem is the mother and Sodom and Samaria are her daughters. Greenberg (1983: 288) is apparently correct when he remarks: 'Since the daughter's depravity derives from bad heredity, her mother's behavior is wholly assimilated to hers (though it is nowhere described to have been so)'. We can regard vv. 44 to 47 as a sub-unit (D1) under the heading: *Like mother, like daughter*.

Verse 48 is a new sub-unit (D2) on the basis of the *Schur*-formula plus the *Gottesspruch*-formula. The theme of Sub-unit D2 (vv. 48-58) is: Jerusalem's bad sisters look 'good' in comparison with her shameless behaviour. The sins of Sodom are named in v. 49. Here 'food in plenty' (שׂבעת־לחם) and 'self-indulgence' (ושׁלות השׁקמ) are used as synonyms (cf. Greenberg 1983: 289). They stand in contrast to גאון, (pride), the complement of היה, and explain it. It is thus at the same time one of the characteristics, but also the cause of pride.

Samaria is used in v. 51 to present Jerusalem as an active subject. 'Your sins are so much more abominable than theirs that they appear innocent in comparison with you', according to the NEB translation of v. 52. Jerusalem gave her sisters the appearance of righteousness (בצדקתך) (feminine infinitive construct of צדק) by pleading for them.

However, in v. 53 Yahweh will change the fortunes (ושׁבתי) of Sodom, Samaria and Jerusalem. Notice the play on words between שׁבתי and שׁבית (captivity). Jerusalem's behaviour was more disgraceful than that of her daughters. Yet she benefitted (נחמ) them through her bad ways (v. 54). She had boasted of her superiority (v. 56). Zimmerli (1979: 351) describes the paradox thus: 'The one who sinned more than Sodom or Samaria defends these sisters before God's judgment of the world and effects their rehabilitation'. Greenberg (1983: 289) notes meaningfully: 'Furthermore, the cases of her sisters being better than hers, their restoration will take precedence over hers (note the order in vv. 53, 55) so that hers can be said to be incidental to theirs ("among them")'. To understand the full humiliating impact of this, we must look at the negative traditions surrounding Samaria and Sodom in tradition criticism. Now it is the arch-nemies Edom and the Philistines who jeer at Jerusalem.

The *Gottesspruch*-formula in v. 58 sets the seal on the punishment for the 'lewd and abominable conduct', which Jerusalem now must bear (נשׂאתימ). The guilt is indicated by the indicative/jussive third-person perfect of נשׂא. The guilt (through the punishment of Yahweh) is a reproach in the eyes of the nations (erstwhile lovers). A recognition of guilt is required, and the acceptance of the accompanying reproach. This is also the conclusion of sub-pericopes D and E. The bridge between D and E is כאשׁר עשׂית (v. 59), 'as you have done', which agrees with כל כאשר עשׂית in v. 54 (cf. vv. 48, 51; and cf. Greenberg 1983: 297).

3.5. *Mercy?*

Sub-pericope E begins in 16.59 with the double emphatic כי (cf. Greenberg 1983: 291) followed by the messengers formula. We find here a reference again to the ברית (covenant) that was made in v. 8 (cf. Greenberg 1983: 291) with an addition, namely 'for ever' (עולם), as well as an alternation between the first and second person. This alternation of the subject between Yahweh and Jerusalem emphasizes Jerusalem's responsibility for its own hopeless condition, as well as the action Yahweh takes to relieve that condition. The second-person verbs (Jerusalem) contrast with the first-person verbs (Yahweh). This is a stylistic characteristic of this sub-pericope.

The idea of זכר (remember) figures strongly in this pericope and refers back to vv. 43 and 22. Zimmerli (1979: 352) strongly emphasises this idea: 'Against Jerusalem's "not remembering" v. 60 sets the gracious "remembering" by Yahweh, through which Jerusalem is to be brought to a right "remembering" (vv. 61, 63) with a sense of its own shame'. In this connection it is meaningful to notice the role played by כלם (vv. 61, 63).

ולא מבריתך (not according to your covenant) in v. 61 makes it clear that Sodom and Samaria are not accepted within the same covenant as Jerusalem, but show a wider covenant (cf. Zimmerli 1979: 353). Yahweh in v. 62 establishes the covenant (בריתי) with Jerusalem, and the basis of this covenant (as well as of the whole pericope) is found in the conventional *Erkenntnis*-formula, which is the basic formula in the book of Ezekiel. This is followed in v. 63 by למען תזכרי ובשׁת (so that you will remember and be ashamed) as the inevitable result of the first-person action of Yahweh in v. 62. The sub-pericope as well as the pericope as a whole is sealed with בכפרי (I cover/close), which formulates the idea of reconciliation as the culmination point. The idea of forgiveness stands in the forefront together with the *Erkenntnis*-formula in v. 62. The whole pericope closes with the *Gottesspruch*-formula in v. 63. Von Rabenau (1955–56: 678) correctly points out that this formula emphasises the authority of the argument 'des göttlichen "Ich"', as coming from Yahweh.

3.6. *Structural Synthesis*

Ezekiel 16 can be structurally analysed as follows:

A Yahweh Discourse

Wortereignis-formula	v. 1	
בן-אדם	v. 2	
messenger formula	v. 3	A
Gottesspruch-formula	v. 14	
waw-adversative	v. 15	
Gottesspruch-formula	v. 19	
Gottesspruch-formula	v. 23	B
summary: הפך	v. 34	
concluding לכן	v. 35	
messenger formula	v. 36	C
Gottesspruch-formula	v. 43	
exclamatic משל + הנה	v. 44	
	v. 47	
	v. 48	D
Gottesspruch-formula	v. 58	
double-emphatic כי +		
messenger formula	v. 59	
Erkenntnis-formula	v. 62	E
Gottesspruch-formula	v. 63	

There are two structures to be seen in Ezekiel 16. One is chiastic:

(vv. 3-14)	A	Yahweh's mercy
(vv. 15-34)	B	Jerusalem's sin
(vv. 35-43)	C	Yahweh's judgment
(vv. 44-58)	D	Jerusalem's sin
(vv. 59-63)	E	Yahweh's mercy

Here, on the one hand, Yahweh's judgment in the middle (C) is emphasized as the centre with B and D as the contributory cause. On the other hand the whole pericope is framed by God's mercy. This structure is intended to emphasize the consequences of Jerusalem's sin.

The diamond structure is climactic and begins and ends in a wedge structure with A and E as the high points.

vv. 3-14	A	Yahweh's mercy
vv. 15-34	B	Jerusalem's sin
vv. 35-43	C	Yahweh's judgment
vv. 44-58	D	Jerusalem's sin
vv. 59-63	E	Yahweh's mercy

Here Yahweh's mercy as the beginning (A) and the ending (E) is emphasized, while it is shown as the result of B and D. I prefer this structure because the *Wortereignis*-formula (A) and the *Erkenntnis*-formula (E) complement each other as the high points. The mercy of Yahweh is emphasized here as incomparable.

4. *Gattung*

The *Wortereignis*-formula, the messenger formula and the *Gottesspruch*-formulas that appear throughout in the pericope underline the fact that we are dealing here with the *Gattung* of the understanding of Yahweh.

Sub-pericope A (vv. 3-14) is rightly regarded by Fuhs (1984: 80) as a *Bildrede* and not an allegory. He is of the opinion that *Märchen* motifs are associated with the foundling child. Garner (1980: 132) thinks that this is a case of personification. Luc (1983: 139) speaks of the metaphor of the abandoned child. Eichrodt (1970: 202) also makes much of the folk-tale motif. In the original story there would be a wizard who saves the child by magic (Eichrodt 1970: 205).

Both Hosea and Jeremiah have similar motifs. This child, however, is adopted. God not only saves the child, he adopts her. He treats her as his own child and not as a slave. 'It is not that she is wonderful, but the care and gifts lavished on her by YHWH', says Greenberg (1983: 301).

I think that A is a *Bildrede*, with vv. 4-6 the picture of the abandoned child, v. 7 that of a plant, and vv. 8-15 that of a bride. There is an easy transition from one picture to the other, keeping in mind the one aim of converging different facets of the same message.

In sub-pericope B (vv. 15-34) we have the picture of fornication, which is a metaphor for idolatry (v. 16), temple prostitution (v. 17) and the resultant sacrifice of children (vv. 20-21). In vv. 26-29 the fornication is a metaphor for Jerusalem's foreign political relations with other countries. This picture of the adulterous woman carries through to v. 35. Sub-pericope C (vv. 35-43) is introduced by the messenger formula (v. 35) and a concluding לכן (v. 37), and it consequently reflects Yahweh's judgment and wrath over Jerusalem's bad behaviour when the adulterous woman is stoned.

In sub-pericope D (vv. 44-58) we again have a *Bildrede* that is developed around a proverb (משל) in v. 44: 'Like mother, like daughter'. This family or household theme is found throughout the whole pericope, for example, in v. 20, where we find children, in v. 46, and in v. 61, where the sisters undergo a surprising transformation (Greenberg 1983: 295).

In conclusion, sub-pericope E (vv. 59-63) is the climax of the divine argument. It begins with the messenger formula and concludes with the *Gottespruch*-formula. The *Erkenntnis*-formula in v. 62 is meaningful, and it confirms that it is possible to talk of the *Gattung* of *Erweiswort*. The *Erweiswort* is about the divine evidence of self-revelation (cf. Zimmerli 1965: 526 and Swanepoel 1987: 33). Thus Yahweh through the *Erweiswort* brings about a personal relationship with him.

To sum up, we can therefore say that the *Gattung* of the pericope is a Yahweh argument consisting of various *Bildreden*, a word of judgment and an *Erweiswort* as a word of salvation.

5. *Sitz im Leben*

Regarding the *Sitz im Leben* there is little clarity. Almost the whole history of Israel is encompassed in this single pericope. Traditionally Ezekiel 1–24 is typified as a judgment prophecy and is therefore dated before the fall of Jerusalem in 587 BCE. The structural analysis has already shown this hypothesis as problematical because the pericope closes with a salvation prophecy climax (cf. sub-pericope E). How can a salvation prophecy be possible before the fall of Jerusalem in 587 BCE? If we look at the centrality of the covenant (ברית) in this section and especially its everlastingness (v. 61), then we must ask the question whether the pericope does not equally well belong in a *Sitz im Leben* after 587 BCE. In this connection it is important to look at Ezekiel 34 and 37 (cf. Swanepoel 1987: 69 and 154). *The terminus ante quem* is at a time when the Babylonian exile belongs in the past, thus 500 BCE, while the *terminus post quem* is about 721 BCE with the fall of Samaria.

6. *Motifs, Traditions and Formulas*

Many motifs appear in ch. 16. Of these the Canaan motif in v. 3 is an interesting example. It is clear that the heathen origins of Jerusalem are here emphasized. Canaan is cursed by Noah in Gen. 9.25. The

Canaan motif also includes the reference to Amorites and Hittites. According to Fuhs (1984: 81), these heathen nations had to be driven out by Israel before they could occupy the land (cf. Deut. 7.1; Josh. 3.10 and 24.11).

The Canaan motif is linked to the abandoned child or foundling child motif in vv. 4-6. Eichrodt (1970: 202) calls it the fairy tale motif. In the original story it would be the wizard who saves the child by magic, but here the hero is Yahweh (cf. Eichrodt 1970: 205). We find the defenceless child also in Hos. 2.2 and Jer. 3.19.

However in Ezekiel 16 there is a drastic change. This is an adopted (heathen) child, whom God not only saves, but even adopts. He treats her as his own child and not as a slave.

Without more ado the *abandoned child motif* passes on to the *plant motif* in v. 7, which emphasizes vitality and growth. This motif uses the language of the creation story in Gen. 2.4-9. It harks back to the *creation tradition* (cf. Fuhs 1984: 81). In its turn the *plant motif* gives way to the *marriage motif* (cf. Fishbane 1984: 139) in vv. 8-14. Zimmerli too (1979: 340) speaks justifiably of 'ceremonies of fetching the bride'. This speaks of an intimate bond between God and humankind. If the first marvel is that Yahweh adopts the child, the second marvel is that he takes the child to wife (cf. Fuhs 1984: 81). Perhaps the plethora of the metaphors needs some explanation.

Zimmerli (1979: 335) rightly observes that in Ezekiel 16 the gap between the metaphor and the fact portrayed can easily disappear, and the reality referred to may arise directly out of the metaphor. There is a directness in the address, and 'from the very beginning everything is set within the realm of an address of accusation. The allegory is a "disclosure of abomination" (v. 2), upon which the threat of judgment can follow in a direct adress to the woman' (Zimmerli 1979: 335). This must have been part of a legal procedure presented as a form of accusation that was both revealing and explanatory. The reader is moved by the kindness and grace of Yahweh as the different metaphors succeeds each other rapidly (one expects an emotional climax), but this expectation is shattered (because of the unfaithful woman) to pave the way for the final climax of the sovereign grace of Yahweh.

The *covenant formula* (v. 8) is closely connected to this and emphasizes what it is about (cf. Greenberg 1983: 254, 277-78), namely, the personal relationship between God and humanity. The theme of the covenant figures strongly in the book of Ezekiel (cf. Ezek. 16.8, 59-62;

17.13-19; 20.37; 34.25; 37.26; 44.7, and especially the formulation in 16.60, namely והקימותי לך ברית עולם (I will establish/maintain my covenant with you for ever).

The plan of hope comes to the fore in the renewing of the Sinai covenant in the *covenant formula*, 'you are my people—I am your God' (cf. Kellermann 1971: 85). This formula does not appear in Ezekiel 16, but the idea certainly does. Therefore we can speak of a *covenantal theme*. Great emphasis is placed on salvation: a new day of salvation has dawned. An important qualification is added in v. 60— the new day of salvation lasts for ever (עולם). The absence of the covenant formula and the (accompanying) stress on the activities of Yahweh demonstrates the inadequacy of Jerusalem.

The motif of the *unfaithful wife* (זני) from vv. 15-34 is not an unfamiliar motif in the OT. We find it, among other places, in Isa. 1.21; 57.8; Jer. 2.20; 3.2, 6, 20; Ezek. 23.3, 8, 11, 12; Hos. 1.2. As has already been demonstrated in the structural analysis, this motif suggests the movement away from Yahweh, how the people try to 'desert' Yahweh in his love. This is also a metaphor for wrong political alliances (vv. 26-29), and for collusion with idols (vv. 17-19).

Even the child sacrifices (vv. 20-22) are related to this. For the children were apparently the products of temple prostitution in the service of Baal. Child sacrifices are also mentioned in Jer. 2.34, 3.24, 7.31, 19.5 and 32.35. They occur in times of great crisis. Eichrodt (1970: 207) shows that this happens when Yahwism merges into Canaanite religions.

Punishment for the unfaithfulness, adultery and child murder follows in v. 36. Here is the shocking exposure of the wife. Greenberg (1983: 286) says, 'This may be the earliest instance of what became a motif of hypersexuality in erotic literature'. The guilty deed (exposure before the lovers) comes back upon the guilty woman as a curse in the form of a punishment (exposure before Yahweh). Hereby both the adultery with the lovers (metaphor) and the immorality with idols (reality) are condemned. Here the sign and the action merge (cf. Zimmerli 1979: 347).

According to v. 38 there are two transgressions: adultery (נאפות) and bloodshed (ושפכת דם). Hence the erstwhile lovers devastate Jerusalem (the Yahweh marriage has run upon the rocks [?]), and Jerusalem returns to its beginning (v. 7), according to Greenberg (1983: 286). The end is like the beginning: in blood (דם). If a woman divorces her husband, she must be naked when she leaves him (v. 39), symbolizing the withdrawal of all her husband's goods (cf. Greenberg 1983: 287).

The punishment for adultery according to Deut. 22.21 and 24 is the stoning of the guilty woman. She is executed by stoning as a public punishment to give expression to the outrage of the community. Her body is also hacked/cut to pieces with their swords (v. 40). Those who execute the punishment are a קהל—a term used for a gathering of armed forces (Ezek. 17.17; 26.7; 32.3, 22; 38.4, 7, 13, 15) as well as of a host of foreign armies that descend upon Jerusalem (Ezek. 27.27, 34).

The motifs around *Samaria* and *Sodom* (vv. 44-58) also deserve our attention. Eichrodt (1970: 217) says that what we find here is a direct personification. The *Sodom motif* is also to be found in Genesis 18, Amos 4.11 and Isa. 1.9. In Gen. 19.5-9 Sodom is linked with sexual immorality. Wevers (1969: 102) points out that Sodom lies south of Jerusalem. 'Sodom is "little" in size not age, since it was destroyed before Judah ever existed', according to Greenberg (1983: 288).

Samaria, on the other hand, lies to the left and north of Jerusalem. In this case it is north of one looking towards the rising sun (cf. Greenberg 1983: 294). Samaria's sin is idolatry, according to 2 Kgs 17.7-18. Greenberg (1983: 288) also says, 'Samaria is "big" in size, not age, younger than Jerusalem, much larger than Judah (for which Jerusalem stands)'.

But the question remains: what is the function of the Sodom and Samaria motifs in this section? Obviously the Ezekiel text (v. 49) is judging self-satisfaction, pride and wealth with regard to Sodom. It is noteworthy that this aspect does not appear in Genesis 19. So it seems more likely that Sodom (and Samaria) are used here in a manner of comparison/metaphorically to emphasize the typical social conditions round about Jerusalem (cf. Zimmerli 1979: 350). What it is saying is that the daughters' (Samaria's and Sodom's) bad behaviour has been learned from the mother (Jerusalem).

In this connection Greenberg (1983: 288) points out that 'daughters' is the designation of smaller towns named in the company of large cities. Ezek. 26.6 with regard to Tyre, as well as Ezek. 30.18 with regard to Tahpanhes, are valid examples. Greenberg (1983: 294) is apparently correct in stating that Jerusalem's sins make the bad sisters' sins look good by comparison with hers. *Her* restoration is also an afterthought to that of the restoration of the bad sisters (cf. the order in v. 53). The behaviour of the sisters receives to a certain extent justification from v. 51.

This brings us to the tradition about Jerusalem, which is never mentioned by name in the book of Ezekiel, but which is always present in the background (cf. Zimmerli 1958: 84). The concept of Zion is used in the name Jerusalem. But because for Ezekiel the Zion tradition had led wrongly to a misplaced faith in Jerusalem's impregnability, he does not use the name of Zion.

The book of Ezekiel prefers to show that Yahweh's presence is the only security for Jerusalem. That is why Fuhs (1984: 82) justifiably believes that it is possible that the lot of Sodom and Samaria can change, because Jerusalem carries their guilt. It is clear that Jerusalem, with regard to the nations, fills a representative role in Yahweh's eyes. Jerusalem is jointly responsible before God for the bad behaviour of Sodom and Samaria.

The covenant theme is in fact ratified by the *Erkenntnis*-formula in v. 62. This formula appears at least 54 times in the book of Ezekiel: 'You/they shall know that I am the Lord'. Through this the recognition of God is revealed as the final goal and the proper conclusion of the *Gotteswort*. The recognition of Yahweh is thus an event that points to an act of Yahweh (cf. Zimmerli 1954: 12). Yahweh's dealings are directed towards humankind (cf. Zimmerli 1954: 14). The act must grip humankind and move towards a recognition, an understanding and an appreciation of Yahweh. Yahweh acts because he wants to attain this appreciation among humankind.

The *Erkenntnis* formula is also in my view the key to the understanding of ולא מבריתך (not according to your covenant). The emphasis is on the second person (Jerusalem) that forms part of the new covenant.

Because Yahweh does good to Jerusalem, he also does good to Samaria and Sodom within a wider covenant. Ostensibly the writer here wishes to place the emphasis on Jerusalem's responsibility for Samaria and Sodom before the Lord. 'Through the judgment God will lead His people so that they will be made ashamed of the overplus of grace shown to them and will be pleased to accept as a daughter the Canaanite Sodom which they had hitherto rejected as too sinful. By such action they will come to recognize their God and know who He is' (Zimmerli 1979: 353).

It is clear that in Ezekiel 16 we find a mixture of different traditions. We find the desert tradition (the abandoned child; cf. also Ezek.

20.10-26) and the Creation tradition (the young plant), as well as the tradition of the occupation of the land (Jerusalem's heathen origins) and the Zion tradition (Jerusalem). All these traditions are used in Ezekiel 16 to bring forth a new understanding, a new realization, a new knowledge of Yahweh. Therefore all these traditions are brought together under the denomination of the *Erkenntnis* formula (v. 62) as the closing formula of the pericope. The *Erkenntnis* formula often functions as the conclusion of a series of Yahweh's deeds (cf. Zimmerli 1954: 10). Yahweh's great acts towards Jerusalem are called to remembrance (actually re-lived). This brings Jerusalem to a right understanding of the eternal covenant.

7. *Redaction Criticism*

As far as redaction criticism is concerned, opinions are divergent Von Rabenau (1955–56: 681) regards 16.1-42 as the original unit The rest would be later redactional additions (Le Roux 1987: 175). Presho (1972: 79) also pays homage to this point of view. According to this view, 16.1-42/43 forms the core theme or 'original word', and vv. 44-58 and 59-63 are then regarded as the core theme developed in a new manner and sent in a new direction. Eichrodt (1970: 217) is outspoken in his belief that 16.54-63 does not originate with Ezekiel. Wevers also (1969: 94) accepts 16.1-43 as the 'original' prophecy. His reason is: 'Not only is the figure of the original story completely abandoned in verses 44ff, but the concept of a restoration to the former estate is completely at odds with the judgement on the adulteress in verses 40-41a'. This idea is strengthened by Clark (1984: 190), who suggests that 16.44-58 is built on 'quotations'.

On the other hand, Lang (1981: 49) regards Ezekiel 16.1-52 as a unit that can be dated from 591 to 588 BCE. Greenberg (1983: 292) divides the pericope into three parts, namely vv. 3-43, vv. 44-58 and vv. 59-63. Each part ends with the *Gottespruch* formula. Thus it seems that there is a difference of opinion about what is 'original' and what is not.

My view is that the structural analysis shows convincingly that the whole pericope forms a meaningful unit. To date any parts earlier or later without sufficient grounds is not a good practice.

In this connection Parunak (1983: 544) points to the relationship between Ezekiel 16 and 17. He describes 16.59-63 as an 'inverted hinge' between 16.1-58 and ch. 17. He bases this especially on the key term ברית, which appears throughout in the chiastic hinge (16.59-63) as well as in both adjacent units (16.1-58 and ch. 17). 'In 16.8 the word refers to a marriage covenant between the Lord and the orphan girl, while in 17.13-19, a political covenant is in view' (Parunak 1983: 545).

This confirms the fact that Ezek. 16.1-63 is the masterpiece of the final redactor(s) of the book Ezekiel. He placed the sub-pericopes in a specific order to attain the desired effect (message).

8. *Final Synthesis*

The *main ideas* in this pericope can be summarized either under the heading of judgment or of salvation. In Ezekiel 16 the pendulum swings from an abandoned child (judgment) to a wild plant (restoration), from young beauty (restoration), and from a bride (restoration), to an unfaithful wife (judgment) who is stoned for her misdeeds, and back to a new covenant (restoration). Ezekiel 16 is a mirror of life for life. Here opposites meet each other: the greatest mercy and the most horrible contempt.

The book Ezekiel exposes here in a gripping way the enormities that can be committed against God. We find also in Ezekiel 16 the pain and anger of personal rejection (cf. Mayo 1973: 24-25), but also the satisfaction which can only be found in an intimate personal relationship with God. Jerusalem's sin against Yahweh is the flagrant breach of precisely this lovely relationship/covenant between the Lord and his child. On the one hand we have the beautiful garments and presents of the Giver, and on the other hand the giving away of these presents to other lovers (the breaching of the covenant). This is to humiliate Yahweh.

Ezekiel 16 does not intend that Jerusalem should think back to the 'good old days'. Those days were in reality evil and bad (Luc 1983: 139). Also, the guilt cannot be laid on something or somebody else, but is placed squarely on the shoulders of Jerusalem. 'Israel wanted to be like the other peoples—it wanted to forget that it had been called into an indissoluble covenant with God' (Fuhs 1984: 85). The punishment is therefore the necessary consequence of the covenant which lays obligations on both parties.

The judgment is a personal judgment of the Covenant God. However, there is no specific judgment linked to a specific sin (cf. Fishbane

1984: 148). So this pericope suggests the reality of Divine Providence on the one hand, but on the other hand the link between sin and judgment. Sin is referred to in metaphorical and poetic language, and not in detail. Ezekiel here prefers to bring home the idea of a sinful inclination/nature of humanity rather than a number of sins. Sin is thus tackled in its core, in its origin.

In this connection it is meaningful to notice that the admission of guilt by Jerusalem (the shaming) will follow after the acquittal. This is because the mercy is so overwhelmingly great. The great mercy of Yahweh overshadows every single act that Jerusalem can commit. But the shame is also the token of a new, pure heart that brings hope for a new future. So with the realization of the reckless past and the broken heart, the objective of the judgment is attained and a new understanding of the Lord is made possible.

This understanding/knowledge of the Lord shows us the personal involvement of Yahweh, in this pericope especially in connection with the judgment. It is saying that Yahweh must also be known in his judgment. His judgment is in the future. It is there to encourage and warn that Yahweh is the mighty God whose judgments will be carried out as they have been announced—a knowledge of Yahweh which is at this stage wanting. Because the judgments are described in advance, those addressed have an anticipatory understanding of this future knowledge (cf. Fishbane 1984: 149). This is precisely the *aim of the pericope*: to bring people to the same intimate knowledge of Yahweh to which unbelievers will also be brought, against their wishes.

There is, however, *an-Other* side: Yahweh's desire to be known. Not because he needs to, but because his name is joined to his people (Zimmerli 1958: 88). The prophet knows this, because his whole being is taken up in this knowledge, but the irony is that those whom he addresses do not come to this realization. Therefore the whole book of Ezekiel is a series of attempts to *make known* the purposes of Yahweh with his children. There is thus no way out.

There remains only one knowledge: the recognition of Yahweh. If you take this reluctantly it will come to you in the form of judgment. The person who accepts it in grace will experience it as salvation. That is why Zimmerli (1958: 90) rightly says, 'Das sola gratia dei, das bei Ezechiel interpretiert wird als ein sola majestas dei, wird darin hörbar'. This honouring of God, which consists of reverence for his Name, is therefore the link between Israel/Jerusalem's critical past, present judgment and future salvation (Luc 1983: 142).

Fuhs's words (1984: 87) are appropriate: 'Shame opens a new way to the love of God. By forgiving all sin God reveals his true greatness. This is the new covenant: forgiveness for all sin and salvation to a new life. The usual order of things, according to which disgrace leads to confession of guilt, thus reverses itself here' (Greenberg 1983: 242).

Jerusalem's joint reponsibility for others (Sodom and Samaria) is therefore also discussed here. The disgrace must be remembered to avoid a repetition of the iniquity. The mercy is so wide that there is even enough for Samaria and Sodom.

By using the Sodom motif (v. 49), self-satisfaction, pride and wealth is judged (cf. also above), and the covenant is extended (v. 61) to urge Jerusalem (believers) to take care of the poor and the underprivileged. Sodom and Samaria are used here by comparison/metaphorically to emphasize the typical social conditions round about Jerusalem. An appeal is thus made to the reader to share the gifts of God (the results of the covenant) with the world (Samaria and Sodom). The existence and renewal of the covenant implies an openness of believers for the need in the world and a readiness to be responsible for those around us. That is an integrated part of our knowledge that Yahweh is the Lord (v. 62).

BIBLIOGRAPHY

Burden, J.J. and W.S. Prinsloo (eds.)
1987   *Tweegesprek met God: Die literatuur van die Ou Testament*, III (Cape Town: Tafelberg).

Clark, D.R.
1984   'The Citations in the Book of Ezekiel: An Investigation into Method, Audience and Message' (PhD dissertation, Vanderbilt University, Nashville, TN).

Eichrodt, W.
1970   *Ezekiel: A Commentary* (OTL; London: SCM Press).

Fishbane, M.
1984   'Sin and Judgment in the Prophecies of Ezekiel', *Int* 38: 131-50.

Fuhs, H.F.
1984   *Ezechiel 1–24* (Würzburg: Echter).

Garner, D.W.
1980   'Forms of Communication in the Book of Ezekiel' (PhD dissertation, The Southern Baptist Theological Seminary, Louisville, KY).

Gowan, D.E.
1985   *Ezekiel* (Atlanta: John Knox).

Greenberg, M.
1983   *Ezekiel 1–20: A New Translation with Introduction and Commentary* (Garden City, NY: Doubleday).

Kellermann, U.
1971   *Messias und Gesetz* (Neukirchen–Vluyn: Neukirchener Verlag).

Lang, B.
1981   *Ezechiel* (Erträge der Forschung, 153; Darmstadt: Wissenschaftliche Buchgesellschaft).

Lemke, W.E.
1984   'Life in the Present and Hope for the Future (Ezek. 33–37)', *Int* 38: 165-80.

Le Roux, J.H.
1987   'Die boek Esegiël', in Burden and Prinsloo 1987: 175-94.

Luc, A.
1983   'A Theology of Ezekiel: God's Name and Israel's History', *JETS* 26: 137-43.

Mayo, J.
1973   'Covenant Theology in Ezekiel', *ResQ* 16: 23-31.

McKeating, H.
1965   'On Understanding Ezekiel', *London Quarterly and Holborn Review*, 36-43.

Parunak, H. van Dyke
1978   'Structural Studies in Ezekiel' (DPhil thesis, Harvard University, Cambridge, MA).
1983   'Transitional Techniques in the Bible', *JBL* 102: 525-48.

Presho, C.
1972   'Distinctive Theological Emphases in the Book of Ezekiel' (PhD dissertation, Queen's University, Belfast).

Rabenau, K., von
1955–56 'Die Entstehung des Buches Ezechiel in formgeschichtlicher Sicht', *Wissenschaftliche Zeitschrift Halle* 5: 659-94.

Swanepoel, M.G.
1987   'Die teologie van Esegiël 33 tot 39' (DD thesis, University of Pretoria, Faculty of Theology [Dutch Reformed Church], Pretoria).

Wevers, J.W.
1969   *Ezekiel* (OTL; Grand Rapids: Eerdmans).

Zimmerli, W.
1954   *Erkenntnis Gottes nach dem Buche Ezechiel—Eine theologische Studie* (Würzburg: Echter Verlag).
1958   'Israel im Buche Ezechiel', *VT* 8: 75-90.
1965   'Special Form- and Traditio-Historical Character of Ezekiel's Prophecy', *VT* 15: 515-27.
1979   *Ezekiel. I. A Commentary on the Book of the Prophet Ezekiel, Chapters 1–24* (Hermeneia; Philadelphia: Fortress Press).

EZEKIEL 27 AND THE COSMIC SHIP

John B. Geyer

ABSTRACT

Ezekiel 27 is reviewed in the context of mythology. This is an oracle against Tyre. The island might have suggested the image of the ship. Tyre's cultural links with Egypt could have evoked the idea of the Cosmic Ship, well known in Egyptian mythology. The materials mentioned in Ezek. 27 indicate links with materials used in the temple at Jerusalem which was modeled on the temple at Tyre. Place names in Ezek. 27 have mythological connotations. The tradition of the Cosmic Ship has been adapted to the prophetic perspective of the downfall of the hero brought about because of hybris.

The purpose of this article is to argue that Ezekiel 27 has to do with a cosmic ship and its role in the overthrow of enemies terrestrial and mythological. A greater concentration of mythological and ritual themes appears to be present than has been admitted in previous studies. Comparison will be made with the Egyptian myth known as the Amduat.

Ezekiel 27 stands within the collection of oracles against the nations in chs. 25–32. In a previous article I have argued that this collection is to be taken along with the collections in Isaiah 13–23 and Jeremiah 46–51, where a common form is followed, and where the basis is mythological.[1] This is not to deny that in places the oracles have historical reference, but it emphasizes that the interest is theological and that the imagery is drawn from creation mythology.

---

1. J.B. Geyer, 'Mythology and Culture in the Oracles against the Nations', *VT* 36 (1986), pp. 129-45. In that article it is argued that Ezek. 25 is not an original part of the collection. In this article the major collections will be referred to as ON(–IJE). A related study has been offered by me in 'Twisting Tiamat's Tail: A Mythological Interpretation of Isaiah xiii 5 and 8', *VT* 37 (1987), pp. 164-79. A further article, 'The Night of Dumah' (a study of Isa. 21.11-12), and a Short Note, 'Mythological Sequence in Job xxiv 19-20', appear in *VT* 42 (1992), pp. 317-39 and pp. 118-20.

In making a comparison with the Amduat, no suggestion is being made that Ezekiel is dependent on the Egyptian myth. Distinct differences will be pointed out between Mesopotamian, West Semitic and Egyptian mythology. The significant fact is that the Ship in Ezekiel 27 has cosmic significance, and the fate of the Ship is described in terms of creation mythology as it appears in other parts of the Old Testament, especially the Psalms. This is in keeping with other myths that are presented in the course of ON–IJE, namely *hēlēl ben šaḥar* in Isaiah 14, or Primaeval Man or the Cosmic Tree in Ezekiel 28 and 31.

Mythology in Ezekiel 27

While the Sea is the natural element in which Tyre is set and over which it trades, it is also a symbol of chaos in the creation mythology. In v. 3 Tyre is introduced as the city enthroned on the entrances of Yam. The absence of the article is significant.[1] Tyre is situated at the gates of Yam's kingdom.

The reader needs to be sensitive to the theological undertones even where there is also a natural reference (*blb ymym*, vv. 4, 6, 27; *mym rbym*, v. 26; *btwk hym*, v. 32; *ymym*, vv. 33, 34).[2] The word *m'mqym* (v. 34) occurs elsewhere only in connection with Rahab (Isa. 51.10) or in liturgical material probably connected with the chaos motif (Pss. 69.3, 15; 130.1). In v. 32 the meaning of the expression *kdmh btwk hym* is by no means obvious. H.J. van Dijk translates, 'like the fortress in the midst of the sea', linking this with Akkadian *dimtu*, 'tower, fortified area',[3] which makes sense for Tyre. Modern translations indicate the difficulties.[4]

---

1. Cf. W. Zimmerli, *Ezechiel*, II (BKAT; Neukirchen–Vluyn: Neukirchener Verlag, 1969), *ad loc.* The *yodh* at the end of *hyšbty* might be the *hireq compaginis* (GKC, §90m) signifying the ruler.

2. Significant passages in which the water and chaos motifs are linked with the destiny of nations were explored by H.C. May, 'Some Cosmic Connotations of *MAYIM RABBÎM*, "Many Waters"', *JBL* 75 (1955), pp. 9-21, an article which deserves more attention than it has received.

3, H.J. van Dijk, *Ezekiel's Prophecy on Tyre (Ez. 26.1–28.19)* (Rome, 1968), p. 85.

4. AV 'like the destroyed'; RV 'like her that is brought to silence'; RSV 'who was ever destroyed... (mg.: Tg. Vg.: Heb. *like silence*)'. NEB has 'with her buildings piled (mg.: prob. rdg.; Heb. obscure)', apparently substituting *krmh*; cf. L.H. Brockington, *The Hebrew Text of the Old Testament* (Oxford, 1973), p. 229. REB evades the difficulty, omitting the phrase without comment.

blb ymym occurs in liturgical contexts at Exod. 15.8 (sg.), Jon. 2.4 and Ps. 46.3. *ymym/ym* parallel with *mym* occurs in ON at Isa. 17.12; 18.2; 23.2-3; Ezek. 27.25-26; 32.2; cf. Exod. 15.8, 10, 19; Ps. 46.3-4; 93.4. The parallelism stands 6 times in ON–IJE, 8 times in the Psalms, 11 times in connection with the creation myth, once in a festal liturgy against the nations (Nah. 3.8), and finally in Isa. 50.2, which describes Yahweh's power over the seas.

The idea of being *enthroned* (*yšb*) is present also in v. 28 and Isa. 14.13. The *mlky 'rṣ* (v. 33; cf. v. 35) occur also in v. 28 and Isa. 14.9, 18 and in liturgical material in Pss. 2.2; 76.13; 89.28; 102.16; 138.4; 148.11; Lam. 4.12. The language is similar to that of Baal 2.i (*CML*, pp. 40-43).

Within the same range are the expressions *klylt ypy* (v. 3), *kllw ypyk* (v. 4; cf. 28.12, 17; 31.3; cf. vv. 8, 9); *yplw...mpltk* (vv. 27, 34; cf. Isa. 14.12; Ezek. 31.12, 13, 16); *yrdw...'l h'rṣ, y'mdw* (v. 29; cf. Isa. 14.11, 15; Ezek. 31.14-17) and *r'š* (v. 28; cf. 31.16 and *rgz* in Isa. 14.19).

Destruction by the (east) wind (v. 26) is characteristic of ON–IJE (Isa. 17.13; Jer. 49.36; 51.1). Van Dijk (p. 82) draws attention to Ps. 48.8, Isa. 27.8, Ezek. 17.10 and 19.12, Jer. 18.17 and Hos. 13.15, Jon. 4.8, and passages such as Isa. 11.15 and 30.28 (against the nations) should also be noted.

The Amduat

Since there are traces that Ezekiel 27 is handling mythological themes, consideration will now be given to an Egyptian mythological text that describes the cosmic ship known as the Bark of Re. This will illustrate the way in which such themes were handled in one tradition and gives a broader perspective from which the material in Ezekiel 27 can be better understood.

A link between the oracles against the nations in the Old Testament and Egyptian mythology and rites has been posited by others, most recently by B. Gosse[1] with reference to the Bremner–Rhind Papyrus[2] which dates from about 310 BCE, though scholars agree that the myth and ritual belong to a much earlier date.

1. B. Gosse, *Isaie 13.1–14.23* (Göttingen, 1988), pp. 27-29.
2. Translations include those by R.O. Faulkner in *JEA* 23 (1937), pp. 166-85, and J.A. Wilson in *ANET²*, pp. 6-7.

This Papyrus is particularly interesting because, especially in Book 26, it links the conflict with creation (the conflict is one in which the primaeval monster snake Apophis attacks Re in his Bark), because the slaying of Apophis is directly linked with the overthrow of the terrestrial enemies of Pharaoh, and because the connection with a daily ritual is explicit.

Attention is directed in this article to the account of the journey of the Bark of Re through the underworld during the Twelve Hours of Night, including the conflict with Apophis, which is given in the *'Imy-Dēt zš n't-jmnt*, *'What is in the Underworld: The Text of the Hidden Chamber'*, which will be referred to as the Amduat. This tale is transcribed in various degrees of completeness in the tombs of the pharaohs and others from the time of Thutmosis I to Ramses IX, and is particularly well preserved in the tomb of Amenophis III (1417–1379 BCE).[1]

In Mesopotamian mythology the Underworld is a dreadful place of dust and mud and darkness. Above all, it is the Land of No Return (Sum. *NU.GI₄A*; Akk. *erṣeti lā târi*). By contrast, the Egyptian Underworld was a land of rejuvenation and rebirth. Re descends to the Underworld in the evening and comes forth renewed in the morning. However, this process is not considered to be automatic. Severe dangers have to be overcome on the way. This is done through knowing the correct formulae. This Underworld realm is known as the Dat.

During the day the god traverses the sky in the Day Bark (*m'ndt*), but during the hours of darkness he travels in the Night Bark (*nt msktt*), which is also known as the Bark of Re (*wj3-n-r*). According to a magic papyrus of the 20th Dynasty, the Night Bark was golden. Re does not disembark. The Bark itself changes from one form to the other. The Bark has the name, 'The one who paves the way' (*dm-w3t*—Mid. Reg., Fourth Hour [p. 86]). In the same Register a towing rope is mentioned for the first time. It is pulled by four gods. The Bark also has a crew which is mentioned in the second scene (Mid. Reg., Ninth Hour [p. 156]), where there are twelve oarsmen, each with an oar in his hand. 'What they have to do is to row Re daily to this place. They stand by the waterway (*nt*) of the Bark which is in

---

1. The edition that has been used in this article is that by E. Hornung, *Das Amduat*, I–III (Wiesbaden, 1963, 1967). All references in this article are to Vol. 2, and the article is wholly dependent on Hornung for translation, notes and commentary.

this place.' In the second scene (Upper Reg., Twelfth Hour [p. 189]) twelve gods hold the tow rope with both hands, their faces turned towards the Bark.

This Bark moves along canals (e.g. Mid. Reg., Sixth Hour [p. 116]) rather than the open sea. When the primaeval water is encountered, it is part of cosmos, the source of life, rather than an element of chaos, though it can be threatening on occasions. The region of the Sixth Hour is called *mdwt*, the Deep, and has the determinative 〰〰. This opens out into the primaeval water Nun, which encloses the world on all sides in an endless stretch, but also runs through it. The threat is encountered in the Upper Register of the Third Hour (p. 64), where reference is made to the flood (*h'pj*) that destroys the enemy. This also is designated as Nun. It attacks the enemies of the god, not the god himself.

But the god does have enemies to face. These (especially Apophis) live on sandbanks, and indeed this Bark has to be pulled over sand and even has to traverse mud (Seventh Hour, introduction, Horizontal line 9 [p. 125]) left behind after the hostile Apophis has swallowed all the water so as to prevent the progress of the Bark. The Bark can be pulled over the sand but it can only get across the mud by magic. The Middle Register of the Fourth Hour (p. 86) describes the Snake domain of *rs'-st3-w* ('the pulling over the sand business'). The Bark changes into a snake so that it can glide more easily over the sand, the bow and stern turned into fire-spitting shining snake heads. Even though the Bark changes into a snake, it is here that the two ropes are produced for the first time. The sand is the desert which, in Mesopotamia also, was an element of chaos, a perpetual threat to cosmos.

Another familiar element of chaos that appears in the Amduat is darkness. Lines 7-9 of the title (p. 2) affirm:

> The beginning is the horn of the west
> the gate of the western horizon;
> the end is the primaeval darkness
> the gate of the western horizon.[1]

The primaeval darkness (*ṭiṭh*) is a region not lighted by Re. It is reserved for the enemies and is at the furthest reaches of the Dat (cf.

---

1. One would expect the eastern horizon to be mentioned, but *kkw-zm3w* has nothing to do with the east. It indicates an absolute boundary in the Underworld that is unconnected with geographical direction.

yrkty br, Isa. 14.15). This is the beginning of a primaeval chaos that surrounds the world, over which neither the gods nor the kings have power. Re does not engage with this chaotic power, but he travels close to the boundaries of being.

In the third scene of the Middle Register of the Tenth Hour (p. 167) there is a falcon-headed snake in a boat, with the inscription, 'He is so constituted in his Bark. He rouses himself against the primaeval darkness.' The Introduction to the Twelfth Hour (p. 184) places Re eye to eye with the primaeval darkness, and the name of the place is 'Rising at dark, appearing at births', from which follows the rebirth of Re. Line 7 of the inscription accompanying the first scene of the Upper Register of the Twelfth Hour (p. 186) makes it clear that darkness binds the dead and light releases them.

The journey of Re through the Underworld is full of threats to the created order. These have to be faced and overcome. The enemies appear in different guises, but they include the military opponents of Pharaoh, the enemies of the gods (criminals?) and the primaeval forces themselves. All these are linked in the unity of creation. The enemies of Re and the enemies of the earthly monarch are one and the same threat.

In the text of the First Hour (p. 33) the gods greet Re with the words: 'You triumph over your enemies (*njkw*); you impose disaster on the punished' (l. 58), and the name of the Hour is: 'The one that shatters the foreheads of the enemies of Re' (l. 76). The Upper Register of the Third Hour (p. 64) states that the gods are there to crush the adversary (l. 6), and the Lower Register (p. 71) records that these gods have to 'roast and slaughter the souls, imprison the shades, bring about the annihilation of the Non-Beings, who are in their place of the Annihilation Posts.[1] They kindle the flames, they burn the enemies through that which is on the point of their swords' (ll. 2-6).

After the fifth scene of the Upper Register of the Fifth Hour (p. 98), the Slaughterers are addressed, who

> belong to the shambles (*nmt*)... May your words arise and may your magic shine (*ssp*). Able (*spd*) be your souls, considerable (*w3s*) be your might. Crushed be the enemies because you destroy the dead and mass-acre the shades of the annihilated. You are the ones who protect Osiris, who prevent a trial because of Onnophris. Sharp be your swords, grue-some be your shambles... so that I may go by you in peace (ll. 3-11).

---

1. *ḥtmjt* is the place where the enemies are expelled from being to non-being.

The first scene in the Lower Register in the Fifth Hour (p. 104) shows four heads wearing the beards of divinity. All of them have the common name *tpw-tk3w* 'Torch Heads', and it is said, 'What they have to do is to destroy and drive back his enemies'. The destruction (*s3m*) is effected through their torches.

The second scene of the Lower Register of the Sixth Hour (p. 121) represents a snake with four human heads (i.e. the sons of Horus), and the inscription states, 'What he has to do is to sip up the shades and extinguish the forms of the enemies who are overthrown in the Dat' (ll. 2-4). This snake is called the *'mw-jrw*, 'the one who devours the forms'. The fourth scene (p. 122) shows nine fire-spitting snake staffs armed with a sword. Connected with them, at the end of the Register, is the god Nun. Re says to them: 'May your faces burn and your swords (*zw*) be sharp so that you may destroy (*3m*) the enemies of Khepri and cut up their shades... Yours it is to protect Khepri, who is the water of Tatenan, the Arisen One' (ll. 4-6).

The main enemy to be overcome is Apophis, and he is encountered in the Seventh Hour. The vertical lines of the introduction (p. 125) assert that Re diverts from Apophis through the magic sayings of Isis and of the Oldest Magician. The name of this Night Hour is 'The one which wards off the *hjw* and beheads the *nh3-hr*'. Both these terms refer to Apophis, who can also be identified with Seth, so that the 37th goddess in the First Hour is called *hsft-zm3 t-sth*. The horizontal lines (11-12) relate that 'it happens that Apophis is dismembered in the Dat in this chamber [although] his place is in the sky', a reminder that Apophis attacks the Bark during the day as well as at night.

The second scene of the Upper Register (p. 127) represents the punishment of the 'enemies', which is to say the dead condemned before Osiris, who is the Underworld Sun god. Three enemies, already beheaded and bound, kneel before the Judge of the Dead. Behind them there is a punishing god. In the inscription the god says to Osiris,

> May your enemies fall under your feet; may you seize those who offended against you! The flames of (the Snake god) 'Living in Forms' are against them. The 'Violent of Countenance' is against them; he massacres them, he roasts them as a roast for himself (ll. 5-8).

The 'Violent of Countenance' (*mds-hr*) is the punishing god. He holds a sword in one hand and a sling in the other.

In the third scene (p. 128) another punishing god holds the end of the halter by which three defenceless prostrate enemies are bound. The inscription reads,

> You whom Osiris bound up and who have rebelled against him of the Dat, may your arms be bound and your nooses be tightened; may your souls be annihilated and your souls be detained. The punisher punishes you with his knife and you never escape his attention.

The aim is to prevent the souls being united with their bodies.

The text of the Middle Register (pp. 131-32) states that the magic of Isis and the Oldest Magician is made to ward off Apophis from Re and describes the sandbank (*ṯw*) of the *nḥȝ-ḥr* in the Dat. 'He fills it with his coils and he is massacred before this god goes past him. This god journeys in this place in the image of the Meḥen (*m sšmw n mḥn*).' The Sun Bark alters course so that Re does not need to go directly by the dangerous Snake until Apophis is rendered harmless.

The second scene (p. 132) shows the much wounded Snake body of Apophis who has already been dismembered by knives and is held neck and tail by a couple of gods. He is found on the sandbank which is called *sḏȝw*. Then 'the one who causes the throat to breathe' slings the lasso about his head while 'the one who is over the knives', the 'Punisher', throws him about at his feet, after Isis and the Oldest Magician have robbed his strength (*pḥtj*) through their magic (ll. 6-9). 'The one who causes the throat to breathe' is the god Selket, *srqt-ḥtjt*, the Scorpion god.

The third scene shows four goddesses armed with knives. According to the inscription, these are the goddesses who punish Apophis in the Dat and divert the blows (*jḥt*—lit. 'things') of the enemy from Re. They carry their knives and every day punish Apophis in the Dat.

Re has armed himself in many ways against the dangerous encounter with Apophis; for example, the Ring Snake (*mḥn*) encircles and protects him in the Bark, and the magic-working gods Isis and Seth (*ḥkȝ w-smsw*) stand by him. The Sun god also conceals a disc ('eye') and alters course for added protection. Apophis blocks the way with his gigantic Snake body, but there is never any real battle. Apophis is bewitched and then easily bound by the other gods. Finally he is annihilated (*ḥtm*). The journey can now continue in peace (*m ḥtp*; cf. commentary, pp. 139-40).

Troubles continue even after the defeat of Apophis in the Seventh Hour. The inscription of the third scene in the Middle Register of the

Eighth Hour records the presence of those who have to dismember the enemies of Re (p. 145).

In the Eleventh Hour (first scene, Lower Reg. [pp. 180-81]) Re gives instructions about the massacre of those who slew his father Osiris, the corpses of the enemies and the bodies of the dead, the over-thrown (*sḫdw*) and the forms of the annihilated. They are cursed by Horus, who says among other things, 'Do not raise yourself, for you have fallen into your graves! May you not escape. May you not flee' (ll. 8-9), and the section finishes with the words: 'Their destruction is commanded every day through the Majesty of the Underworld Horus' (ll. 18-19). The second scene of the Lower Register of the Twelfth Hour makes it clear that Apophis is still a threat to Re (p. 191).

At most gates Re is greeted by the resident gods. In the closing text of the First Hour (p. 33) the gods say among other things, 'You tri-umph over your enemies (*nkjw*); you impose disaster on the punished' (l. 58; cf. also pp. 55-56, 74). In the third scene of the Middle Register of the Fifth Hour (p. 101) the goddesses offer the greeting, 'Re comes in peace to the Dat. The way is opened for Re in his Bark, which is in the earth as his body. His enemies are destroyed for you...You triumph and your enemies are driven away.'

The entire drama of the Amduat is linked with concepts of the creation of the universe. The Superscription of the first part of the Middle Register of the First Hour (p. 17) refers to 'The Two Realities' that draw (*st3*) the god in the Night Bark. 'The Two Realities' (*m3 'tj*) are elsewhere represented as two goddesses, and they indicate the duality inherent in the cosmos rather than two separate beings. At the end of the journey (Introduction to the Twelfth Hour, vertical lines [p. 184]) Re 'goes out of the Dat, lies down in the Day Bark and steps forward (*ḫ'j*) out of the thighs of Nut' (l. 5), where Nut represents the primaeval water of life and fertility. The cosmic dimension of the situation appears again in the second scene of the Upper Register of the Twelfth Hour (p. 189), where twelve gods stand with their legs reaching over the gigantic body of the Snake, through which they pull the Bark. In the first scene of the Lower Register of the Twelfth Hour (p. 191) the totality of the primaeval gods is present, with the excep-tion of the paired Amun/Amaunet.

The Amduat indicates that during the course of the Night journey law and order in the world are confirmed. In the third scene of the Middle Register of the Sixth Hour (p. 118) Re is found confirming the kings of Upper and Lower Egypt in their offices.

The structure of the cosmos is preserved through this daily ritual. This is made clear in the first scene of the Upper Register of the Ninth Hour (p. 154), where Re says, 'May you do your duty for Osiris, that your worship for the Lord of the West may be declared (*sw3š*), and let him triumph over his enemies every day. It is the Judgment Court of the Gods that interrogates on behalf of Osiris every day. What you have to do in the Dat is to fell the enemies of Osiris' (ll. 7-8). The destruction of the enemies 'every day' is commanded in the first scene of the Lower Register of the Eleventh Hour (p. 181, ll. 18-19).

Analysis of Ezekiel 27

1. *Outline and Structure*

The image is not clearly held throughout. First of all Tyre is introduced as the city enthroned on the entrances of Yam. In the second part of the verse, though it is not explicit, is the theological indictment of hybris. Tyre has said that she is perfect in beauty—which she is, according to v. 4. It might be that the image of the ship is introduced in v. 3, *BHK* and *BHS* reading *'nyh* for *'ny*,[1] 'You have said, "I am a ship, perfect in beauty"'.

Verses 5-7 record the materials imported from various nations for the construction of the vessel, and vv. 8-11 record the various nations from which the crew has been assembled. Verse 9b interrupts this flow with mention of the way in which all trading ships contribute to Tyre's commerce, and this links up with v. 25.

Verses 12-24 list the various wares traded by Tyre, together with the countries from which they are imported. This section is generally regarded as an insertion of material different from the rest of the chapter, though, as H.J. van Dijk says, 'on insufficient grounds'.[2] The most obvious difference is that while the rest of the chapter is clearly written in poetic metre, vv. 12-24 are not so obviously poetic. But vv. 12-24 have a rhythm and may be intended as poetry, an indication of which is the regular repetition of phrases used like a drum beat to mark the stages of the list:

1.	Cf. Zimmerli, *Ezechiel*, II, *ad loc.*
2.	Van Dijk, *Ezekiel's Prophecy*, p. 75.

v. 12	*sḥrtk*
	ntnw 'zbwnyk
v. 13	*rklyk*
	ntnw m 'rbk
v. 14	*ntnw 'zbwnyk*
v. 15	*rklyk <strt ydk>*
v. 16	*sḥrtk*
	ntnw b'zbwnk
v. 17	*rklyk*
	ntnw m'rbk
v. 18	*sḥrtk*
v. 19	*b'zbwnyk ntnw*
	bm 'rbk hyh
v. 21	*sḥry ydk. . . sḥryk*
v. 22	*rklyk*
	ntnw 'zbwnk
v. 23	*rkltk*
v. 24	*rklyk*

There is a close connection in thought and language between vv. 9-24 and the remainder of the chapter. G.A. Cooke[1] listed words and phrases that are repeated in both parts:

kllw ypyk	vv. 4, 11
'zbwyn	vv. 12, 14, etc., 27
mrb klḥwn	vv. 12, 18, 33
m 'rb	vv. 13, etc., 9, 34
sḥrym	vv. 12, 15, etc., 36

Cooke explains this phenomenon as a deliberate attempt by the later author (vv. 9b-24) to link his material with the poem. Yet the fact that both sections are painting the picture of a world power, that they both produce names, some of which belong more in the mythological realm than the historical, and that they both list materials that are associated with the construction of the temple are all reasons for accepting the chapter as an integral unit from whatever sources its parts may have been brought together.

The wreck of the ship by an east wind is described in vv. 26-27. Verse 28 is curious and introduces some confusion. It might be translated:

---

1. G.A. Cooke, *The Book of Ezekiel* (Edinburgh, 1936).

> At the sound of the cry of your helmsmen
> the common ground (?) shakes.

We are then told (v. 29) that 'rowers, sailors and helmsmen' go down from their ships and stand '*l-h'rṣ*. These are not the survivors of the ship Tyre unless they were equipped with lifeboats. *yrdw...'l-'rṣ* recalls '*l-š'wl twrd* in Isa. 14.15 and similar phrases in mythology. The *y'mdw* does not seem to belong, and one would expect '*l* for '*l* if it did. Whatever is going on in these two verses, 'they' then become the chorus singing the lament, which is standard in the myths under review, finishing with the same words as Ezek. 28.19.

2. *Names and Substances*
An outstanding feature of Ezekiel 27 throughout is the collection of proper names and the list of substances, both those used for the construction of the ship and those that were the wares traded by Tyre. On examination, these are seen to have links with mythological traditions and, as far as the substances are concerned, they are much in keeping with the materials used in the construction of the temple in Jerusalem.

3. *Proper Names*
Thirty-six proper names of towns or states appear in Ezekiel 27; of these, 13 occur in the first section (vv. 5-11), and 23 in the trade list (vv. 12-23). This is excluding the name of Tyre itself, though Tyre is not without significance. The name of Tyre occurs 46 times in the Old Testament, of which nearly half (20) are in ON–IJE. Two conclusions may be drawn from this fact. One is that geographical names will obviously occur in particular contexts, and the names of Israel/Judah's immediate neighbours can be expected to occur in oracles concerned with nations more frequently than elsewhere. The second possible conclusion is that the name of Tyre is not so widely spread through the Old Testament as might be expected. Analysis of the occurrence of the other names bears out the fact that the 36 places mentioned are sparsely distributed in the Old Testament and frequently belong together in other contexts.

Clues as to the provenance of these names emerge from the occurrence of *lbnwn*. This is mentioned in v. 5 as the place from which wood was imported for the ship's mast. There is nothing curious about this either geographically or historically. But the distribution of *lbnwn* in the Old Testament should be noted. It is found again in ON–IJE at

Isa. 14.8 and Ezek. 31.3, 15, and elsewhere in an oracle against a foreign nation,[1] in oracles against Israel or Judah[2] and in oracles of promise to Israel.[3] It is found in poetry.[4] The wood is valued for the temple building,[5] which has more significance for Ezekiel 27 when the list of wares in the following section is considered. It occurs in the enthronement Psalm 29 (vv. 5, 6) and the royal Psalm 72 (v. 16; cf. also Ps. 92.13). It is associated with the House (Temple?) of the Forest of Lebanon.[6] Like *śnyr*, it is associated with Hermon (almost certainly a cult resort) in Josh. 11.17 and 13.5, and also with Seir (Josh. 12.7). It occurs in the spurious lists,[7] the dubious nature of which is highlighted by more historical references.[8]

This evidence suggests that although *lbnwn* was (and is!) a historical site it had particular emotional overtones that were brought into play, especially in oracles of doom or promise concerning the nations, including Israel/Judah.

The traditional use of the names is brought into sharper focus by consideration of the other items in the list. Fifteen of the names occur also in the lists in Genesis 10 and 1 Chronicles 1, three of them occurring only in Ezekiel 27 and the lists (*'lyšh*, v. 7; *'wzl*, v. 19; *r'mh*, v. 22), and one of them occurring in the lists and the Gog–Magog tradition (*twgrmh*, v. 14; Ezek. 38.6). The names occur in poetry: *śnyr*, v. 5;[9] *q d r*, v. 21;[10] *šb'* (vv. 22, 23);[11] in liturgy: *bšn*, v. 6;[12] *tršyš*, v. 12 (Ps. 48.8), and in a royal Psalm (Ps. 72.10).

The majority of the occurrences of all the names falls in the oracles about the nations or about Israel/Judah. *ywn* and *tbl* (v. 13) are men-

1. 2 Kgs 19.23 // Isa. 37.24; Isa. 10.34; Nah. 1.4; Zech. 11.1 (or against Judah?).
2. Isa. 2.13 (or against another nation?); 29.17; 33.9; Jer. 18.14 (proverb?); 22.6, 20, 23; Ezek. 17.2; Hab. 2.17.
3. Isa. 35.2; 40.16; 60.13; Hos. 14.6, 7, 8; Zech. 10.10.
4. Ps. 104.16; Cant. 3.9; 4.6, 8, 11; 5.15; 7.5. It is also found in fable: Judg. 9.15; 2 Kgs 14.9 // 2 Chron. 25.18.
5. 1 Kgs 5.13, 20, 23, 28 (*bis*); 2 Chron. 2.7 (*bis*), 15; Ezra 3.7.
6. 1 Kgs 7.2; 10.17, 21; 2 Chron. 9.16, 20.
7. Josh. 9.1; Judg. 3.3.
8. Deut. 1.7; 3.25; 11.24; Josh. 1.4.
9. Cant. 4.8.
10. Cant. 1.5; Ps. 120.5; cf. *mšk*, v. 13.
11. Job 6.19; Ps. 72.10, 15.
12. Ps. 68.16, 23.

tioned together in Isa. 66.19, where favour is promised to the nation. Of particular note are the eight place names in the Gog–Magog tradition: *prs*, v. 10; *pwt*, v. 10; *tršyš*, v. 12; *tbl*, v. 13; *mšk*, v. 13; *twgrmh*, v. 14; *ddn*, vv. 15, 20; *šb'*, vv. 22, 23. Of these, *tbl* occurs in ON–IJE at Ezek. 32.26 (+ *mšk*), in the lists Gen. 10.2 and 1 Chron. 1.5 (also with *mšk*) and Isa. 66.19 (with *lwd*); *mšk* (v. 13) is similar; *twgrmh* occurs elsewhere only in the lists Gen. 10.3 and 1 Chron. 1.6; *ddn* occurs 10 times: 4 times in ON–IJE plus Ezek. 25.13, in an oracle against nations (Jer. 25.23), and in the lists (Gen. 10.7; 1 Chron. 1.9, 32).

One sixth of the names (6:36) are *hapax legomena*: *hylk* (NEB Cilicia) and *gmdym* in v. 11; *ḥlbwn* and *ṣḥr* in v. 18; *knh* and *klmd* in v. 23. Some of these may be traceable to faulty transmission. There must have been thousands of places that are no longer known by name to us. Van Dijk suggests that *gmdym* refers to dwarfs (*gōmed* 'short cubit'). M. Elat[1] has made an impressive reconstruction of the text to show that v. 19 may be translated, 'Also Dan and Yawan traded for your wares from Uzal', and that these places were to be found in Anatolia. But to be able to give geographical or historical identity to some, or all, of the places mentioned does not in itself explain the list. It remains mysterious; the Gog–Magog tradition suggests that this is deliberately so. The poetic allusions, particularly those in the Psalms, suggest that the use in ON–IJE in general, and Ezekiel 27 in particular, is traditional rather than factual. Modern scholars, struggling to treat the list as factual, have failed to reach a comprehensive explanation.

In the light of all this, *prs* stands out as exceptional. Apart from Ezekiel 27 and the Gog–Magog tradition, it is found frequently in Esther, Daniel, Ezra, Nehemiah and 2 Chronicles, and so is in perfect keeping with the Persian period to which it refers. This does not necessarily give the date of Ezekiel 27. It may appear here in an attempt to bring the oracle up to date, and it may have replaced an earlier *kwš* (cf. Ezek. 30.5; etc.). *šb'* (vv. 22, 23) is a good example of the way in which history and tradition combine. Closely connected with the queen (1 Kgs 10.1, 4, 10, 13 // 2 Chron. 9.1, 3, 9, 12), it has never been finally decided where it lay, and that makes very little difference to the legend in which it is embedded. It was a romantic title conjuring up the mysteries of the east (or the south or wherever).

---

1. M. Elat, 'The Iron Export from Uzal (Ezekiel xxvii 19)', *VT* 33 (1983), pp. 323-30.

The names in Ezekiel 27 are not intended to do much more than that. The attempt to read the chapter in a matter-of-fact way is misleading.

4. *Substances*

Fifty-three substances are mentioned altogether in the poem and the list. These may be considered all together, since, from this point of view, no significant difference exists between them.

Nine of the words used are *hapax legomena*, so no further comment can be made on them except to say that if this were a list of well-known products they might be expected to appear elsewhere in the Old Testament. The fact that they do not so occur might suggest that the author's mind was elsewhere—for example on some cultic or mythological theme. The nine are: *mprś* (v. 7); *swsym wpršym wprdym*, to be treated as a unit (v. 14); *hbny* (v. 15; an Egyptian loan word found in Ugaritic[1]), and all the substances in v. 24 except *hbl*, namely *mkll*, *glwm*, *brm* and *'rwz*, which last is possibly an adjective (see the versions).

A further five words appear in secular contexts and never (in the Old Testament) have reference to sacral functions. These are: *trn* (v. 5), *šn* (vv. 6, 15), *rqmh* (vv. 7, 16, 24), *r'mh* (v. 16) and *hblym* (v. 24). However, no fewer than 30 substances are connected elsewhere with the temple (or ark or tabernacle), and this suggests that the image in the author's mind was the sacred place as he knew it best, in Jerusalem, along with its associated traditions, and these he has transferred to Tyre, which he might have known, or have justifiably thought, to be similar to the temple in Jerusalem.[2] This stands even though the author was using the symbolism of a merchant ship and its wares (hence the five substances not known to have connections with sacred places).

The list is presented below under headings indicating objects with which the substances are elsewhere associated.

The Temple. *rwšym* (v. 5) were used for panelling the large chamber of Solomon's temple (2 Chron. 3.5). *'rz* (v. 5) was used for David's palace, making the king ashamed that the ark was housed only in

1. *UT* 2102.6; cf. van Dijk, *Ezekiel's Prophecy*, p. 78.
2. Tyre was much involved in the building of the temple in Jerusalem and was the dominant partner; cf. J.K. Kuan, 'Third Kingdoms 5.1 and Israelite–Tyrian Relations during the Reign of Solomon', *JSOT* 46 (1990), pp. 31-46.

curtains; it was then used for Solomon's temple and its altar (e.g.
1 Kgs 6.18) and for the postexilic temple (Ezra 3.7). It was used for
sacrifice (Lev. 14.4, 49; Num. 19.6) and by those who made idols
(Isa. 44.14). It appears in hymnody and myth.[1] *bqd* occurs elsewhere
only with reference to the temple.[2] *brzl* (v. 12) was used in the temple
according to 1 Chron. 22.14, 16; 29.2; 2 Chron. 2.6, 13. Strangely, it
was used for the sarcophagus of Og (Deut. 3.11), but it is prohibited
in the construction of altars (Deut. 27.5; Josh. 8.31; 1 Kgs 6.7), which
was due to the nature of the 'living stone' rather than any objection to
the substance that was not to be used on it. It is associated with curse
(Deut. 28.23; cf. v. 48), but also with blessing (Deut. 33.25). It is
holy when placed under ban (Josh. 6.19, 24).

Temple Furnishings and the Like. luh (v. 5) is used frequently of the
tables of stone given to Moses (e.g. Exod. 24.12; 31.18; Deut. 4.13);
also of the material for the trolleys in Solomon's temple (1 Kgs 7.36).
ns (v. 7) is used of an altar (Exod. 17.15) and of the bronze serpent
(Num. 21.8-9). It also occurs in ON–Isa. 13.2; 18.3; Jer. 50.2; 51.12.
'bn yqrh (v. 22) appears again in ON–Ezek. 28.13 and as part of the
temple adornments (1 Chron. 29.2; 2 Chron. 3.6). *bws* (v. 16) is an
emblem of grandeur (Est. 1.6; 8.15), otherwise mentioned only in
connection with attendants of the ark (1 Chron. 15.27) and the veil
(2 Chron. 3.14). The places where it was processed are noted
(1 Chron. 4.21).

The Tabernacle. qrš (v. 6) is otherwise used only in connection with
the tabernacle.[3] In the case of *šš* (v. 7), the majority of references is
to the tabernacle and its court.[4] As to *tklt* (vv. 7, 24), apart from the
dress of Samaria's lovers the Assyrians (Ezek. 23.6) and its association with royalty (Est. 1.6; 8.15), all references are to the tabernacle
(Exod. 26.36), the breastplate and ephod (Exod. 28.39), to the covering for objects in the sanctuary[5] or to the covering for idols (Jer.
10.9; note the reference in the same verse to silver from Tarshish).
'rgmn (vv. 7, 16) is very similar to *tklt* and is associated with it in

1. Pss. 29.5; 92.13; cf. ON–Isa. 14.8 and Ezek. 31.3.
2. 2 Kgs 12.6-13; 22.5; 2 Chron. 34.10.
3. Exod. 26.15; 35.11; 36.20; 39.33; 40.18; Num. 3.36; 4.31.
4. Exod. 26.1; 27.9; 39.28. It is also used of the ephod: Exod. 28.6.
5. Num. 4.6; cf. also Num. 15.38; 2 Chron. 2.6; 3.14.

some places. There are references to the covering for the altar,[1] the tabernacle,[2] the ephod (Exod. 28.39) and, along with *tklt*, to idols (Jer. 10.9) and royalty (Est. 6.1; 8.15). *mksk* (v. 7) is an unusual, possibly unique, use of piel participle. of *ksh* (cf. ON–Isa. 14.11). The noun *miksek* should perhaps be read. This is used of the tabernacle.[3] *ksp* (v. 12) was used for the decoration of the tabernacle[4] and the veil.[5] *nḥš* (v. 13) is used for the tabernacle,[6] the temple,[7] its vessels,[8] its platform,[9] its pillars,[10] its altar,[11] its 'Sea',[12] and the 'Serpent' in the wilderness.[13] It constitutes members of heavenly beings[14] and of mountains seen in vision.[15] It forms part of Goliath's armour[16] and also David's.[17] *zhb* (v. 22) was used for the construction of the ark, the tabernacle and their furnishings,[18] the ephod,[19] the breastplate,[20] the lampstand,[21] the gold altar,[22] the rosette for Aaron's turban,[23] the inner shrine to house the ark and its fittings,[24] and furnishings for the temple,[25] as well as the construction of idols.[26]

1. Num. 4.13; cf. 2 Chron. 3.14 + *tklt*.
2. E.g. Exod. 26; 27.
3. Exod. 26; 35.11; 40.19; cf. Num. 4.
4. Exod. 26.19, 21, 25.
5. Exod. 26.32.
6. Exod. 26.11; 27, *passim*.
7. 1 Chron. 22.3.
8. 1 Kgs 7.47.
9. 2 Chron. 6.13.
10. 1 Kgs 7.14-16; 2 Kgs 18.4; 25.17.
11. Exod. 27.2, 3, 4; 1 Kgs 8.64; 2 Kgs 16.14; 2 Chron. 1.5, 6; 4.1; 7.7; Ezek. 9.2.
12. 1 Chron. 18.8.
13. Num. 21.9.
14. Ezek. 1.7; 40.3; Dan. 10.6.
15. Zech. 6.1.
16. 1 Sam. 17.5, 6.
17. 1 Sam. 17.38.
18. Exod. 25.26.
19. Exod. 28.6-22.
20. Exod. 28.13.
21. Num. 8.4.
22. Exod. 40.5, 26; Num. 4.11.
23. Lev. 8.9.
24. 1 Kgs 6.20, 30.
25. 1 Kgs 7.48.
26. 1 Kgs 12.18; Ps. 135.15.

The High Priest's Breastplate. As well as *tklt* (see under Tabernacle), *npk* (v. 16) is used of the breastplate and of that only,[1] along with ON–Ezek. 28.13, which probably depends on the breastplate.

Anointing Oil. *qdh* (v. 19) is mentioned otherwise only as an ingredient of sacred anointing oil (Exod. 30.24). *qnh* (v. 19) is mentioned in connection with sacrifice (Isa. 43.24) and as an ingredient of sacred anointing oil (Exod. 30.23). It is also the term used for the branches of the temple lamp (Exod. 25.31). *bśm* (v. 22) is used in the sacred anointing oil (Exod. 30.23; 35.28).

Sacrifice. *hth* (v. 17) constituted one of the regular sacrifices.[2] *šmn* (v. 17) is used as an oblation,[3] sacrifice[4] and also for anointing.[5] *yyn* (v. 18) occurs in ON–Isa. 16.10, 22.13, Jer. 48.33 and 51.7. It is forbidden on entrance to the sanctuary,[6] but is recognized as a sacrificial offering.[7] *kr* (v. 21) is associated with sacrifice as a symbol of the destruction of the nations.[8] *'yl* (v. 21) has a regular place in the sacrificial system.[9] *'twd* (v. 21) is presented in sacrifice,[10] though it is spurned by some;[11] it is associated with the slaughter of the nations.[12]

Symbols of Yahweh. *mgn* (v. 10) occurs also in ON–Isa. 21.5 and 22.6, in Jer. 46.3, 9, in the Gog–Magog tradition,[13] and in other oracles against nations.[14] It occurs in poetry.[15] Its most common usage is

---

1.   Exod. 28.18; 39.11.
2.   Exod. 29.1; cf. 34.22; Ezek. 45.13.
3.   Gen. 28.18; 35.14.
4.   Lev. 2.1, 6; Ezek. 45.24; 46.5, 7, 11, 14.
5.   Exod. 30.25; 31.11; 37.29; Lev. 8.2; 21.10; Ps. 133.2.
6.   Lev. 10.9; Ezek. 44.21.
7.   Exod. 29.40; Lev. 23.13; Num. 15.5, 7, 10; 28.14; cf. Gen. 14.18; 1 Sam. 1.14; 1 Chron. 9.29.
8.   Isa. 34.6; Ezek. 39.18; ON–Jer. 51.40.
9.   Exod. 29.13; Lev. 5.15; 9.2; 16.3, 5; Num. 7.15; etc.; Ezek. 43.23, 25; 46.6; Ps. 66.15.
10.   Num. 7; Ps. 66.15.
11.   Ps. 50.9; Isa. 1.11.
12.   Isa. 34.6; Ezek. 39.18.
13.   Ezek. 38.4 and in 38.5 with *kwb'*.
14.   2 Kgs 19.32 // Isa. 37.33; Nah. 2.4; Ps. 76.4.
15.   Judg. 5.8; 2 Sam. 1.21; Cant. 4.4.

either as a symbol of Yahweh or an object associated with him.[1] It occurs in the House of Forest of Lebanon,[2] otherwise as a military term only in 1 Kgs 14.26, 27; Ezek. 23.24; Neh. 4.10 and 1–2 Chron. (10 times); Job 14.26; possibly also Prov. 6.11; 24.34. Problematic are Hos. 4.18 (probably a reference to Yahweh) and Job 41.7 (mythological?). *kwb'* (v. 10) occurs in the Gog–Magog tradition with *mgn* (Ezek. 38.5); it belongs to the armoury of Yahweh (Isa. 59.17) and Goliath (1 Sam. 17.5). It has a military use in 2 Chron. 26.14 and in ON–Jer. 46.4. *hdr* (v. 10) is most frequent in liturgical texts connected with Yahweh or the king.[3] *qrn* (v. 15) also occurs in ON–Jer. 48.25, Ezek. 29.21. It is a symbol of Yahweh[4] and of worship[5] and is connected with the altar.[6] It is a symbol of the king[7] and his anointing.[8]

There remain nine words whose provenance is equivocal, words that could be used in a 'religious' sense, that is to say, connected with rites and rituals, but which might equally be used in a natural or secular sense (this is also true of some of the 30 words in the previous list, but a concentration of their usage in ritual contexts and their being linked together in Ezekiel 27 suggests more positively the author's intention to describe the temple under the figure of the ship).

'lwn (v. 6) is associated with sacred places and with idolatry,[9] *(h)bdyl* (v. 12) stands in apposition to *h'bn* in Zech. 4.10, a symbol held by Zerubbabel as messianic ruler. It has been suggested that the word might be pointed as hiphil of *bdl* and have the sense 'dividing'.

'wprt (v. 12) occurs in Exod. 15.10 as an image of the way in which Egypt sank as a result of Yahweh's action at the Reed Sea. *npš*

---

1. Gen. 15.1; Deut. 33.29; 2 Sam. 22.3, 31, 36 // Ps. 18.3, 31, 36; Prov. 30.5; Pss. 3.4; 7.11; 28.7; 33.20; 59.12; 84.10, 12; 89.19; 115.9, 10, 11; 119.114; 144.2; cf. Pss. 35.2; 47.10; Prov. 2.7.

2. 1 Kgs 10.17 // 2 Chron. 9.16.

3. Pss. 8.6; 21.6; 29.4; 45.4, 5; 90.16; 96.6; 110.2; 111.3; 145.5, 12; 149.9; 1 Chron. 16.27; cf. Isa. 2.10, 19, 21; 35.2; Mic. 2.9; Job 40.10.

4. 2 Sam. 23.3 // Ps. 18.3; Hab. 3.4.

5. 1 Chron. 25.5.

6. Exod. 29.12; Lev. 4.7; 1 Kgs 1.50; 2.28; Amos 3.14; Ezek. 43.15; Ps. 118.27.

7. 1 Sam. 2.10; 16.1; Ps. 132.17; cf. 1 Sam. 2.1.

8. 1 Sam. 16.13; 1 Kgs 1.39.

9. Gen. 35.8; Hos. 4.13; Isa. 6.13; 44.14.

'dm (v. 13) is a comparatively rare phrase.[1] Only in 1 Chron. 5.21 does it have the same sense as Ezek. 27.13 (slave/captive). A list of slaves is called *spr npš* in *UT* 2106.1-2.[2]

'škr (v. 15) occurs elsewhere only of the tribute paid by Tarshish, Sheba and Seba (Ps. 72.10). *kdkd* (v. 16) is used elsewhere only of a (mythologically) restored Jerusalem (Isa. 54.12; cf. 54.16). *dbš* (v. 17) is not to be burnt as an offering to Yahweh (Lev. 2.11), but it is a standard symbol of the promised land.[3] *ṣry* (v. 17) occurs in ON–Jer. 46.11 and 51.8; it is otherwise to be found only in Gen. 37.25; 43.11 and Jer. 8.22. *ṣmr* (v. 18) was not to be worn in the sanctuary (Ezek. 44.17). It is once said to have been used in divination (Judg. 6.37).

A tenth substance might be added to this list with *r'mt* in v. 16, elsewhere only Job 28.18 and Prov. 24.7—but on this see NEB and W. McKane.[4] Van Dijk (p. 79) draws attention to *UT 'nt* III 1-2 (= *CML* 3 C 1-2, p. 48): *[t]št rimt lirth*. He says that the singular 'coral' is a collective noun, the *-ō-* pointing to Phoenician vocalization. Has the Old Testament suppressed an intimate adornment of the goddess?

Not all the substances are associated with the temple in Jerusalem. Some of them are not even acceptable there. The fact that some of them are associated with idolatry does not exclude the possibility that the author is thinking of the temple in Tyre. The fact that some of the substances are not known to have been associated with worship does not preclude the conclusion that the author was thinking principally of the temple. The concentration of articles well known as part of the paraphernalia of the temple suggests that that is what he had in mind. The image he used was that of a merchant ship, and he included articles other than those associated with worship as he thought appropriate.

The sea, though always feared, had also a benevolent aspect for seafaring people. A. van Selms compares an Egyptian text dealing with a shipwrecked sailor and the Ugaritic texts *UT* 129, 137 and 68 (= *CML* 2 iii, 2 i, pp. 37, 40). In the Egyptian text the sea-god gives the sailor a shipload of goods. Van Selms concludes, 'None of the epic

1. Gen. 9.5; Num. 19.13 (both *h'dm*); Lev. 24.17; Num. 9.6, 7; 19.11; 31.55, 40, 46; 1 Chron. 5.21.
2. Quoted by van Dijk, *Ezekiel's Prophecy*, p. 76.
3. Lev. 20.24; Deut. 6.3; 11.9; 26.9, 15.
4. W. McKane, *Proverbs* (London, 1970).

texts discovered at Ugarit deals with seafaring but the Egyptian story is an indication that the sea, far from being the universally abhorred chaotic force, could also be pictured as a great and good god'.[1]

Comparisons

Now that the two mythologies have been set out, they may be compared.

1. The most striking difference is that the sea appears as a threatening element in Ezekiel. The sea does not appear at all in the Amduat, where sand and desert are the most threatening features of the natural world. In the Egyptian tradition any reference to water is generally as the source of life and fertility. The flood (*ḥ'pj*) is an element that destroys the enemy but protects the god.

2. A notable element in ON–IJE is the Lament passage. This also occurs in the myths where the lament becomes a taunt (Isa. 14.9-11; Ezek. 27.29-36; 31.15). Where the lament occurs in myth, it usually marks the point at which the god (hero or anti-hero) is greeted in the Underworld, often without enthusiasm (cf. *Descent of Istar*, ll. 28-37; *CML* 5 ii 17-22). A remarkable feature of the Amduat is the way in which Re is greeted at the gates of the various Hours. He is always greeted with adulation. The contrast is wholly in keeping with the Old Testament use of myth, where the one who should end up as the glorious god ends up as the defeated, humiliated tyrant.

3. In the Amduat a crew of twelve oarsmen is mentioned and there is also mention of twelve gods who pull the tow rope. Much attention is given to the crew in Ezekiel, where the crew is drawn from many countries, some of which are known only from mythology. This accentuates the cosmic dimension of this Ship.

4. The primaeval darkness (*ṭiṯh*) is a region not lighted by Re. It is reserved for the enemies and is at the furthest reaches of the Dat. Re does not engage with this chaotic power, but he travels close to the boundaries of being. In view of the mythological significance of the sea in Ezekiel 27, *hyšbty 'l-mbw't*

---

1. A. van Selms, 'The Fire in Yammu's Palace', *UF* 3 (1971), pp. 249-52.

ym in v. 3 comes to have a similar significance. Tyre stands at the boundaries of chaos.

5. Frequent references are made in the Amduat to rituals that are to be carried out daily, and it becomes clear that the whole progress of the Bark is closely monitored in worship. In fact, what the Amduat is about is the right ordering of the cosmos expressed through temple liturgies. The construction of the Ship shows that Ezekiel also had the temple very much in mind. He speaks of the fate of Tyre but he does so in terms that link this oracle with the other myths used in ON–IJE. He speaks of the God who brings order out of chaos and who does so by subjugating the rebel people.

STRUCTURE, TRADITION AND REDACTION IN EZEKIEL'S DEATH VALLEY VISION[*]

Leslie C. Allen

ABSTRACT

This study analyses Ezek. 37.1-14 from the perspectives of structure, tradition history and redaction. Structurally there is a double movement in the vision account from a negative orientation to a positive one; this is matched by a single movement in the accompanying oracle of salvation. In terms of tradition history this movement echoes the metaphorical credal statement that Yahweh both kills and makes alive, in order to affirm his positive purpose to restore his exiled people. Redactionally the passage functions as an elaboration of the gift of Yahweh's spirit promised earlier in Ezek. 36.27a.

The degree to which the vision of dry bones has gripped the religious imagination is evident in expressions as culturally diverse as the Dura-Europos synagogue paintings and black American preaching.[1] In this article a concerted attempt is made to explore the meaning of this powerful text in Ezek. 37.1-14 from three perspectives, one synchronic and two diachronic.

Structure

M.V. Fox, in a valuable rhetorical study of this pericope, has played down the value of formal structural analysis, in a desire to focus on the persuasive force of discourse and thus to align Old Testament rhetorical criticism with the extra-biblical discipline.[2] His general

---

[*]   An earlier draft of the material relating to structure and redaction was read as a paper at the 1989 Annual Meeting of the Pacific Coast Region of SBL.

1.   For the latter, see F.C. Watkins, '"De Dry Bones in de Valley" (Ezek. 37, 1-10)', *Southern Folklore Quarterly* 20 (1956), pp. 136-49.

2.   'The Rhetoric of Ezekiel's Vision of the Valley of the Bones', *HUCA* 51 (1980), pp. 1-15 (1-4).

point is well taken: complex static patterns could hardly have been appreciated by an audience. However, it needs to be borne in mind that in its present form Ezek. 37.1-14 functions as a literary text, which permits rereading and so appreciation of fine points. Fox went on to admit that analysis of the structure of a unit of discourse may have some value. As we shall see, it helps to reveal not only the relation between the various parts of a unit, but also its dynamic development.

Various scholars have tried their hand at uncovering the structure of the passage. An overview of their rather different conclusions will be presented before a fresh analysis that builds upon their work is offered. H.V.D. Parunak made a good start by observing symmetrical elements that dominate the piece.[1] He divided vv. 1-14 into two main parts, two symmetrical 'symbolic panels' in vv. 3-8 and 9-10, prefaced by a heading in vv. 1-2 and followed by an interpretative oracle in vv. 11-14. He found the structural focus of the passage in the two panels. They exhibit triple parallel structuring consisting of (1) divine command with three repeated features (an introductory 'and he said to me', 'son of man', and 'prophesy...and say') in vv. 2-6 and 9, (2) report of prophetic obedience in vv. 7a and 10a, and (3) narrative description of the result of the prophecy in vv. 7b-8 and 10b. Elements of this central structure stretch back and forward to frame the pericope; the third element of description is anticipated in the heading of vv. 1-2, while the first element of divine command is repeated in vv. 11-14.

Next, M. Fishbane has claimed chiasm as the key to the structure.[2] According to him there are three double elements, ABCC'B'A'. The first and last, in vv. 1-2 and 14, consist of a combination of terms, the 'spirit' (רוח) of Yahweh and hiphil forms of the verb נוח with Yahweh as subject, ויניחני 'and he set me down' and והנחתי 'and I will settle' (A–A'). The next elements are the fulfilment of Ezekiel's prophecy over the dry bones and its interpretation in national terms (B–B') in vv. 3-10 and 12-13. The central elements of the chiasm are the interpretation of the vision in v. 11a and what he describes as an idiomatic focus to the vision provided in v. 11b (C–C'); both anticipate the interpretation

1. 'Structural Studies in Ezekiel' (PhD dissertation, Harvard, 1978; Ann Arbor, MI: University Microfilms International), pp. 479-81.

2. *Biblical Interpretation in Ancient Israel* (Oxford: Clarendon Press, 1985), p. 452.

that follows. Fishbane has drawn attention to the significance of the parallelism between the A–A′ elements. Ezekiel's experience of being 'set down' in the valley by Yahweh turns out to be a model for that of Israel's being 'set down' in its own land by Yahweh. What was to be done for the community was first done in the person of the prophet, so that his experience functions as a guarantee of national restoration.

C. Westermann has offered a double analysis.[1] First, dividing the passage into two parts, vv. 1-10 and 11-14, he discovered a parallel sequence inset in the former, a sequence of commissions and consequences in vv. 4-5/7 and 9/10, after the basic vision in vv. 1-3 and before the presentation of its meaning in vv. 11-14. This analysis is similar to Parunak's, with less exposure of his element of description. True to his longstanding concern for form, Westermann judged a form-critical structuring also to be important. He found a central role for v. 11b as a fragmentary declaration of communal lament, while vv. 1-10 and 12-14 function as expressions of an oracle of response. Both Fishbane and Westermann have given a central role to v. 11. They echo an emphasis expressed by W. Zimmerli, that v. 11 is the nucleus of the whole pericope, looking both back and forward.[2]

Both scholars seem to have uncovered vital structural elements from their different perspectives. If one looks afresh at the pericope in the light of their labors, reusing some of these elements and utilizing further features, a consistent structure emerges. Verse 1a seems to function as the introduction, lying outside the structure of the unit as a whole. The body of the text consists of a threefold sequence, whose elements grow progressively shorter, in vv. 1b-8a, 8b-10 and 11-14. The sequence of elements is ABCBCA′–ABCA′–AB. A represents negative description, B divine speech, C prophetic reaction, and A′ positive description.

The first part, vv. 1b-8a, falls into two segments, vv. 1b-3 and 4-8a. The former consists of three elements, the first of which is a negative description of bones so devoid of life that they are 'very dry' (vv. 1b-2, A). The vividness of the visionary scene is emphasized by the two uses of 'behold' in v. 2. There follows a divine speech in v. 3a (B), prefaced by the introductory formula 'and he said to me' and begin-

1. *Prophetische Heilsworte im Alten Testament* (FRLANT, 145; Göttingen: Vandenhoeck & Ruprecht, 1987), pp. 133-34.

2. *Ezekiel* (Hermeneia; 2 vols.; Philadelphia: Fortress Press, 1979, 1983), II, p. 257.

ning with the vocative 'son of man'. The divine speech consists of a
question, to which a prophetic answer is given in v. 3b (C). The negati-
vism in vv. 1b-2 seems to dominate this first segment. Ezekiel's laconic
reply may be taken as a reinforcement of the negative description:
'You know that these bones—so dry and lifeless—will not and cannot
live'.[1]

The second segment of vv. 1b-8a is composed of vv. 4-8a. Three of
the elements of the first segment reappear, with variety of order and
content. First comes divine speech (B), in vv. 4-6. It essentially consists of an oracle of salvation that is a two-part proof saying, in which
the particle 'behold' is pointedly reused in a positive context. The
oracle is prefaced with the introductory formula already used for the
divine speech of v. 3. It is prefaced with a commission to prophesy, a
call to attention and a messenger formula. Prophetic transmission of
the oracle (C) follows in v. 7a. Finally there is positive description
(A′) in vv. 7b-8a, which studiously includes two uses of 'behold', in a
happy counterpart to the grim usage in v. 2. Overall, the relation
between the two parts, vv. 1b-3 and 4-8a, seems to be that of a negative prelude to a positive, transforming event. Within vv. 1-10 the
content of vv. 1b-8a is marked by incompleteness, in that the oracle of
revival has only partially been fulfilled. Yet structurally this portion is
self-contained and represents a distinct phase that comes to an end
with v. 8a.

Verses 8b-10 present a second part that, while developing the story
line, includes the same elements as vv. 1b-8a but in a shorter compass.
A brief negative description (A) paves the way, in v. 8b.[2] There
follows divine speech (B) in v. 9, which comprehensively recapitulates
in its preliminary features the cases in vv. 3a and 4-6: the introductory formula (// vv. 3, 4), the commission to prophesy (// v. 4), the
address 'son of man' (// v. 3) and the messenger formula (// v. 5). The
call to attention in v. 5 is left out of this recapitulation, with a brevity
that may echo the overall conciseness of vv. 8-10 in relation to vv. 1b-

---

1. 'The prophet's reply should probably be paraphrased: "You know the answer
to that. Of course they can't live!"' (P.C. Craigie, *Ezekiel* [Daily Study Bible;
Philadelphia: Westminster Press, 1983], p. 260). Cf. W.E. Lemke, 'Life in the
Present and Hope for the Future', *Int* 38 (1984), pp. 165-80 (178-79).

2. P. Höffken ('Beobachtungen zu Ezechiel xxxvii 1-10', *VT* 31 [1981],
pp. 305-17 [308 n. 10]) has drawn attention to the change in the mode of description
at v. 8b, from visual experience to interpretation.

8a. The actual oracle is of a different kind from that in vv. 5-6; it is now an oracle of command for the רוח, here the world-sustaining life-force, to presence itself and fulfil the work of reanimation. There follows in v. 10 prophetic transmission (C) which matches that of v. 7a, with stylistic variation.[1] Finally comes positive description (A') in v. 10b. Overall, vv. 8b-10 has echoed the elements already used in vv. 1b-8, but telescoped them, as is not uncommon in literary repetition.

The third part, in vv. 11-14, is briefer still in terms of the number of elements. Prophetic reaction is lacking, and so is the positive narrative description featured in vv. 7b-8a and 10b. The part is wholly made up of divine speech (B), which takes the form of a disputation. Imbedded within it is an element of negative description (A), in v. 11. It consists of interpretation of the dry bones described in vv. 1b-2 and a complementary quotation of the exiles' lamenting despair. Its attention-drawing particle 'behold' noticeably echoes v. 2. In reply to this negative feature, the divine speech moves in vv. 12-13 to an oracle of salvation, a two-part proof saying in vv. 5-6. It too contains 'behold', now corresponding to that in v. 5. One may add that it also alludes to its double presence within the positive description of vv. 7b-8a, at v. 8a. What is promised in the oracle of vv. 12-13 naturally corresponds to what was performed in the vision, as well as to what was promised there. The divine speech is initiated by elements already familiar to the reader: in v. 11 the introductory formula (// vv. 3, 4, 9) and the vocative address (// vv. 3, 9) and in v. 12 the commission to prophesy (// vv. 4, 9) and the messenger formula (// vv. 5, 9). Prophetic formulaic language used in the two sections of the vision narrative is here gathered up and reused in this interpretative section. Structurally one might have expected the piece to conclude with v. 13. However, in v. 14 there follows as a seeming climax a further oracle of salvation, again a two-part proof saying, which is capped by an asseveration formula and a divine-saying formula.

Support for this structural analysis comes from a pair of inclusions evident in the passage. The first of the three sections of the pericope was defined as vv. 1b-8a; in fact the double usage of 'behold' in both the initial negative description and the final positive description provides a nice framework for it. The second section, vv. 8b-10, is marked

---

1. R. Rendtorff (*TDNT*, VI, p. 799) has compared the hithpael of the verb 'prophesy' with the use at 13.17, where it characterizes a misused psychic gift of mediating life or death. Here the prophetic word shares this immense potential.

by a contrasting border, ואין רוח בהם 'but there was no breath in them'
and ותבוא הרוח בהם 'and breath came into them' (8b, 10).

There are a number of other examples of inclusion in this stylistically rich pericope. What Fishbane regarded as the first and last steps
in a chiasm may at least be viewed as an envelope for the pericope, in
vv. 1 and 14. The first two sections together make up the visionary
part of the passage. D. Baltzer has noted that it is marked off by the
parallel double usage of מאד 'very' in vv. 2 and 10.[1] The repetition
accentuates the contrast between the negative and positive descriptions
in which they are set. Smaller portions of text are also delineated by
inclusion. P. Höffken has observed that within the oracle of salvation
in vv. 5-6 the first part of the proof saying has its own inclusion,
בכם רוח וחייתם, '...in you breath and you will live', which serves to
focus on the gift of new life.[2] Parunak has drawn attention to the
extensive inclusion that marks the oracle of salvation in vv. 12-13: 'I
will open your graves and bring you up from your graves', and the
resumptive 'when I open your graves and bring you up from your
graves'.[3] Tight bonding and differentiation are achieved by all these
examples of inclusion, and among them are pointers to a structural
break between v. 8a and 8b.

Cognizance may be taken of a number of cases of word repetition
and wordplay, mainly serving as stylistic links between parts. Wordplay
is characteristic of vision oracles, and so one is not surprised to find it
here. The word repetition is not of a straightforward kind, but applies
the same terms to different contexts. The first and third parts are
loosely linked by two examples of this patterning. First, the divine
bringing of breath (אני מביא 'I will bring', v. 5) is echoed in the
bringing of the exiles to the land of Israel (והבאתי 'and I will bring',
v. 12). Secondly, the divine bringing up of flesh upon the bones is
capped by the bringing up of the exiles from their virtual graves (והעליתי
'and I will bring up', vv. 6, 12). Wordplay also unites these parts: ותקרבו
'and (the bones) joined' (v. 7) finds an echo in קברותיכם 'your graves'
(vv. 12, 13). Another instance of wordplay bridges the second and third
parts: פחי 'breathe' (v. 9) and אני פתח 'I will open' together with בפתחי
'when I open' (vv. 12, 13). Counterpointing of this same pair of stems
occurs in Jeremiah's vision of the tilting cauldron and its explanatory

1. *Ezechiel und Deuterojesaja* (BZAW, 121; Berlin: de Gruyter, 1971), p. 109.
2. Höffken, 'Beobachtungen', p. 306.
3. 'Structural Studies', p. 483.

oracle in Jer. 1.13-14. Mention may also be made of consonantal assonance that occurs within the second part: ‏(ב)הרוגים האלה ויחיו‏ 'these slain
ones, that they may live' and ‏(על-) רגליהם חיל‏ '(upon) their feet, a host'
(vv. 9, 10). The transposed consonants stylistically emphasize the
radical transformation Yahweh would bring about, whereby victims
of divine judgment were to become recipients of salvation and strength.

The third part deserves closer structural examination. In general the
lament is obviously matched by the following oracle of salvation, with
appropriate correlation of forms. The three clauses of the lament
correspond to the three clauses of the divine response, but only
loosely. In fact, the third clause in v. 11 matches the second clause in
v. 12, for two reasons. First, the double pronominal reference in
‏נגזרנו לנו‏ 'we are cut off for ourselves' is nicely answered by that of
‏והעליתי אתכם מקברותיכם‏ 'and I will bring you up from your graves'.
Secondly, the metaphors of graves and of being cut off (in death) are
closely associated concepts in a lament context, as Ps. 88.6(5) illus-
trates: ‏כמו...שכבי קבר...נגזרו‏ 'like...those who lie in the grave... they
are cut off'. The second clause in the lament seems to correspond to
the first one in the oracle. The emotional expression of dead hope,
‏ואבדה תקותנו‏ 'and our hope is perished', is answered by a new hope,
Yahweh's opening of their graves. One may note here not only the
matching of the two final terms in the Hebrew, as nouns with suffixes
that relate to the exiles, but also the echo of the death-laden verb in
the term 'graves', and the irruption of dynamic activity on Yahweh's
part to deal with the passive situation of the exiles. The first statement
in the lament and the third one in the oracle function as flanges. The
initial lament clause 'our bones are dried up' has its own role to play,
as a metaphor of disorientation that expresses a low quality of life.
Reinterpreted in terms of the metaphor of death expressed in the third
clause ('we are cut off'), it has formed the basis of the preceding
vision, as the references to dry bones in vv. 2 and 4 reveal. The interpretation of the vision commences with the basic factor revealed at the
start of the vision. The third statement in the oracle of v. 12 concerning restoration of the exiles to their own land is an important
element in the interpretation. It grounds the metaphor of new life in
Ezekiel's general positive agenda of a new exodus. By implication it
serves to identify the bringing up from the graves with the actual
phase of exodus, which is then followed by the phase of entry into the
promised land. Verse 21 is comparable, where the exodus phase is

flavored by the symbolism of taking sticks (לקח 'take', vv. 16, 19, 21). The mention of entry into the land finds reinforcement in v. 14 within the second salvation oracle.

Tradition

Hopefully the reason for this complex structuring will become evident from a consideration of Ezekiel's use of tradition history. It must be said that there is much in 37.1-14 that correlates with material elsewhere in the book. For instance, the overall form of the unit is similar to that of 36.16-32 in consisting of both a private communication of Yahweh to the prophet and a public oracle. In form-critical content, although not in the order of its components, it is especially close to 11.1-13. There a vision and a disputation that consists of divine interpretation of the vision, a commission to deliver an oracle and the actual oracle are followed by a visionary account of the effect of the oracle and a question asked by the prophet.[1] The two stages of reanimation in the vision have been compared by Zimmerli to the two phases of Ezekiel's eating the scroll in 3.1-3, which both consist of divine command and prophetic compliance.[2] F. Hossfeld has observed that the reference to the 'slain' (הרוגים) in v. 10 echoes the use of the verb in 9.16, 21.16(11) and 23.10, 47 in contexts of divine judgment against Israel.[3] At a climactic point in the vision the term is deliberately used to categorize the exiles as virtually 'slain', victims of Yahweh's punishment for their sins.

Yet it is also clear that the pericope draws upon earlier traditions. Commentators generally see in the two stages of reanimation narrated in the vision the influence of Gen. 2.7; the fact that the verb 'breathe' (נפח) is common to both passages supports the derivation.[4] Yahweh is engaged in a work of new creation. Baltzer has found in the divine command of v. 9 a reference to the power of the creative word in Genesis 1.[5] But what of the conception of death and new life? The

1. See especially Höffken, 'Beobachtungen', pp. 310-12.

2. *Ezekiel*, II, p. 257; cf. *Ezekiel*, I, pp. 135-36.

3. *Untersuchungen zu Komposition und Theologie des Ezechielbuches* (Forschungen zur Bibel, 20; Würzburg: Echter Verlag, 1977), p. 380. He also cited the usage in foreign oracles at 26.6, 8, 11, 15; 28.9.

4. See, e.g., Zimmerli, *Ezekiel*, II, p. 261.

5. *Ezechiel*, p. 112.

very question of v. 3 appears to indicate that a belief in physical resurrection was not yet current to provide the basis for a positive answer. Scholars have usually been content to ground the conception in the lamenting citation of the exiles' despair in v. 11, with examples from the Psalms of disorientation described in terms of a living death.[1] If the citation supplies the negative imagery, one can go on to relate the gift of new life to the reorientation that Yahweh brings about. 'You have brought up my being from Sheol', exclaims the giver of thanks (Ps. 30.4[3]; cf. 86.13). But may one find a more specific parallel? Hossfeld, who views vv. 11b-13a as a separate unit from vv. 1-10 and so cannot ground the latter in the imagery of v. 11, has included in his extensive study of vv. 1-14 a section on the tradition history of the vision. He has found the source of its imagery of new life after death in the literal resurrection of the dead boy through the prophet Elijah in 1 Kgs 17.17-24.[2] In his section on semantic analysis he noted that both there and in the vision the verb חיה 'live' has an ingressive sense, 'come back to life'.[3] Even more significantly he also cited as a semantic parallel the interrelated sayings in 1 Sam. 2.6 and 2 Kgs. 5.7 concerning God's power to kill and bring back to life.[4]

Here surely is a likely traditio-historical source for the transformation in the vision. Deut. 32.39, 1 Sam. 2.6 and 2 Kgs 5.7 are all examples of a merismus that couples Yahweh's omnipotent power both to inflict death and to bestow life.[5] In view of its particular contexts, it is apparently used not of literal death but metaphorically of Yahweh as the originator of both disorientation and reorientation.[6] In the first case it is expressed in hymnic language, 'I put to death and bring to life', and is followed by 'I wound and I heal'. The second case is a similar affirmation: 'Yahweh puts to death and brings to life'.

---

1. For a recent study of death in the Psalter, see C.C. Broyles, *The Conflict of Faith and Experience in the Psalms* (JSOTSup, 52; Sheffield: JSOT Press, 1989), pp. 84-95. The imagery appears to be restricted to individual psalms.

2. *Untersuchungen*, p. 390.

3. *Untersuchungen*, pp. 376-77.

4. *Untersuchungen*, p. 377.

5. See J. Krašovec, *Der Merismus im Biblisch-Hebräischen und Nordwestsemitischen* (BibOr, 33; Rome: Biblical Institute Press, 1977), p. 118; K.-J. Illman, *Old Testament Formulas about Death* (Åbo: Åbo Akademi, 1979), pp. 164-68. Cf. Wisd. 16.13: 'For you have authority over life and death; you bring down to the gates of Sheol and back again'.

6. Cf. A.D.H. Mayes, *Deuteronomy* (NCB; London: Oliphants, 1979), p. 392.

The text continues with examples of God's providential dual activity, impoverishing/enriching and demoting/promoting. In its setting of thanksgiving the focus is on the second element: Yahweh who inflicts deathlike disorientation also restores to a new quality of life. In the third case both the emphasis on the second of the two elements and the metaphorical nature of the terminology are clear: 'Am I God to put to death and to bring alive, that this person sends to me to cure a man of his leprosy?'

Let us recall at this point that Ezekiel made use of a series of Achilles' heel metaphors to corroborate his message of coming divine judgment. These metaphors first empathetically shared the misplaced optimism of the exiles and then took a very logical tangent toward pessimism.[1] Thus Tyre is a magnificent ocean-going merchant ship— but in traditional Israelite thinking do not ships tend to be wrecked (ch. 27)? The prince of Tyre has all the glory of the fabulous primaeval man in Eden—but did he not fall (ch. 28)? Pharaoh possesses the power of the mythological chaos monster—but did it not lose to its divine enemy (chs. 29 and 32)? In the prophet's message of salvation here the same thing seems to be happening in reverse. The exiles' despair cited in v. 11 is depicted in a visionary metaphor that fully assents to their pessimism: 'Can these bones live?' Who indeed could give an affirmative answer? In the terms of 33.10, 'How can we live?' Yet the bones do come back to life. Just as Ezekiel used older cultural concepts as models to support his theme of unforeseeable judgment, so here the implicit basis for salvation appears to be the traditional hymnic quality of the national God to give triumph over the tragedy he sends.[2] Yahweh puts to death *and* brings back to life. The 'slain', victims of just punishment at his hand, are destined to enjoy an amazing new lease on life. The double process of reanimation itself reflects the prophet's twofold agenda of first empathizing with the exiles' mood and then contradicting it. Fox has delightfully compared 'the magician

---

1. Cf. C.A. Newsom, 'A Maker of Metaphors—Ezekiel's Oracles against Tyre', *Int 38* (1984), pp. 151-64 (157).

2. In this free adaptation of the hymnic formula, הרג 'slay' functions as a synonym of המית 'put to death'. Note too the hiphil of עלה 'bring up (from Sheol)' in 2 Sam. 2.6, as in vv. 12-13 here. Illman (*Old Testament Formulas*, pp. 164, 166) has observed that alongside the formulaic phrasing of 'put to death/make alive' there are freer instances that employ the qal of חיה 'live' in a perfect consecutive construction (Exod. 1.16; Esth. 4.11)—which is what occurs here in vv. 5, 6, 14.

who invariably "fails" once or twice in attempting the grand finale in order to intensify suspense and to focus attention on the climactic success to follow'.[1] In fact the magician is also reinforcing the evident impossibility of the trick in the minds of the audience. The double process of reviving expressed in the two structural sections of the vision concedes the difficulty of the enterprise and accentuates the power of God. Like the hero in Paul Gallico's *The Man Who Was Magic*,[2] Yahweh was a real magician.

Also woven into the visionary account is the traditional concept of the prophet as inaugurator of the future he prophesies for the people.[3] 'I have hewn them through the prophets, I have slain them by the words of my mouth', declared Yahweh through Hosea (Hos. 6.5). Yet not only a negative future was unleashed by the prophets. Jeremiah was set 'over nations and kingdoms, to pluck up and break down... to build and plant' (Jer. 1.10; cf. Ezek. 36.36). In all three parts of the pericope, structural emphasis is laid on the role of the prophet in bringing about Yahweh's positive work.[4] As in 11.4-12, Ezekiel's prophetic word controls the development of the vision.[5] He was to function under God as the agent of renewal. This role served both as an assurance to the prophet and as an assertion to the people regarding the authority and authenticity he possessed as proclaimer of salvation, as truly as when he had predicted the judgment that had now been fulfilled.

Redaction

Scholars have varied in the amount of redactional material they have detected in 37.1-14. Perhaps surprisingly Zimmerli has here refused to see any.[6] Others have discovered in redaction criticism the answer to a discrepancy between the vision and its interpretation—a scene of

---

1. Fox, 'Rhetoric', p. 11.
2. London: Heinemann, 1966.
3. Cf. J. Lindblom, *Prophecy in Ancient Israel* (Philadelphia: Fortress Press, 1965), pp. 117-20.
4. Fox's description of Ezekiel in the vision as a largely passive spectator has rightly been criticized by R.W. Klein (*Ezekiel: The Prophet and his Message* [Columbia: University of South Carolina Press, 1988], p. 155 n. 9).
5. Cf. Zimmerli, *Ezekiel*, I, p. 258.
6. *Ezekiel*, II, p. 257.

unburied bones gives way to a graveyard. Accordingly A. Bertholet, G. Fohrer and J.W. Wevers have envisaged an original unit of vv. 1-12aα and 14, which has been supplemented with the first oracle of salvation in vv. 12aβ-13 that contains the awkward 'graves'.[1] More recently a rather more radical expedient has found favor: to envisage the combination of two independent units—an interpreted vision and a disputation—and then their supplementation with either v. 14 or vv. 13b-14. Thus Baltzer has taken the vision of unburied bones in vv. 1-10 along with the interpretation in v. 11 ('These bones are all the house of Israel') as a unit separate from the divine introduction in the rest of v. 11 and the graves-based oracle of vv. 12-13. The fresh oracle of v. 14, which uses רוח in the sense of 'spirit' (rather than 'breath' or 'life force') and makes it Yahweh's, is a subsequent comment on vv. 6 and 12-13. It is linked with the redactional 36.26-28, which employs רוח in the same way as here.[2] Hossfeld has largely followed Baltzer's analysis except that he has aligned v. 11a as a whole with vv. 1-10, rather than only the interpreting clause, envisaging the redactional addition as vv. 13b-14.[3] He diluted the basic similarity between vv. 1-11a and v. 11b by claiming that the references to 'dry bones' within vv. 2 and 4 were redactional additions to bind vv. 1-11a more closely to the next, juxtaposed unit. He drew attention to the omission of the normal אדני 'Lord' in the divine-saying formula in v. 14.[4]

Zimmerli has brushed aside as unnecessary the concern about change of imagery from unburied bones to properly interred remains.[5] His instinctive reaction against envisaging two units may be supported by objective arguments. First, in view of the lament style of the quotation

1. A. Bertholet, *Hesekiel* (HAT; Tübingen: Mohr [Paul Siebeck], 1936), p. 126; G. Fohrer, *Ezechiel* (HAT; Tübingen: Mohr [Paul Siebeck], 1955), pp. 209-10; J.W. Wevers, *Ezekiel* (NCB; London: Nelson, 1969), pp. 277, 279.

2. *Ezechiel*, pp. 101-108. He has been followed by A. Graffy, *A Prophet Confronts his People* (AnBib, 104; Rome: Biblical Institute Press, 1984), pp. 83-84.

3. *Untersuchungen*, pp. 367, 369. He followed G. Jahn, *Das Buch Ezechiel auf Grund der Septuaginta hergestellt* (Leipzig: E. Pfeiffer, 1905), p. 255, and more recently by J. Garscha, *Studien zum Ezechielbuch: Eine redaktionkritische Untersuchung von 1–39* (Bonn: Lang, 1974), p. 222, in taking v. 13b as the start of the redactional addition. Both Baltzer and Hossfeld construe המה 'they' at the end of v. 11a with v. 11b, in order to supply a subject at the beginning of their new unit.

4. *Untersuchungen*, p. 387.

5. *Untersuchungen*, p. 387.

in v. 11, it is pertinent to refer to the free mixing of metaphors to describe the experience of disorientation in the psalms of lament and thanksgiving. For instance, there is free movement from a figure of drowning to that of a trap in Ps. 124.4-5, 7 (cf. Pss. 57.2, 5, 7 [1, 4, 6]). Accordingly it is wooden to differentiate on this score between the prophetic vision and the divine oracle, which comment from slightly different perspectives on the deathlike disorientation of v. 11b. Secondly, one must take seriously the stylistic coherence of the passage suggested above, especially the parallel elements and wordplay. Thirdly, the role of the prophet in the vision as agent of divine salvation for the exiles matches the prophetic formulations and the actual message of salvation in the interpretative material. Fourthly, a warning needs to be sounded against confusing form criticism and redaction criticism.[1] The existence of unredacted 'mixed' Psalms is a perennial caution against this not infrequent confusion. There is no reason why a vision and a disputation cannot coexist from the beginning in a prophetic piece.[2]

Zimmerli also dismissed as unnecessary the assignment of vv. 13b-14 to a redactor's hand.[3] He explained vv. 12-14 as an expanded proof saying and was able to cite other examples in the book of Ezekiel. However, he admitted elsewhere that at times what looked like an original expanded proof saying might on other grounds turn out to be primary material redactionally expanded.[4] In this case the factor of inclusion permits v. 13b to be taken with what precedes, so that Baltzer's limitation of the alleged supplement to v. 14 may be judged preferable. Certainly in terms of structure vv. 11-13 supplies what one expects to find in correspondence with the previous two sections of the unit. The extra oracle of salvation or proof saying in v. 14 gilds the structural lily. What then is the role of v. 14? The answer lies in the wider literary setting of this pericope. Baltzer, Garscha and Hossfeld all made reference to 36.27 and ascribed v. 14 or vv. 13b-14

---

1. Graffy (*A Prophet*, p. 84) identified form and structure as 'the principal reasons' for division into two units, with the change in metaphor as a supplementary reason. By 'structure' he meant form-critical structure.

2. One might add, fifthly, that R. Bartelmus has argued strongly for the unity of v. 11, against Baltzer and Hossfeld ('Textkritik, Literaturkritik und Syntax: Anmerkungen zur neueren Diskussion um Ezek. 37, 11', *BN* 25 [1984], pp. 55-64).

3. Bartelmus, 'Textkritik'.

4. *Ezekiel*, II, p. 97.

to the same redactional hand that they found in the context of 36.27.[1]
Zimmerli himself assigned 36.23bβ-38 to the 'school' of Ezekiel,[2]
while in a recent commentary[3] I have judged 36.24-38 to be redactional. U. Cassuto once suggested that the similarity of 36.27 and 37.14
was the reason why 37.1-14 was placed after ch. 36.[4] His insight may
be developed in a redactional direction. Verse 37.14a is remarkably
like 36.27a: ואת־רוחי אתן בקרבכם 'and my spirit I will put within you'
appears to be echoed by ונתתי רוחי בכם 'and I will put my spirit in
you'. The change of preposition and verbal construction may be
explained as deliberate assimilation to ונתתי בכם רוחי in v. 6 in order to
allude to specific material within 37.1-13. The continuation with וחייתם
'and you will live' and a recognition formula in both vv. 6 and 14 is
further evidence of a recapitulating intent.

This virtual quotation from 36.27 in v. 14 needs to be linked with a
parallel echoing of 36.27b in 37.24b: ועשיתי את אשר־בחקי תלכו ומשפטי
תשמרו ועשיתם 'and I will cause that in my statutes you walk and my
ordinances you observe and do' is resumed by ובמשפטי ילכו וחקתי
ישמרו ועשו אותם 'and in my ordinances they will walk and my statutes
they will observe and do them'. The reversal of the objects is typical
of literary resumption of earlier material.[5] In the case of 37.24b,
Zimmerli has seen it as the start of a redactional expansion in vv. 24b-
28.[6] Rightly so, most probably, but more remains to be said about the
redactional process. 37.14a and 37.24b seem to function as final
captions to 37.1-13 and 37.15-23. These captions deliberately refer
back to the two halves of 36.27. The editorial function of 37.1-13 in
its present position is to throw light on the gift of the spirit in 36.27a.
That of 37.15-23 is to clarify a means by which Yahweh would bring
about the obedience of 36.27b, namely via a Davidic king who would
impose order among God's people, uniting southern and northern
elements with his royal staff or scepter. In turn 37.14a represents an

1.   Baltzer, *Ezechiel*, p. 108; Garscha, *Studien*, p. 222; Hossfeld, *Unter-*
suchungen, p. 401.
2.   *Ezekiel*, II, pp. 245-46, 248.
3.   *Ezekiel 20–48* (WBC; Dallas: Word Books, 1990).
4.   *Biblical and Oriental Studies*. I. *Bible* (Jerusalem: Magnes, 1973), p. 239.
5.   Cf. in principle S. Talmon in F.M. Cross and S. Talmon (eds.), *Qumran and*
the History of the Biblical Text (Cambridge, MA: Harvard University Press, 1975),
pp. 359-68. It is a further example of what Talmon called 'inverted distant parallelism' used in inner-biblical quotations.
6.   *Ezekiel*, II, pp. 272-73.

editorial rounding off of the unit of vv. 1-13, which uses the vision
with its ninefold occurrence of רוח 'breath/spirit' as an illustration of
the restoring power of God in 36.27a. It intends to focus particularly
on the reference to the giving of the רוח in v. 6, but its identification
as Yahweh's spirit seems to echo Ezekiel's own empowering in v. 1.

Hossfeld observed that in both 36.27 and 37.14 reference to renewed
occupation of the land follows.[1] The redactor apparently used the
unusual verb הניח 'settle' in order to recall the setting down of Ezekiel
in v. 1, thereby creating not only a structural inclusion but also the
role-modeling intent detected by Fishbane, which the skewing factor
of redaction makes more likely than it would be in an unredacted text.[2]
The formula of asseveration that is woven into the recognition
formula, אני יהוה דברתי ועשיתי 'I Yahweh have spoken and will act',
serves to reinforce the twin components of promise and event present
in the vision. The interpretation of vv. 11-13 necessarily focused on
promise; the asseveration formula allows both components to surface
in a final reference. There is a nice stylistic echo of דבר יהוה 'the word
of Yahweh' in v. 4, which in the rest of the vision and in the interpretation lacks a matching counterpart. There is much evidence in the
book of Ezekiel that the redactor(s) had an eye for literary style. Here
an opportunity is taken for a slight stylistic improvement that yields a
satisfying climax by adding the last piece to a structural jigsaw. The
closing signature of the divine saying formula accords with a feature
of redactional work in the book, the claim of prophetic inspiration

---

1. *Untersuchungen*, p. 386. The change from ארץ 'land' to אדמה in 37.14 is
doubtless to be explained by to the influence of the latter term in 37.12; cf. also 36.24.

2. Fox refused to see inclusion in the double use of רוח, since it would hardly
be detectable to an auditor and since the term functions so differently that the repetition has no rhetorical value ('Rhetoric', p. 14 n. 18). Fishbane's larger inclusion and
explanation, when set in a redactional perspective, serve to answer his second point.
If v. 14 is redactional, his first point is invalid. Höffken has reasonably asked
whether the verb means 'settle', as in Isa. 14.1, or 'allow to stay', as in Jer. 27.11
('Beobachtungen', p. 315 n. 26). He took it in the latter sense and intriguingly saw
in vv. 12 and 14 two different acts of God, corresponding to the two in vv. 8 and
10. However, if v. 14 is taken as primary, it should most probably be regarded
form-critically as the closing part of an expanded proof saying, as Zimmerli took it.
Then v. 14 continues the subordinate clauses of v. 13, as further acts after bringing
the exiles up from their Sheol of disorientation. Yet in v. 12 the next step is return to
the land, to which one accordingly expects a reference in v. 14.

and divine authority in valid continuation of the work of Ezekiel himself.

An attempt has been made to analyze this pericope from three perspectives in order to shed light on its meaning. In terms of structure there is a double movement from a negative orientation to a positive one in the vision report; it is matched in the accompanying oracle. In terms of tradition history this movement relates to the credal affirmation that Yahweh both kills and makes alive, which is echoed in order to confirm his positive intent to restore his people. Redactionally the pericope functions as an elaboration of the gift of Yahweh's spirit promised in 36.27a.

Part III

MINOR PROPHETS

IN PRAISE OF DIVINE CAPRICE:
THE SIGNIFICANCE OF THE BOOK OF JONAH*

Alan Cooper

ABSTRACT

'Deliverance', as the author of Jonah depicts it, is neither a reward for merit nor a tempering of justice with mercy. It is, instead, a free and gracious act of divine love. The wellspring of this concept of deliverance is not covenant faith, but personal religion. This understanding of the message of Jonah is defended by a close reading of the critical passages in Jon. 3–4, and by an examination of intertextual relationships between Jonah and some of the other Minor Prophets.

I

The Book of Jonah gives common sense a battering. At almost every turn, it seems to refute some unspoken assumption, something taken for granted about the way things work in the world. A prophet commissioned to go to the east would not flee to the west; people drown when they are tossed into a tempestuous sea; if God announces that he is going to destroy a city, it is as good as destroyed; the Assyrians would not change their entire way of life because of a five-word admonition from a Hebrew prophet—except (in all four cases) in the Book of Jonah. Practically everything in the book confutes normal expectation—its characters, its plot, and even its language. Its fictive world is far removed from the everyday world descried by experience and common sense.[1]

* I would like to thank my former students, Rabbi R.M. Rosenberg and Rabbi E.W. Torop, for their responses to the ideas contained in this paper. I also benefitted from keen critical readings of earlier drafts by my friends, Drs M.V. Fox, B.R. Goldstein and B. Halpern.

1. See S. Stewart, *Nonsense: Aspects of Intertextuality in Folklore and Literature* (Baltimore: Johns Hopkins University Press, 1980), pp. 3-46. In her words, 'nonsense most often results from what may be seen to be a radical shift... away

One of the classic confutations of the 'real world' in all literature, of course, is Jonah's sea voyage in the belly of a great fish. This incredible adventure is spun out of the literalization or inversion of a metaphor,[1] specifically the metaphor of Jon. 2.3-4 ('From the belly of Sheol I cried out'). The effect of such inversion is to 'present a critique and a denial of univocal meaning and the ideology of univocal meaning found in common sense'[2]—not a bad precis for the entire Book of Jonah, in my view. Yet it is out of the book's befuddlement of its readers that its profound theological message emerges, as I intend to show in this paper.

It can hardly be fortuitous that two astonishing instances of unpredictable plot-reversal (*peripeteia*) in the Bible happen to involve the prophet Jonah. In 2 Kgs 14.25-27, God permits the expansion of Israel's borders, 'according to the word that his servant Jonah uttered', despite the nation's persistent sinfulness (14.24). And in Jon. 3.10, God reverses the evil decree that Jonah had pronounced against Nineveh in 3.4. The thematic link between these two events was already noted in the Babylonian Talmud, where R. Naḥman b. Yiṣḥaq is quoted as saying, 'Just as evil was transformed[3] into good for Nineveh, so was evil transformed into good for Israel during the days of Jeroboam b. Joash' (*b. Yeb.* 98a).

In each instance, the change of fortune entails the falsification of a prophetic threat of destruction. The reversal of Jon. 3.4 is self-evident.[4]

---

from a contiguous relationship to the context of everyday life...' (p. 33).

1.   Examples of this phenomenon are legion in everyday discourse, and are often a source of humor. When cartoon characters become furious, they turn red and breathe fire, their ears emit steam, and the tops of their heads blow off—all literalizations of commonly used metaphors. On these and other metaphors of anger, see G. Lakoff, *Women, Fire and Dangerous Things: What Categories Reveal about the Mind* (Chicago: University of Chicago Press, 1987), pp. 380-97.

2.   Quoting Stewart, *Nonsense*, p. 77.

3.   R. Naḥman uses the niphal of *hpk*, as does Jon. 3.4.

4.   I am assuming for the moment that Jon. 3.4. is unequivocally negative. Yet according to Rashi and Isaac Abravanel, for example, *nehpāket* might have two senses: either Nineveh will be 'overthrown', or it will be 'transformed' for the better. Nineveh's response to the oracle will determine which of the two senses is effectuated. This view has been adopted recently by E.M. Good, *Irony in the Old Testament* (Philadelphia: Westminster Press, 1985), pp. 48-49; B. Halpern and R.E. Friedman, 'Composition and Paronomasia in the Book of Jonah', *HAR* 4 (1980), pp. 79-92, esp. pp. 87, 89. For an arbitrary rejection of it, see H.W. Wolff, *Obadiah and*

It is less frequently noted that the prophecies of Amos against Jeroboam, recounted in Amos 7.9 and 11 (the latter being Amaziah's report of Amos's speech), are contradicted by the favorable notice in 2 Kings 14 and, by inference, must have been at variance with Jonah's predictions. As M. Cogan and H. Tadmor remark, 2 Kgs 14.27 'evidences awareness of a prophetic word contradicting that of Jonah'.[1] A midrash suggests that Jeroboam was rewarded because he repudiated Amaziah's charge against Amos: 'Was not Jeroboam an idolater? Yes, yet God chose him to save Israel because he refused to accept slander of the prophet Amos.'[2] The sixteenth-century homilist Moses Alshekh explains that by sparing Amos's life, Jeroboam brought about the annulment of Amos's prophecies, and the fulfillment of Jonah's.[3]

In each case, the Bible seems to supply God's motive for sparing the condemned people. I say 'seems to' because, upon closer examination, the purported motives evanesce, or at least raise more problems than they solve. I intend to argue that these problems are the crux of the Book of Jonah—and not the contrast between Israel and the gentile nations, the clash between universalism and particularism, the tension between divine justice and mercy, or the dilemma of false prophecy, to name the four themes that have dominated discussion of the book for two millennia.[4]

Jonah (trans. M. Kohl; Minneapolis: Augsburg, 1986), p. 149.

1. *II Kings* (AB, 11; New York: Doubleday, 1988), p. 161 (see also p. 164).

2. *T. d. Eliyy.* 17 and parallels. See W.G. Braude and I.J. Kapstein, *Tanna Debe Eliyyahu* (Philadelphia: Jewish Publication Society, 1981), pp. 233-34.

3. M. Alshekh, *Sefer Mar'ot ha-Sove'ot* (repr. New York: Joseph Weiss, 1979), *ad* 2 Kgs 14.26. Alshekh's position is consistent with a common attitude towards prophecy, namely that prophecies of destruction are contingent upon the human response to them. Such prophecies may therefore be annulled without prejudice to the prophet who pronounced them. Promises of good fortune, on the other hand, are invariably fulfilled. On the latter point, see *b. Ber.* 7a (bot.); *b. Šab.* 51a. On the general principle, see Maimonides, *Hilkhot Yesodei ha-Torah* 10.4 (trans. H.M. Russell and J. Weinberg [New York: Ktav, 1983], pp. 26-27); Levi ben Gershom, *Milḥamot ha-Shem* 2.6 (trans. S. Feldman [Philadelphia: Jewish Publication Society, 1986], II, pp. 59-60).

4. For basic orientation, see E. Bickerman, 'Les deux erreurs du prophète Jonas', *RHPR* 45 (1965), pp. 232-64; *idem, Four Strange Books of the Bible* (New York: Schocken Books, 1967), pp. 3-49; L. Schmidt, *'De Deo': Studien zur Literarkritik und Theologie des Buches Jona...* (BZAW, 143; Berlin: de Gruyter, 1976), pp. 4-130; J. Magonet, *Form and Meaning: Studies in Literary Techniques in*

According to 2 Kgs 14.26-27 (contrary to the aforementioned midrash), God perceived the abject helplessness of Israel, and 'resolved not to blot out the name of Israel from under heaven' (NJPSV).[1] A similar pretext is apparently adduced for the rescue of Nineveh: its inhabitants 'do not yet know their right hand from their left' (Jon. 4.11). The thrust in both cases seems to be that the helpless, the ignorant, or those who are not responsible for their actions (like those renowned 'beasts' of Jon. 4.11) benefit from God's mercy.[2]

The problem with that motive for divine mercy is twofold. In the first place, it is contradicted by other descriptions of the human characters. Amos depicts an Israel that exults in its military successes (Amos 6.13), and is anything but forlorn: 'They lie on ivory beds, lolling on their couches, feasting on lambs from the flock and on calves from the stalls' (6.4). One might suggest that God's perception of Israel is at odds with Israel's self-perception, but that would be special pleading in favor of harmonizing Amos with 2 Kings 14. And that suggestion would not explain why God should choose to construe *this* particular instance of Israelite sinfulness as helplessness.

The contrast between the professed divine motivation and human action is even more blatant in Jonah. In response to Jonah's word, the Ninevites embark on a course of action that is so commendable that it has been taken for satire:[3] they repent (Jon. 3.5-8). In effect, they act

the Book of Jonah (Sheffield: Almond Press, 1983), pp. 85-112; A. Preminger and E.L. Greenstein, *The Hebrew Bible in Literary Criticism* (New York: Ungar, 1986), pp. 467-78. On the history of interpretation in general, see the works listed in Wolff's bibliography (*Obadiah and Jonah*, pp. 91-92, §10).

1.   The passage bristles with difficulties. For a recent discussion, see Cogan and Tadmor, *II Kings*, pp. 107, 160-64.

2.   Cf. J. Licht, *Storytelling in the Bible* (Jerusalem: Magnes, 1978), pp. 121-22. Licht suggests that God 'spares His creatures for the simple reason that He likes them to exist'. That suggestion raises an obvious question: why, then, does he destroy them?

3.   See J.A. Miles, Jr, 'Laughing at the Bible: Jonah as Parody', *JQR* 65 (1974-75), pp. 168-81; J.S. Ackerman, 'Satire and Symbolism in the Song of Jonah', in B. Halpern and J.D. Levenson (eds.), *Traditions in Transformation: Turning Points in Biblical Faith* (Winona Lake, IN: Eisenbrauns, 1981), pp. 213-46; *idem*, 'Jonah', in R. Alter and F. Kermode (eds.), *The Literary Guide to the Bible* (Cambridge, MA: Harvard University Press, 1987), pp. 234-43, esp. 238-39. Note also T. Eagleton's recent characterization of Jonah as a 'surrealist farce' ('J.L. Austin and the Book of Jonah', in R. Schwartz (ed.), *The Book and the Text: The Bible and Literary Theory* [Oxford: Basil Blackwell, 1990], pp. 231-36).

out Amos's admonition to 'seek the Lord and live' (Amos 5.6). This hardly represents the behavior of helpless, ignorant or irresponsible people. And their motivation for repentance is sophisticated: 'Who knows but that God may turn and relent?' (Jon. 3.9). In 3.10 God 'perceives' (*r'h*, as in 2 Kgs 14.26) what the Ninevites have done, and reverses his evil decree. For a moment, it even seems as if God has renounced his threat *because* of the Ninevites' repentance, but that causal nexus is immediately severed by both Jonah (4.2) and God (4.11). According to Jonah, mercy arises out of God's character, which the prophet defines by a purposeful revision of Exod. 34.6.[1] When God accounts for his behavior, however, he refers neither to the Ninevites' repentance, nor to Jonah's characterization of him (4.11).

The dissonance between God's actions and his putative motive(s) is exacerbated by a second consideration: the redemption of both the Northern Kingdom and Nineveh was abortive. The 'transformation of evil into good' was reversed in both cases. Israel persisted in its evil ways and was wiped out (2 Kgs 17). The Ninevites repented, and lasted long enough to serve as the agents of Israel's destruction before meeting their doom (Nahum). The destinies of the two beneficiaries of divine 'mercy' were thus intertwined until the demise of both.

It should be clear from the forgoing remarks that I reject the notion that 'Jonah has no connection with the grand sequence of sacred history'.[2] Such a claim may serve the interests of critics who would divorce Jonah from its canonical context, and read it as an isolated, self-contained entity. My view, however (to be elaborated below), is that *only* an intertextual reading can do justice to the book. It seems obvious to me that, as B.S. Childs observes, the reader of Jonah 'has in his canon the book of Nahum!'[3] (and, I would add, Amos and 2 Kings as well). I would apply that observation to ancient and modern readers alike, and suspect that it was already in the mind of the editor of the Book of the Twelve Minor Prophets.

---

1. I shall return to this topic below. See the important discussions by M. Fishbane, *Biblical Interpretation in Ancient Israel* (Oxford: Clarendon Press, 1985), pp. 335-50; T.B. Dozeman, 'Inner-Biblical Interpretation of Yahweh's Gracious and Compassionate Character', *JBL* 108 (1989), pp. 207-23.

2. Licht, *Storytelling*, p. 124.

3. *Introduction to the Old Testament as Scripture* (Philadelphia: Fortress Press, 1979), pp. 425-26.

It is easy, then, to sympathize with I. Abravanel's explanation of Jonah's anger, apropos of Jon. 4.1:[1]

> He never thought that the decree against [the Ninevites] would be reversed, for even though they had turned away from their wicked deeds, they persisted in their idolatry... Why, then, did God renounce the punishment that he had planned to bring upon them?... So that they might become the 'rod of his anger' [Isa. 10.5] and the 'weapons of his wrath' [Isa. 13.5], in order that he might take vengeance against Israel by means of them.[2] The prophet protested against God in his heart: Why should it be his intention to destroy Israel for idolatry, while pardoning Nineveh for the same offense?

The question that Abravanel puts in Jonah's heart is precisely the question of the Book of Jonah, but it needs to be rephrased in a more general way: why does God allow a wicked nation to prosper, only to destroy it later on for the selfsame wickedness?

The point is not to contrast God's treatment of Jews with his treatment of gentiles, but simply to ask why God seems to be so inconsistent and unpredictable. Is his behavior motivated in some comprehensible way? The Book of Jonah and 2 Kings 14 provide three possible answers to that question: (1) God spares the helpless; (2) God is 'compassionate and gracious, slow to anger, abounding in kindness, renouncing punishment'; (3) God eschews the punishment of those who repent. All three of those answers are rendered problematic,[3] particularly granting the validity of intertextual reading. Even within the stories themselves, Israel and Nineveh are not portrayed as particularly helpless. In the larger canonical context, it becomes clear that God did not utterly renounce their punishment; he only put it off for a while.[4] Finally, while the repentance of the Ninevites did not save

---

1. All citations of Abravanel are from the Warsaw (1862) edition, where the commentary on Jonah can be found on pp. 119-30. The commentary on the Latter Prophets was first published in Pesaro in 1520.

2. For a modern commentator who derives Jonah's pathos from his prophetic knowledge of Israel's future destruction by Assyria, see H. Gese, 'Jona ben Amittai und das Jonabuch', *Theologische Beiträge* 16 (1985), pp. 256-72.

3. For a diametrically opposed opinion on this point, see T.E. Fretheim, *The Message of Jonah: A Theological Commentary* (Minneapolis: Augsburg, 1977), p. 129. Fretheim asserts the *validity* of all three answers.

4. Abravanel discerns God's true intention by interpreting Jonah's prophecy esoterically. 'Forty days more' (3.4) turns out to mean 'in 120 years', for 'days' = 'years', and the numerical value of the Hebrew word for 'more' ('*ôd*, i.e. 70 + 6 + 4

them in the end, a remnant of Israel, which never repented, survived.

Why should the Book of Jonah raise three explanations of divine behavior that are subject to contradiction or falsification? Because, in my view, that is the point of the book! God's actions are uncanny and inexplicable; he is absolutely free to do as he chooses. More importantly, for the postexilic author of the Book of Jonah,[1] divine freedom manifests the only tolerable alternative to the failed conditional covenant—the covenant that had literally compelled God to destroy Israel.[2]

Divine freedom is often propounded as a theme of the Book of Jonah,[3] but I do not think that it has been understood in all its ramifications. In a popular introduction to Jonah, K. Pfisterer Darr writes,

> Central to the Book of Jonah are the concepts of divine freedom and
> mercy in the face of repentance. The story is, in fact, illustrative of the
> perspective found in a text like Jeremiah 18.7-8,[4] wherein Yahweh says:
> 'If at any time I declare concerning a nation or a kingdom, that I will pluck
> up and break down and destroy it, and if that nation, concerning which I

= 80) must be added to the explicitly mentioned forty!

1.   Perhaps also for the authors of Lamentations and Job. See my articles, 'The Message of Lamentations', in J. Lassner and P. Machinist (eds.), *The Hebrew Bible: Sacred Text and Literature* (Detroit: Wayne State University Press [in press]); 'Reading and Misreading the Prologue to Job', *JSOT* 46 (1990), pp. 67-79.

2.   I accept the scholarly consensus that places the composition of Jonah in the late fifth or early fourth century. On the reassessment of covenant in exilic and post-exilic Israelite thought, see D.J. McCarthy, 'Covenant in Narratives from Late OT Times', in H.B. Huffmon *et al.* (eds.), *The Quest for the Kingdom of God: Studies in Honor of G.E. Mendenhall* (Winona Lake, IN: Eisenbrauns, 1983), pp. 77-94; P.D. Hanson, 'Israelite Religion in the Early Postexilic Period', in P.D. Miller, Jr, *et al.* (eds.), *Ancient Israelite Religion* (Philadelphia: Fortress Press, 1987), pp. 485-508; S.D. Sperling, 'Rethinking Covenant in Late Biblical Books', *Bib* 70 (1989), pp. 50-73.

3.   See, e.g., Wolff, *Obadiah and Jonah*, p. 177, on God's 'completely free grace'. Schmidt comments (*'De Deo'*, p. 129) that the Book of Jonah 'vermag zwar von ihrem Ansatz her die Freiheit Gottes zu wahren, auch das in der volkstümlichen Weisheit gelegentlich nicht der Fall gewesen sein mag'. See also Magonet, *Form and Meaning*, p. 112; J. Blenkinsopp, *A History of Prophecy in Israel* (Philadelphia: Westminster Press, 1983), p. 271.

4.   So already the ninth/tenth-century Karaite commentator Daniel al-Qumisi, in his *Pitron Sheneim-Asar* (ed. I.D. Markon; Jerusalem: Mekize Nirdamim, 1957), p. 42.

have spoken, turns from its evil, I will repent of the evil that I intended to do to it'. God exercises freedom to pronounce judgment against, and be moved by compassion toward, Nineveh.[1]

What Darr calls 'freedom' is not freedom at all. God acts in a clearly motivated way, under compulsion, in fact. He condemns the Ninevites for their wickedness (Jon. 1.2), but then he *must* spare them because of their (and his) adherence to the formula in Jeremiah 18. Jonah's objections, in this light, appear silly, or, worse, turn him into a hard-hearted Jew.[2]

Then, too, if the Ninevites were saved because of their repentance, what hope is there for those who do not repent? The logic of Jeremiah 18 ineluctably condemns them. The author of Jonah, in turn, condemns that logic. As A. and P.E. Lacocque observe in their provocative study of Jonah,[3]

> The author of Jonah had the amazing boldness to show the 'anti-Jonah' in the persons of the wicked Ninevites. To the Jonah who hungered for certainty they opposed the ultimate uncertainty of 'perhaps' [Jon. 3.9]. They thus opened an immense possibility, namely, that God might choose extravagance over determinism...

In this view, God is free to save (or, as the Lacocques neglect to mention, to destroy) whomever he pleases, in whatever manner he chooses. The adroitly paired storm wind (1.4) and desert scirocco (4.8),[4] tempest (1.4) and hot sun (4.8), Phoenicians (1.6) and Assyrians (3.9), great fish (2.1) and tiny worm (4.7)—all do God's bidding, with the

1. K.P. Darr, 'Jonah', in B.W. Anderson (ed.), *The Books of the Bible* (2 vols.; New York: Scribner's, 1989), I, pp. 381-84 (quotation on pp. 382-83).

2. Darr also remarks that 'Jonah's story refutes any notion that Israel alone deserves divine mercy, whereas the other nations of the world merit only divine justice' ('Jonah', in Anderson (ed.), *The Books of the Bible*, p. 383). Similarly, Wolff, *Obadiah and Jonah*, p. 177. These are but modern reworkings of the kind of interpretation that Bickerman demolished. Cf. the salutary remarks in Blenkinsopp, *History of Prophecy*, p. 271.

3. A. Lacocque and P.-E. Lacocque, *The Jonah Complex* (Atlanta: John Knox, 1981), pp. 90-100, 125-27 (quotation on p. 127). The authors' 'in-depth reworking' (*Jonah: A Psycho-Religious Approach to the Prophet* [Columbia: University of South Carolina, 1990]) arrived after the present article was completed. On the issue under discussion, see esp. pp. 122-25.

4. On this symmetry, see the sensitive remarks of G.H. Cohn, *Das Buch Jona im Lichte der biblischen Ezrählkhunst* (Studia Semitica Neerlandica, 12; Assen: Van Gorcum, 1969), pp. 54, 59-60.

sole purpose of teaching Jonah what he knew all along, namely that 'deliverance is the Lord's' (2.10).

'Deliverance', as the author of Jonah depicts it, is neither a reward for merit nor a tempering of justice with mercy.[1] It is, instead, a free and gracious act of love. As such, it is a worthless people's only hope for survival. And the wellspring of this concept of deliverance is not covenant faith, but the simple trust in God's love and fear of his wrath that are the hallmarks of 'personal religion'.[2]

I intend to defend this understanding of the message of Jonah in two ways: by proposing a new interpretation of the critical passages in Jonah 3–4, and by examining one aspect of the intertextual relationship of Jonah with some of the other Minor Prophets, especially Micah and Nahum, the two books that follow Jonah in canonical order.

II

Since the pioneering article by N. Lohfink,[3] it has become common for scholars to regard the two episodes in Jonah 3–4 as a narratorial unity, their complex textual pre-history notwithstanding. The linchpin of any unified reading, as Lohfink observed, is the interpretation of 4.5, which establishes some sort of temporal relationship between the two episodes. My view, itself admittedly not free of difficulties, is that 4.5bβ establishes the *simultaneity* and *complementarity* of the two accounts.[4]

The stories about Nineveh and Jonah, in other words, illuminate and confound one another. Each one supplies vital details that the other is lacking, so that neither one is comprehensible except in the light

---

1. Contrast Cohn (*Das Buch Jona*, pp. 87-88), who sees this as the central theme of the book.

2. On the emergence (or, perhaps, re-emergence) of personal religion in postexilic Israel, see McCarthy, 'Covenant in Late OT Times', in McCarthy *et al.* (eds.), *The Quest for the Kingdom*, pp. 86-88. I use the term 'personal religion' in the sense delineated by T. Jacobsen, *The Treasures of Darkness: A History of Mesopotamian Religion* (New Haven: Yale University Press, 1976), pp. 147-64. I have discussed the concept in relation to the theology of the Book of Lamentations in my article, 'The Message of Lamentations' in Lassner and Machinist (eds.), *The Hebrew Bible*.

3. 'Jona ging zur Stadt hinaus (Jona 4, 5)', *BZ* NS 5 (1961), pp. 185-203; cf. Wolff, *Obadiah and Jonah*, p. 163.

4. Simultaneity in narrative has the advantage of disrupting ordinary narrative temporality, and thus disorienting the reader. See Stewart, *Nonsense*, pp. 146-70.

of the other. In the end, Jonah's strange encounter with God brings about the deconstruction and re-mystification of the superficially simple tale of Nineveh's repentance and salvation.

At the heart of the matter is an analogy cum wordplay, which centers on God's ability to do what he wants by means of seemingly unpromising agents. Thus, Jonah (the agent) is to Nineveh (the one acted upon) as the *qîqāyôn* (4.6)[1] is to Jonah. This analogy is not merely signalled by the wordplay *YÔNâ/qîqāYÔN*.[2] The *qî*- element in the plant name also evokes Jon. 2.11, where the fish 'vomits' (*wayyāQĒ'*) Jonah out onto dry land.[3] And God describes the *qîqāyôn* as having had a lifespan of a single day (4.10b), which corresponds to the amount of time that Jonah had spent in Nineveh (3.4), despite that city's enormous size. Jonah's physical presence was as ephemeral for Nineveh as that of the *qîqāyôn* was for Jonah.

With this analogy in mind, we can follow the two story-lines as they overlap and intertwine. Both stories begin with the human characters in a state of 'evil' (*rā'â*). Jonah prophesies against Nineveh, the 'great city' whose 'evil' has come to God's attention (1.2; 3.3-4). Having prophesied, Jonah experiences a 'great evil' himself (4.1).

The Ninevites' initial response to Jonah's word is to believe it; they take it to be reliable (*wayya'ᵃmînû*)[4] and of divine origin (3.5). Jonah, in contrast, asserts that God is *un*reliable, in his reformulation (4.2) of one of the divine attributes listed in Exod. 34.6aβ-b:

---

1. I do not gloss this word because, as Good rightly observes, the identity of the plant is irrelevant (*Irony in the Old Testament*, pp. 51-52).

2. It also should be noted that NYNWH (Nineveh) contains the same consonants as YWNH (Jonah).

3. So, rightly, Halpen and Friedman, 'Composition and Paronomasia', pp. 85-86.

4. In general, *wayya'ᵃmînû* has been grievously overinterpreted (e.g. Wolff, *Obadiah and Jonah*, p. 150). I would understand it here in its simplest sense, 'to consider trustworthy, reliable'. For discussion, see A. Jepsen, ''āman', *TDOT*, I, (1977), pp. 293-309. Unfortunately, Jepsen also overinterprets in the present case (pp. 304-305). W. Rudolph takes the simpler view: 'Trotz der ungenügenden Ausrichtung der Botschaft trauen sie [the Ninevites] dem Boten des unbekannten Gottes und nehmen die Warnung ernst' (*Joel–Amos–Obadja–Jona* [KAT, 13/2; Gütersloh: Gerd Mohn, 1971], pp. 358-59). But even Rudolph feels compelled to contrast Nineveh's receptivity to the divine word with Israel's deafness to it.

Exodus	Jonah
'erek 'appayim	_'erek 'appayim_
we̊rab ḥesed	_we̊rab ḥesed_
we'e̊met	_we̊nihām 'al-hārā'â_

Instead of being 'reliable' (_'e̊met_),[1] Jonah's God 'renounces evil' (_nihām 'al-hārā'â_). The substitution is both intentional and polemical[2]— renunciation of evil, from Jonah's perspective, connotes unreliability. And the prophet's characterization of God seems to be accurate in context. The _possibility_ that God's word is not truthful gives hope to the Ninevites (3.9; _mî-yôdea'_); the _certainty_ that it is not moves Jonah to despair (4.2-3; _yāda'tî_).[3] The paradox here is disorienting; Jonah's sure knowledge that God will spare Nineveh is taken for unbelief, while Nineveh's hope in a false God manifests a true faith.

After staking out their basic positions concerning God's reliability, both the Ninevites and Jonah take action. As Ackerman has observed, Jonah and the Ninevite king can be construed as 'antitypes'.[4] The following parallel plot summaries will extend and amplify that point:

Nineveh (Jon. 3.5-10)	Jonah (Jon. 4.2-6)
The Ninevites fast and mourn.	Jonah prays; he demands to die.
Jonah's word reaches the king; the king gets up (_wayyāqom_) from his throne	Jonah leaves the city; he sits down (_wayyēšeb_).
The kings puts on sackcloth (_wayKaS SaQ_), and sits (_wayyēšeb_) in the dust.	Jonah erects a _SuKKâ_, and sits (_wayyēšeb_) in its shade.

1. I am assuming that _'mn_ and _'e̊met_ are cognate. See Jepsen, '_'āman_', pp. 309-10.

2. So, rightly, Cohn, _Das Buch Jona_, p. 99 n. 2. Dozeman ('Inner-Biblical Interpretation') unaccountably misses this point altogether.

3. I follow the opinion of Eliezer de Beaugency that, at the time of his utterance in 4.2-3, Jonah 'did not know of [the Ninevites'] repentance' (_Kommentar zu Ezechiel und den XII kleinen Propheten_ [ed. S. Poznański; Warsaw: Mekize Nirdamim, 1909], p. 159 [_ad_ Jon. 4.1]). He cannot, therefore, have been ascribing God's mercy to that repentance. Rather, 'it turns out that I struggled and broke my body and had my strength exhausted along the way for nothing, for I realized that you would renounce the evil even without repentance' (_idem_, _ad_ Jon. 4.3).

4. 'Satire and Symbolism', pp. 239-40, following Magonet, _Form and Meaning_, pp. 19-20.

The Ninevites mourn, fast, and turn
away from their wickedness (*rā'â*).

The Ninevites pray; they hope to live.

God sees (*r'h*) what the Ninevites   Jonah waits to see (*r'h*) what will
have done.   happen in the city.

God decides not to do the evil (*rā'â*)   God provides a *qîqāyôn* to save
that he had promised to do.   Jonah from his evil (*rā'â*).

                                          Jonah rejoices.

This plot summary may be abstracted further, and condensed into
three parallel plot elements:

1. The human character is in a state of evil.
2. The human character acts to counter the state of evil.
3. God unilaterally reverses the state of evil.

Jonah impugns God's reliability, builds himself a shelter,[1] and then
waits passively. The Ninevites, in contrast, believe God, and put on an
extravagant display of piety as they attempt to avert their fate. The
point of contact between the respective actions of Jonah and the
Ninevites (plot element 2) is the word play *KSh SaQ(Qîm)* (3.6, 8) //
SuKKâ (4.5). Jonah 'sits' (*yŠB*) in the shade of his hut while the
Ninevites 'repent' (*ŠwB*). *Yet the outcome is the same in both cases*:
God rescues both Nineveh and Jonah from the 'evil' that besets them.
The Ninevites repent, and God spares them; Jonah cavils, and God
'saves' him too.

We hear nothing about Nineveh's reaction to God's reversal of its
fate. The possibility envisioned in Jon. 3.9 // Joel 2.14 seems to have
been realized.[2] As for Jonah, his rescue from evil makes him happy
(4.6), and his story, too, seems to have reached a satisfactory resolution.

And then the worm turns. The following morning, God arranges
for the demise of the *qîqāyôn* (4.7). The sun beats down on Jonah's
head and, once again, the prophet wishes to die (4.8).[3] Now it is time

---

1. See Cohn's important discussion of the contrast between Jonah's *sukkâ* and
the God-given *qîqāyôn* (*Das Buch Jona*, pp. 87-88); also Ackerman, 'Satire and
Symbolism', pp. 240-42; Lacocque and Lacocque, *The Jonah Complex*, pp. 87-90.
I am sympathetic to the efforts of Ackerman and the Lacocques to find allusions to
the Temple here, especially in the light of Isa. 4.5-6.

2. See Dozeman, 'Inner-Biblical Interpretation', pp. 213-16.

3. It does not seem to occur to Jonah that he might return to his *sukkâ*, perhaps

for God to teach him a lesson. But what is that lesson?[1] The usual view is well summarized by Darr:[2]

> ... God remonstrates this prophet [*sic*], who cares more for infallible prophecy and mechanical justice than for mercy in the face of whole-hearted repentance. If Jonah pitied the plant (himself?), which he had no part in creating, should not God feel pity for a repentant city with many thousands of human and animal inhabitants?

Although that widely proffered view embodies a valuable teaching, I do not think that it is the lesson of Jonah, for at least three reasons.

First, even assuming that Jonah did resent his prophetic 'loss of face',[3] there is not the slightest indication that he begrudged the Ninevites their salvation, nor does he express any opinion about the proper divine response to human initiative.[4] Jonah's prayer in ch. 2 manifests the ethos of personal religion: one cries out and hopes that God will respond (2.3). Acts of piety serve as offerings of thanks, not as attempts to win God's favor in a time of crisis (2.10).[5]

Secondly, God never says that he was merciful to the Ninevites because of their repentance. That is an inference derived from reading

because its shade (*ṣēl*) was lacking in redemptive power (*maṣṣîl*).

1.   Cf. the anonymous Bible critic cited by Augustine, *Epistulae* 102, 30 (*apud* Giancarlo Rinaldi, *Biblia Gentium* [Rome: Libreria Sacre Scritture, 1989], pp. 402-403): 'Then what is the purpose of the gourd which sprang forth above the disgorged Jonas? What was the reason for its appearance? Questions such as these I have seen discussed by Pagans amidst loud laughter, and with great scorn.'

2.   Darr, 'Jonah', in Anderson (ed.), *The Books of the Bible*, p. 382.

3.   See especially Bickerman; also, e.g., M. Sternberg, *The Poetics of Biblical Narrative: Ideological Literature and the Drama of Reading* (Bloomington: Indiana University Press, 1985), p. 320. I refrain from discussing Sternberg's interpretation in detail because I cannot share one of his basic premises: that the *reader* arriving at Jon. 3.1 expects Nineveh to be destroyed, and is shocked by the reversal (p. 319). *This* reader never did, not even as a child. I am, in general, uncomfortable with Sternberg's arrogation of the epithet 'the reader'; the first person would be more honest.

4.   Jonah is not portrayed as ruthless or homicidal—he acts to save the sailors, even though it seems to mean certain death for him (1.12). Jon. 1.15 is another verse like 3.10, in which it is possible, but not necessary, to infer a cause-and-effect relationship between the two clauses.

5.   Cf. Elizer de Beaugency, *Kommentar*, p. 158 (*ad* Jon. 2.2): 'There are prayers in Scripture that are pleas, and others that express praise and thanks, for example, "and Hannah prayed" [1 Sam. 2.1], which consists entirely of praise and thanks, and this one [i.e. Jonah 2]'.

Jon. 3.10 as a statement of cause and effect,[1] but that reading is not necessarily correct. Jonah's alternative is to assert that it is in God's nature to 'renounce evil' (4.2),[2] without explicating the relationship (if any) between human action and divine response.

Thirdly, the *a fortiori* reasoning allegedly found in God's statements in 4.10-11 makes no sense. God is supposedly saying, in effect, 'if you (Jonah) would spare that insignificant plant (for your sake), then naturally I (God) should spare all those people and animals (for my sake [?])'. In this view, Jonah's self-absorption is contrasted with God's magnanimity. The speciousness of the analogy becomes painfully evident, however, when someone (Abravanel, in this case) tries to elucidate it:[3]

> God reproved [Jonah] and got to the heart of the matter when he said, 'You cared about the plant'. In other words, you cared about something that was not the work of your hands, that 'you did not work for and did not grow', for something that was considered worthless because it 'appeared overnight and perished overnight'. If that is the case, then how can 'I not care about Nineveh, that great city', that wondrous work of my hands that is a great and mighty edifice, unlike the plant?

Is the idea that God likes the big things that he makes more than the little things? Or that people have no right to grieve for the loss of good things that they did not make for themselves? Such notions, in my view, represent misreadings of the relationship between 4.10 and 4.11—not least the preposterous idea that God was responsible for the construction of Nineveh, and might regret its loss for that reason.

Abravanel's continuation confuses the issue even further. He has God say to Jonah:

> You cannot argue that you did not care about the plant for its own sake, but, rather, for the benefit that it provided you with, namely the shade, because Nineveh provides me with acknowledgement and glorification that are like the shade.

At least Abravanel recognizes (as most commentators do not) that the story depicts the plant not as something worthless, but as the agent of

---

1.   See Bickerman, *Four Strange Books*, pp. 45-48; Fishbane, *Biblical Interpretation*, pp. 346-47.

2.   See Eliezer de Beaugency, *Kommentar*, p. 159 (*ad* Jon. 4.2).

3.   For a modern restatement of Abravanel's position, see, e.g., A.J. Hauser, 'Jonah: In Pursuit of the Dove', *JBL* 104 (1985), pp. 21-37, esp. p. 37.

Jonah's salvation (4.7). Nevertheless, he fails to show that the Ninevites provide God with an analogous benefit, no matter how many of them there are. They are not, after all, agents of benefaction like the *qîqāyôn*, but beneficiaries of divine mercy, like Jonah in ch. 4.

When Jonah grieves for the plant that had shaded him, God says to him, 'As for you, you cared about the plant, which you did not work for and which you did not grow, which appeared overnight and perished overnight' (4.10). The point is not that Jonah's caring was trivial or self-absorbed. It is, rather, that God, the one who *did* 'work for' and 'grow' the plant (so to speak) in order to give Jonah shade and respite (4.6), also destroyed it without compunction, thus reducing Jonah to his previous sorry state (4.3 // 4.9). Jonah cared about the plant, and rightly so; God did not.

Now Nineveh, like Jonah, has also been granted respite from 'evil', but God's treatment of Jonah is cold comfort for them. What God says to Jonah about the 'great city' is clearly parallel in construction to what he had said about the plant:

Jon. 4.10	Jon. 4.11
'attâ ḥastâ	*wa'^anî lō' 'āḥûs*
'al-haqqîqāyôn	*'al-nîn^ewēh*

The universal assumption that 4.11 is interrogative ('Should I not care about Nineveh?') flies in the face of the parallelism with 4.10. That assumption, apparently based on an exegetical a priori, represents just one possibility; it is neither necessary nor inevitable. God's utterance also can be translated as a simple declarative: 'As for me, I do not care about Nineveh'. The implication would be that God cares no more about that huge city full of ignoramuses and beasts than he had about the *qîqāyôn*. Their repentance means nothing to him, and he has kept his real reason for sparing them (if, indeed, he had one) to himself.

The Book of Jonah itself gives no grounds for choosing between the interrogative and declarative renderings of 4.11, since it simply ends here.[1] My preference for the latter is based on reading Jonah in the light of Nahum. In the immediate context of Jonah, however, the point of the ambiguity is to suggest that God's treatment of Nineveh, when scrutinized, might be just as unintelligible to the human observer as

---

1. As the Lacocques remark concerning the 'open-endedness' of Jonah (*The Jonah Complex*, pp. 99-100), 'It seems... that it is one of the important features of the book that it does *not* bring the plot to a veritable end'.

his treatment of Jonah.[1] God buffets the prophet about against his will, makes him prophesy and then falsifies his word, rescues him from his pathetic emotional condition and then condemns him to it once more. One can infer that Nineveh's situation is no less absurd, and that it is, therefore, fraught with insecurity.

III

The ending of Jonah leaves the ultimate fates of its principal actors undetermined. What will become of Jonah and Nineveh? Jonah seems to be consigned to death, since the threat of 4.7-9 has not been countered. Jonah does not react to God's words in vv. 10-11, nor does God state his intentions concerning the prophet. As for Nineveh, nothing has occurred to disturb the apparent equilibrium attained in 3.10.

The denouement of Jonah, in my view, takes place *outside the book*. The book's full significance emerges only in the light of its canonical setting—especially in relation to the prophetic books (Hosea–Nahum) that are concerned primarily with the Assyrian crisis. The assemblage begins with the first announcement of divine judgment against Israel, and ends with the destruction of Assyria. I propose that the *Book* of Jonah (as opposed, perhaps, to its constituent parts), was never intended to be read apart from that canonical context. An intertextual reading of the book is, therefore, both valid and necessary.

The prophets who address the Assyrian threat struggle mightily to understand the nature of God's wrath and love, and Jonah contributes to that discussion by way of interpretation and elaboration.[2] First and foremost, one notes five midrashic adaptations of the attribute formulary in Exodus 34. The following are the relevant texts (all except for

1. So already Eagleton, who comments that 'God's mercy is indeed a kind of absurdity' ('J.L. Austin and the Book of Jonah', in Schwartz [ed.], *The Book and the Text*, p. 236).

2. It should be obvious that I am not interested in the historicity or the literary history of the components of the 'Book of the Twelve', but in the way that they function together as parts of a unified collection. See, provisionally, D. Schneider, 'The Unity of the Book of the Twelve' (PhD dissertation, Yale University, 1979); much more work needs to be done. I am aware of two new works on the topic, neither of which was available to me when I was writing this paper: P. House, *The Unity of the Twelve* (JSOTSup, 97; Sheffield: JSOT Press, 1990); J. Nogalski, 'The Use of Stichwörter as a Redactional Unification Technique within the Book of the Twelve' (Doctoral dissertation, University of Zürich, 1991).

the Nahum excerpt cited according to NJPSV, with the allusion to Exod. 34.6-7 emphasized in each case):

1. Take words with you and return to the Lord. Say to Him: '*Forgive all guilt (kol-tiśśā' 'āwōn)* and accept what is good. Instead of bulls we will pay [the offering of] our lips'... I will heal their affliction, generously will I take them back in love; for my anger has turned away from them (Hos. 14.3, 5).

2. Rend your hearts rather than your garments, and turn back to the Lord your God. For *He is gracious and compassionate, slow to anger, abounding in kindness, and renouncing punishment.* Who knows but He may turn and relent, and leave a blessing behind for meal offering and drink offering to the Lord your God (Joel 2.13-14)?

3. '... Let everyone turn back from his evil ways and from the injustice of which he is guilty. Who knows but that God may turn and relent? He may turn back from his wrath, so that we do not perish.' God saw what they did, how they were turning back from their evil ways. And God renounced the punishment He had planned to bring upon them, and did not carry it out. This displeased Jonah greatly, and he was grieved. He prayed to the Lord, saying, 'O Lord! Isn't this just what I said when I was still in my own country? That is why I fled beforehand to Tarshish. For I know that *You are a compassionate and gracious God, slow to anger, abounding in kindness, renouncing punishment*' (Jon. 3.8–4.2).

4. Who is a God like You, *forgiving iniquity and remitting transgression (nōśē' 'āwōn wᵉ'ōbēr 'al-peša')*; who has not maintained His wrath forever against the remnant of his own people, because He loves graciousness! He will take us back in love; He will cover up our iniquities, You will hurl all our sins into the depths of the sea. You will keep *faith* [*'ᵉmet*] with Jacob, *loyalty* [*ḥesed*] to Abraham, as You promised on oath to our fathers in days gone by (Mic. 7.18-20).

5. The Lord is a passionate, avenging God; the Lord is vengeful and fierce in wrath. The Lord takes vengeance upon his enemies, he rages against his foes. *The Lord is slow to anger and of great forbearance ('erek 'appayim ûgᵉdol-kōaḥ), but the Lord does not remit all punishment (wᵉnaqqēh lō' yᵉnaqqeh)* (Nah. 1.2-3a).

The 'historical' question of the Book of Jonah—what will become of Jonah/Israel and Nineveh/Assyria—is subsumed in the canonical context (where the historical reality of Assyria is not an issue) to a theological question: what moves God to shape human destiny for good or for ill? Exod. 34.6-7 serves as a fixed point of reference for various answers to that question.

The first text cited above belongs to the sublimely equivocal conclusion of Hosea (chs. 13–14). The Israelites are utterly guilty and have forgotten God (13.1-6). God, therefore, will slaughter them (13.7-11). He spared them despite previous iniquity (13.12-15a), but now he will destroy them (13.15b–14.1). The people are admonished to return (14.2-4), and God declares, finally, that he will redeem them because of his love for them (14.5-9). The tension between God's justice and his love is manifest—divine anger is motivated by human sin; divine love, on the contrary, may or may not be contingent upon human action. The restoration prophesied in Hos. 14.5-9 may never have taken place, but the text does not blame that failure on the absence of repentance.

The contingent character of salvation is taken up in Joel 2.12-14. Israel does not want a god who is 'reliable' (as in Exod. 34), but one who 'renounces punishment'. Reliability means the inevitable fulfilment of an oracle of destruction (Joel 2.1—'The day of the Lord has come!'); it is essential, however, that God be willing to reverse his decree. First Joel suggests that such reversal *might* be effectuated by repentance (2.14), then he tries to demonstrate that it certainly is, the beginning of 2.19 strongly implying cause and effect. Joel 2.19 looks like a midrash on Hos. 2.24[1] that seeks to counter Hosea's vacillation and unclarity. In order to accomplish that, Joel explicates the restoration envisioned by Hosea in terms of a causal link between Israel's repentance and God's mercy.

That causality is put to the test by the Book of Jonah, with Nineveh serving as the test case. The very use of Nineveh, together with the plain unreality of the city's repentance (animals in sackcloth),[2] indicates the hypothetical thrust of the story. A single question with three mutually exclusive answers brings the problem of Jonah to a head:

---

1. Note the use of *'nh* and the sequence 'grain and wine and oil' denoting restoration in both texts. The context of Hos. 2.24 (vv. 18-25) suggests unilateral divine action; in Joel 2.19, restoration is God's response to all the fasting and praying in vv. 15-17.

2. The penitent beasts of Jonah represent the same kind of literary play as the big fish, namely the literalization of such poetic turns of phrase as Joel 1.20a, 'The very beasts of the field cry out to you'. One might also imagine a midrashic play on Exod. 34.7aα, taking *'ªlāpîm* to mean 'beasts' instead of 'thousands'.

Question: Should God spare repentant Nineveh?

> Answer 1—the answer of Joel: *yes*, because the God who 'renounces evil' reverses his decree for the sake of those who repent.
>
> Answer 2—the answer of Jonah the prophet: *no*, because the God who 'renounces evil' is not being 'true' to his word.
>
> Answer 3—the answer of the Book of Jonah: God does as he pleases, and it is folly to try and justify or rationalize his behavior.

The author of Jonah recognizes the error of Joel, who has merely substituted one mechanistic view of God for another. Naturally one would like God to forgo destruction and work salvation at every opportunity, but that is not the way things are. If an oracle of doom is reversible according to some formula, then, logically, so is a promise of restoration—the contrary view of the Jewish tradition notwithstanding. And *any* formula that requires God to be just in a mechanical way is likely to work against Israel in the long run; the Exile is proof of that.

On the other hand, the position of the prophet Jonah (the character as distinct from the author of the book) is also untenable. It is just as erroneous to say that God *cannot* reverse his decree as it is to say that he *must*. And thus, as the Lacocques realized, the Ninevites hold the only theologically respectable position, on the slippery ground of *maybe*.

If we recontextualize the views of Joel and Jonah within the Assyrian crisis, we are compelled to draw two absurd conclusions: God must save the hated Ninevites because they have repented; and, he must destroy his beloved Israel because their demise has been prophesied, yet they have not repented. Absurd conclusions, obviously, are derived from false premises. The incomprehensible ending of the Book of Jonah—Nineveh saved and Jonah condemned—is the *reductio ad absurdum* of a false theology.

God cannot be constrained by a mechanistic formula, nor can he be predicated by any set of attributes. Such formulas and attributes constitute no more than vague guidelines, tentative gropings towards an understanding of God's character. Israel's hope, in fact, abides in their *un*truth, in the extent to which God's capricious and unrequited love will motivate his behavior (the point, after all, of Hosea). The dark side of that view is that God's destructive wrath might be just as arbitrary and unconstrained, as in the case of the *qîqāyôn*. One hopes and prays for God's love, while recognizing that nothing is certain.

And that is the point of Mic. 7.18-20, which provides the real reso-lution of the Book of Jonah. Again, as in Jonah, the focus is on the meaning of the divine attributes *rab ḥesed we'emet*. Jonah (the character) intimates that insofar as God allows his *ḥesed* to alter his course of action, he is not a God of *'emet*. Micah, like the author of the Book of Jonah, recognizes divine caprice as a boon for Israel. God annuls Israel's punishment entirely out of *ḥesed*; neither repentance nor acts of expiation are required (Mic. 7.18). God simply tosses Israel's sins into the sea, Mic. 7.19 explicitly alluding to Jon. 2.4. And God's love is not at odds with his truth. Rather, *'emet* and *ḥesed* are one and the same thing; thus the parallelism of Mic. 7.20.

Just as God saves Israel, he also wipes out Nineveh. The bizarre conclusion of the Book of Jonah is, finally, turned topsy-turvy with a vengeance by the Book of Nahum. Where his enemies are concerned, then, God is not *rab ḥesed*, but *gedol-kōaḥ*, 'fierce in wrath' (Nah. 1.3).[1] He does not care about Nineveh, and he does not remit the punishment of those he hates. God's wrath is just as inexplicable and uncontrollable as his love, but that, too, is part of what it means for him to be freely and truly God.

---

1. Note the intertextual allusions of Nah. 1.3-4 to the tempest language of Jon. 1-2.

JONAH: A BATTLE OF SHIFTING ALLIANCES

Timothy L. Wilt

ABSTRACT

Jonah's first chapter contains many elements of ancient Near Eastern battle accounts. The whole book has several lexical similarities with the holy war account in Joshua 10.1-27 and is structurally parallel to it. However, there are also key semiotic oppositions between the two accounts, including the role reversals in Jonah where insider becomes adversary, outsiders become allies, and victory is expressed in terms of mercy rather than massacre. Thus, Jonah may be viewed as the *terminus ad quem* of the transformation of the war oracles that began in the second half of the eighth century.

Introduction

Much has been written about the literary parallels between Jonah and other prophetic literature, key Torah narratives, and the Psalms.[1] Further appreciation of Jonah's literary richness and message may be gained through considering its similarities to biblical and other ancient Near Eastern battle accounts and its parallels in literary structure and lexical references with the particular account of a battle recorded in Josh. 10.1-27. Comparison with the Joshua narrative makes the ironic reversals in Jonah's depiction of human relationships with the divine warrior even more poignant—insider becomes adversary, outsiders become allies, and victory is expressed in terms of the warrior god YHWH's mercy rather than massacre. Thus, Jonah may be viewed as the terminus ad quem of the transformation of the war oracles that began in the second half of the eighth century.

Battle Motifs in Jonah

In this section, we focus on the elements in the first chapter of Jonah that are common to biblical and other ancient Near Eastern battle

---

1. E.g. Lacocque 1981: 10-16; Magonet 1976: 65-84; Sasson 1990: 168-201.

reports: flight, divine use of celestial weapons, seeking of divine guidance, terror, confusion, crying out for deliverance, and offering of vows and sacrifices. Although each of these elements could be referred to in other kinds of narratives, their ensemble in a text of sixteen verses strongly suggests the battle setting.

Jonah's Flight as a Prelude to Battle

At the outset of the narrative, YHWH commissions Jonah to go and prophesy against Nineveh, but instead he flees (ברח) in the opposite direction. In the Hebrew scriptures, the two words most often translated by the English 'flee' are ברח and נוס. The former refers to flight before physical violence breaks out, whereas the latter refers to flight after an initial outbreak of violence. Thus, for example, David usually flees (ברח) from Saul before there is combat between them;[1] only once does he flee (נוס) from Saul, after Saul throws his spear at him (1 Sam. 19.10).

Though the person who flees (ברח) has not yet engaged in open conflict, she/he flees because of being in an oppressive situation and/ or, by far most frequently, because of being in danger of being killed.[2] Naturally enough, the one from whom one flees is the one responsible for the oppression and the threat to life. While the fleer might wish to have a more amicable relationship with the oppressor (as David would wish to have with Saul in 1 Samuel), the oppressor's actions do not allow for this.

While Jonah might have wished for a more comfortable relationship with YHWH, YHWH's command disallows this. Jonah, his life threatened in view of that great and evil power to which the oppressive YHWH would send him, must run if he is to save his life. There seems no more reason to accept Jonah's after-the-fact explanation to YHWH of why he fled (4.2) than to accept Jacob's explanation to Laban (Gen.

---

1. 1 Sam. 19.12, 18; 21.1; 21.10; 22.17; 27.4.
2. Flight because of an oppresive situation: Hagar from Sarah (Gen. 16.6-7), Jacob from Laban (Gen. 31), Israel from Egypt (Exod. 14.5).

Flight because of threat to the fleer's life: Jacob from Esau (Gen. 27.43), Jacob from Laban and his sons (implied by Gen. 31.1-2, 7b, 29a), Moses from Pharaoh (Exod. 2.5), Jotham from Abimelech (Judg. 9.21), David from Saul (1 Sam. 19–27) and from Absalom (2 Sam. 15.14), Absalom from David (2 Sam. 13), Hadad from Joab (1 Kgs 11.12), Jeroboam from Solomon (1 Kgs 11.40), Uriah from Jehoiakim (Jer. 26.21), and Zedekiah and his soldiers from the Babylonians (Jer. 39.4).

31.31) of his flight which contrasts with his previous explanation to
Rachel and Leah (Gen. 31.4-11).[1]

If the oppressor chooses to pursue the fleer and is able to catch up,
the stage is set for a confrontation which may result in either reconciliation (e.g. Gen. 31.43-55; 1 Sam. 24, 26) or further conflict (e.g.
Exod. 14; Jer. 26). Jonah is pursued and a battle ensues.

Divine Use of Celestial Weapons

In several ancient Near Eastern traditions, one deity was both god of
war and god of the storm.[2] Accordingly, the storm and elements
associated with storms were commonly used by non-Israelite deities in
earthly battles, as they were by YHWH (Weinfeld 1984). In Jonah,
YHWH's weapon, wind, is the same instrument he used against the
Egyptian army during the exodus (14.21; 15.8, 10).

Seeking Divine Guidance

Oracles were sought to determine whether or not one should go to

---

1.   Awareness of the many traditions about prophets' fearful response to and/or
resistance of YHWH (e.g. Exod. 3.6–4.14; Isa. 6; Jer. 1.4-8; 20.9), the persecution
of prophets who speak out against evil and/or announce judgment (e.g. 1 Kgs 13.4;
18.4a; 19.2; Jer. 1.1-2; 20.10; 26; 37.14-15; Amos 7.11-13), and prophets' flight
from danger (e.g. 1 Kgs 17.3; 18.4b-14; 19.3; Jer. 26.21) makes it natural to
assume that Jonah flees out of fear of his task. Explicit reference to fear is reserved
for development of the characterization of the sailors' response to YHWH's actions
and revelation which has been pointed out, e.g., by Alexander (1988: 106-109) and
Magonet (1976: 106-109). These observations are evidence against Sternberg's
(1985: 318-20) position that a narrative gap must be filled within the narrative itself,
leading him to take at face value Jonah's explanation for his flight. Of the gap in ch.
1, where Jonah's reason for fleeing is not given, Sternberg says: 'Why does Jonah
flee...? The narrator does not say, but apparently only because the reason is self-
evident: Jonah is too tender-hearted to carry a message of doom to a great city'
(p. 138). This explanation of what the reader would infer seems far-fetched in view
of the absence of biblical accounts of prophetic tenderness towards wicked, pagan
cities.

2.   Kang 1989: 26, 32, 37, 50, 54, 68, 77, 96. With regard to who might have
been the god of the sailors with whom Jonah travelled, Sasson has this to say:
'...any sea tempest...must include heavy black clouds, lightning, and thunder: one
and all weapons of a storm god...the sailors were likely Phoenicians and as such
would have worshiped..."Baal (is) Heaven" as their main god...This god's
propensity for shipwrecking those he despises is...cited in...a treaty between
Assyria's Esarhaddon and the king of Tyre...' (Sasson 1990: 118).

war or respond to the aggression of an adversary,[1] or on how a war should be fought (Judg. 20.18; 2 Sam. 5.23). Lots were one of the ways in which this divine word could be obtained.[2] While the oracles would normally be consulted before the onset of a battle, there could also be consultation during the course of a battle.[3] In Jonah, the sailors, struggling for their lives, seek a divine word by casting lots and thereby learn via Jonah that they have been caught up in a battle with a divinity.

Terror

Reference to divinely inspired terror was a common component of ancient Near Eastern battle reports.[4] In Jonah, the sailors feared (וייראו) the storm from the outset, but, upon learning that Jonah was fleeing from the god of the sea, fear turned to terror (וייראו יראה גדולה).

Confusion and Panic

The terror felt by those losing a battle because of a divinity's intervention could be but a prelude to confusion and panic and self-inflicted loss.[5] Although the technical word המם used to refer to divinely-inspired confusion does not occur in Jonah 1, there are several images of confusion: the raging of the sea is ever-increasing (vv. 4, 11, 13); the ship, no more controllable than Sisera's chariots which YHWH put into confusion (Judg. 4.15), comes close to breaking apart (v. 4); and the sailors cry out to their gods in fear and throw cargo into the sea (v. 5). Along with these explicitly stated elements of confusion, there is also the situational element of disarray in which ally turns into

---

1.   Non-Israelite traditions: Kang 1989: 42, 57, 98; Biblical records: e.g. 1 Sam. 14.36-37; 23.2.

2.   Kang 1989: 57; 1 Sam. 14.18, 36-37; 14.41-42.

3.   Kang 1989: 57, 79; perhaps Josh. 10.8.

4.   'Victory in battle is always attributed to the terrifying power of the gods (ANET, 281b); this has a paralyzing effect upon the opponents, leaving them in confusion and weakness... (ANET, 289b)' (Jones 1989: 301). Von Rad (1991: 46-47) lists several references to an enemy's terror stemming from YHWH's alliance with Israel: e.g. Exod. 15.14-16; 1 Sam. 4.7-8.

5.   The Egyptian god Seth was the god of confusion as well as the god of war and of the storm (Kang 1989: 96). Some examples (from the list of von Rad 1991: 48-49) of biblical references to divinely inspired confusion in a battle situation are: Exod. 23.27; Josh. 10.10; Isa. 5.11.

adversary—the one who should be with YHWH is fleeing from him, thus the captain and the sailors who sought alliance with Jonah (v. 6) must distance themselves from him, thereby becoming YHWH's allies.

Of course, the sea setting itself is the most important image of not only confusion but *chaos*, as reflected in ancient Near Eastern traditions of a supreme god's battle against watery chaos.[1] But the superiority of YHWH to neighboring gods is indicated in Jonah. YHWH, god of the heavens, is not simply one who struggles against and defeats chaos; rather, he is the maker of the sea and, as the narrator shows, he is as able to manipulate that principal element of chaos (chs. 1–2) as he is able to manipulate elements on the dry land (ch. 4).

Crying out for Deliverance

In biblical narratives, when the Israelites cry out (זעק or צעק) to YHWH, it is almost exclusively in the context of military conflict.[2] The cry may go up after an extended period of oppression[3] or it may go up in the midst of battle.[4] The sailors in Jonah are like those of this latter situation, in which their battle seems doomed unless the divinity intervenes, or rather, in this case, unless the divinity ceases fire.[5]

Offering of Vows and Sacrifices in the Wake of Victory

In preparation for battle, soldiers would undergo purification rituals, and make vows and sacrifices.[6] The sailors of the Jonah account

---

1. 'Yam...Baal's "fundamental" opponent...is the prince of the sea, and the sea...is the primordial element of chaos' (Grønbæk 1985: 31). Before creating the world, the Babylonian Marduk must battle against Tiamat, who is a 'personification of the sea and its powers' (Jacobsen 1968: 105).

2. The Jonah account is the only one in which non-Israelites are referred to as calling out (זעק or צעק) to a divinity. In Judges, the cry to YHWH is always followed by his raising up a person to deliver them in victorious battle against a military opponent.

3. E.g. Judg. 3.9, 15; 4.3; 6.6, 7; 10.10.

4. Exod. 14.10, where those in flight are pursued by the Egyptian army; Isa. 7.8, 9, where YHWH responds to the cry by using thunder as a weapon; 1 Chron. 5.20; 2 Chron. 13.14; 32.30.

5. Cf. the curse in the treaty between Esarhaddon and the King of Tyre: 'May Baal...raise an evil wind against your ships...may a strong wave sink them in the sea' (*ANET*[3], 534, cited in Sasson 1990: 118).

6. Biblical references in von Rad 1991: 42; other ancient Near Eastern references in Kang 1989: 62, 63.

obviously had no occasion to do such before their encounter with YHWH and the prophet. But in great fear of YHWH, they offered sacrifices and made vows after the sea became calm.[1]

Jonah and Joshua 10.1-27

We may go beyond the identification of various similarities between Jonah 1 and other battle narratives and compare the book of Jonah with one specific battle narrative. Jonah parallels the account of a battle in Josh. 10.1-27 in lexical references, semiotic relationships and narrative structure.

Lexical Parallels

The most striking lexical similarity between the two stories is their use of גדול. Although this is the most frequently used qualitative adjective in the Hebrew Scriptures, Jon. 1.1–2.1 and Josh. 10.1-27 stand apart from all other narrative passages in the Hebrew scriptures in both the number of occurrences of this adjective and the variety of lexical references which it modifies. A list of the modified references can be made to prefigure other observations that will be made about the parallels between these two passages:

	Joshua 10	*Jonah 1*
Key city:	Gibeon (v. 2, twice)	Nineveh (v. 2)
Heaven-sent weapon:	(hail-) stones (v. 11)	wind (v. 4)
		storm (vv. 4, 12)
Tools of confinement:	rocks (vv. 17, 27)	fish (2.1)
Result of YHWH's		
intervention:	defeat (v. 10)	fear (vv. 10, 16)
	destruction (v. 20)	

Chart 1: *Occurrences of* גדול

גדול might be as appropriately labelled a 'leitmotif' of the Joshua account as it has been with regard to the Jonah narrative;[2] YHWH

---

1. References to ANE post-battle sacrifices are to be found in Jones 1989: 301 and Kang 1989: 49.

2. This is a key theme in the *hortatory* passages of Deuteronomy. Note especially 4.32-38, where there is a cohesive density of גדול occurrences (five, in reference to the exodus event, deeds accompanying it, YHWH's fire, YHWH's strength, and the nations driven out by Israel) similar to that in the two narrative passages that we are

battles with great means, for great people, and with great results (Lacocque 1981: 8; Sasson 1990: 72).

Other lexical parallels between the two narratives, reflecting similarity in plot, are found in the following verbal references:

Semantic domain	*Joshua 10*	*Jonah*
flight	נוס (vv. 11, 16)	ברח (1.3, 10; 4.2)
attack (נכה)	(vv. 4, 10, 20, 26)	(4.7, 8)
casting down	שלך (vv. 11, 27)	טול (1.4, 5, 12, 15)
		שלך (2.4)
downward descent (ירד)	(vv. 11, 27)	(1.3, 3, 5; 2.6)
fear (ירא)	(v. 2)	(1.10, 16)

Chart 2: *Predicative Parallels*

Despite the obvious parallels here, the irony involved in the Jonah narrative is indicated by considering the two accounts with regard to the agents and objects associated with these events.

In the Joshua account, YHWH, Joshua and Israel act in harmony against the enemy. Thus, it is they (or one of them on behalf of the others) who 'strike' and 'cast down', and it is the enemies who fear for their lives, take flight, and are forced downward. But the rebellious Jonah flees downward and is then cast downward like the five kings who fled and were cast downward, or at least ground-ward, into the cave.

When they learn with whom Jonah is allied, the sailors experience terror as did the king of Jerusalem when he learned of Gibeon's alliance with Israel. But whereas the non-Israelites resist and are slaughtered through the chosen representatives of YHWH, the non-Israelites in the Jonah account are saved through ridding themselves of YHWH's chosen representative.

Parallels in Text Structure

The two narratives have parallel structures at various levels. The similarities of structure at the overall text level reinforces the impression of similarity in genre. The similarities at lower levels enable further appreciation of the contrast between how things stand between YHWH, his insider representatives, and outsiders *now*, in the time of Jonah's original postexilic audience, and how they stood *then*, when YHWH and his people fought together in holy wars against pagan outsiders.

considering. Also, Deut. 9.1-2 refers to great nations, great cities and great people.

High-Level Parallels

The basic structure of both accounts is:

	Joshua 10	*Jonah*
Setting	10.1-5a	1.1-3
Battle	10.5b-11	1.4-16
Miracle report	10.12-14	1.17-2.10
Closure of primary battle account	10.15	2.10
Follow-up and lesson	10.16-26	3–4
Closure	10.27	4.11

Chart 3: *Text-Level, Structural Parallels*

The narrative begins by setting the stage for the conflicts to occur. A report is then given on how the battle is fought and who the victor is. In both accounts, the divine use of a common element of nature (hail in Joshua, wind in Jonah) is shown to have been a key factor in the battle.

But the report on the battle which involved a relatively common-place divine weapon (see the section on celestial weapons, above) is followed by reference to a much less common, perhaps unique (see below), manipulation of nature that underscores the extent to which YHWH has been involved in the battle. The Joshua narrator comments directly on this intervention, exulting in the greatness of Joshua as well as of YHWH, while the Jonah narrator depicts Jonah as producing the psalm of praise.

Following this interlude the narrative tension is diminished, but the extent to which YHWH gives victory is demonstrated, and an object lesson accompanied by a moral is given.

Lower-Level Parallels

Lower-level comparisons of the texts further reveal parallels in structure, but the difference in the way that the structural slots are filled indicates a considerable contrast in perspective on the various aspects of YHWH's alliances. In the following we will consider the most salient parallels within each of the basic segments diagrammed above. The appendix contains an even more detailed outline of the parallel texts.

Setting. The settings of both accounts may be outlined as follows.

	Joshua 10	Jonah 1
Inciting moment	10.1-2	1.1
Call for allied action	10.3-4	1.2
Response to the call	10.5a	1.3

Chart 4: *Setting Components*

In both stories the inciting moment, the event that sets the stage for the narrative's conflicts, is the reception of a word concerning an adversary, a great (גדולה) city.[1] The reception of the word concerning the great city causes great fear. The Joshua narrator states this reaction explicitly (v. 2a); the Jonah narrator *shows* this reaction by referring to Jonah's flight (as noted above).

The call for allied action is an adversary's response to the fearful word in Joshua, but it becomes part of the fearful word to the insider Jonah. The Jerusalem king Adoni-Zedek calls out to his allies, four other kings, for help in attacking those allied with the Israelite god; YHWH entrusts his ally Jonah with the divine word of judgment to attack Nineveh, whose evil reflects their non-alignment with YHWH.

In Joshua, the four kings respond to Adoni-Zedek's call just as he had desired, and the stage is set for a battle in which the distinction between allies and adversaries is clear-cut. Jonah also moves out—but to flee in the direction opposite to where he has been called to go. The kings' unified action takes them up (עלה); Jonah's rebellion takes him down (ירד) on a descent that will not end until he is at the 'roots of the mountains' (1.3, 3, 5; 2.6). Thus, in the Jonah account, an initial alliance turns into a civil war and a battle against the rebel is necessitated before the battle against the original adversary continues.

The Battle. The following chart indicates the similarities of the two battle accounts.

---

1. The Joshua narrator underscores the greatness of Gibeah by modifying it twice with גדולה in the two clauses explaining Jerusalem's great fear. In Jonah, Ninevah will be referred to as (ה)עיר (ה)גדולה three more times (3.2, 3; 4.11). These are the only places in the Hebrew Scriptures where there is repeated reference to a specific city as גדולה. In Moses' Deuteronomic exhortation to the children of Israel, there are three references to ערים גדלת as part of the image of the imposing task of the conquest, possible for the Israelites only because YHWH is fighting for them (1.28; 6.10; and, especially, 9.1).

The Battle	Joshua 10	Jonah 1
Attack	10.5	1.4a
Call for help	10.6	1.6
Response	10.7	—
Oracle	10.8	1.7-10
Battle scene	10.9-11a	1.4-15
Deaths and calm	10.11b, 15	1.15

Chart 5: *Battle Components*

In Joshua, the battle begins when the five kings lay siege against isolated Gibeon whose only hope is that the people in league with YHWH will respond to their call for help. But in Jonah the battle begins when YHWH hurls his weapon against the one who is supposed to be in league with him but who has made the sailors unwitting allies in his only battle tactic, flight. The sailors soon see that they have no hope but to call for help, divine help.

The Gibeonites send to their sworn ally to gain deliverance; the captain goes to his inert ally in the ship's hold so that 'we might not perish'. In both accounts, those calling for help begin their addresses by denouncing inaction and then tell what must be done and why. While the Gibeonites' plea is given only in terms of human, military assistance, the captain of Jonah's ship realizes that the battle for their lives involves a divine element. What he does not realize, however, is that the god whom he is ordering Jonah to 'call out to' (קרא אל) is the one who had ordered Jonah to 'call out against' (קרא על) a pagan power, and that his call for Jonah to work in alliance with the sailors, who have already made frantic calls to their gods (v. 5), is also a call to make good of a divine alliance against which Jonah has revolted, thereby enmeshing the sailors in the battle.

Joshua, in respect of his alliance, responds to the Gibeonite call as the four kings had responded to the Jerusalem king's call. In contrast, no mention is made of Jonah's response: how can he call out to the one from whom he is fleeing? Rather, the scene shifts to the sailors who must resort to divination.

In both accounts, the divine word concerning the battle comes after the battle has already begun. But while the Joshua account portrays YHWH as speaking directly to Joshua, the sailors must first throw lots, then interrogate Jonah for further clarification. The word to Joshua from YHWH is 'do not fear'; the word to the sailors from Jonah is an ambiguous 'I fear' and the sailors in turn 'fear a great fear'. Joshua

need not fear because YHWH has put the enemy 'in their hands'; but
the sailors have plenty of reason to fear since they now recognize that
Jonah's presence has put them in the hands of the one who made the
sea as well as the dry ground, and that their alliance with Jonah—
which they refuse to take lightly (1.11-14)—has brought them into the
midst of a civil war, and on the wrong side. Indeed, the intensity of
the sailors' fear upon learning of this uncertain alliance (Jonah is
fleeing yet claims to fear/worship YHWH) is like that of the king of
Jerusalem who 'feared greatly' when he heard of Gibeon's alliance
with Israel (v. 2).

While there is less correspondence between the sequence of
elements in the battle scenes (the fifth component of Chart 5) than in
what has been observed up to this point, there are several referential
parallels. We have already mentioned the images of confusion in the
Jonah account. The Joshua account records the classic element of holy
wars in the Near East: the military panic/confusion (המם) sent from
God. In Jonah, however, since YHWH is battling against an individual,
rather than the group with whom Jonah finds himself, there is no need
to add any more confusion to the sailors' plight than what is already
present simply from the intensity of their battle against the storm. The
image of the raging sea and the plunging ship correspond to Joshua's
more prosaic reference to the 'great attack'.

More saliently parallel are the accounts of the attempted flight and
the divine cut-off.[1] The armies of the five kings flee from (מפני) the
Israelite soldiers, thus, as shown by the divine sanction in v. 8 and the
agent of 'confuse' and 'attack' in v. 9, away from YHWH. Similarly,
Jonah is fleeing from (מלפני) YHWH.[2] The direction of the flight is
downward, in both narratives. Though this might be an incidental
detail in the Joshua account, it is vested with theological significance in
Jonah (Magonet 1976: 17; Sasson 1990: 80, 187; Wolff 1986: 112).

Then comes a classic attack from heaven: the divinity takes an
element of the sky and hurls it down upon the fleer. His weapon is no

---

1. That Jonah's flight was not simply a prelude to the battle but also an integral
part of it may be signalled by the participial form of ברח in v. 10, rather than the perfect, which could have signalled that he had fled but now recognized such flight to be
impossible. The participial form could be taken to indicate that his flight is an
ongoing process.

2. This same prepositional phrase is used in reference to flight in battle in
2 Chron. 19.18.

skimpy one: whether hail-stones from heaven or wind, it is גדול, 'great'.

In both accounts, focus on the agent of the fusillade, as well as his opposition to their attempt to flee, is provided by the fronting of YHWH to sentence-initial position.[1] Though YHWH has been referred to by name twice in the Joshua account (both times as subject of the clause) and three times in the Jonah account, this is the first time in both accounts that his name occurs in the sentence-initial position. Indeed, it is the first time that any subject appears in that position.

The climatic part of the Joshua account ends with a comment on how many died from the hailstones cast down by YHWH. That of the Jonah account ends with depiction of Jonah being cast down to his apparent death in the sea by the sailors (v. 15) but also by YHWH (2.4). Verse 16 shows that this one death was all that was sought: all others survived and worshipped the one who was the source of the threat to their lives.

The Fantastic Event. In both accounts, the narration slows down to report and comment on a fantastic, unique[2] miracle: the stopping of the sun in Joshua and the deliverance via a fish in Jonah. The presentation of these events may be compared in several respects (see Chart 6, below).

The key semiotic opposition is between the references to elements associated with the region of God's dwelling place and life and those associated with the region of death. The positive signs of the Joshua account underscore the glory of the Israelite victory; the negative signs underscore the depth of the prophet's plunge away from God.

1.   Josh. 10.11b: ויהוה השליך עליהם אבנים גדלות; Jon. 1.4: ויהוה חטיל רוח־גדולה אל־הים.

2.   The references to the divine casting down of hail (Josh. 10) or wind (Jonah) have many parallels in biblical and ancient Near Eastern literature (as shown, for example, in Weinfeld 1984). But there are few, if any, parallels to the stopping of the sun and the salvation via a fish. The only near-parallels that Weinfeld (1984: 146-47) suggests, concerning the stopping of the sun miracle, are the reference in Hab. 3.11, which may be borrowing the image from the Joshua account, and a wish expressed in the Iliad that 'the sun set not... until I have cast down... the hall of Priam'— which is not followed by a report that the sun did actually stop.

Ben-Yosef (1980: 113) points out that though 'the fish, or water-monster, swallows a man' is a folk motif found in various parts of the world, 'From the point of view of the element of a *benevolent* fish... the story of Jonah is unique, especially in the cultural milieu where it originated' (my emphasis).

	Joshua 10	*Jonah 1.17–2.10*
Battle situation:	YHWH against enemy of Israel (outsiders)	YHWH against prophet of Israel (insider)
Witness:	Israel	None but the victim/ delivered one
Natural elements referred to:	Sun, moon, heaven (up, positive, association with God's abode)	Fish, roots of mountains, Sheol, and so forth (down, negative, association with death)
Purpose:	Defeat of enemy	Salvation of rebel
Call to God:	'Joshua spoke to YHWH'	'I called out to… YHWH'
God's response:	YHWH heard a human voice	'He heard my voice'
Result:	Victory	Deliverance

Chart 6: *Referential Components of the Fantastic Events*

Thus, though the fantastic events in both battles occur for the benefit of those originally leagued with YHWH, the first is a great victory for, and witnessed by, the Israelite nation and their leaders, whereas the second is a hidden act of deliverance of a rebel who finally surrenders. However, a key link between the ignominious rebel and the great holy-war commander is that they both called out to YHWH and YHWH heard their voice.

Follow-up and Lesson. Though the greatness and victoriousness of YHWH's work in battle has been shown, the battle does not end. Joshua commands his troops, 'Don't stop!', and Jonah is once again commanded by YHWH to do what had prompted his rebellion: the pursuit of the enemy is to continue.

However, there is quite a difference in strategy. The Israelites were to attack their enemies from the rear and prevent them from entering their cities. In contrast, Jonah, equipped with YHWH's word, is to walk into the midst of the enemy's city. The Israelite soldiers' continuance, in keeping with their orders, results in an overwhelming defeat of the enemy. Jonah's weapon—a word of judgment from his warrior God—overwhelms the enemy but with the result that they believe God, cry out to him for mercy, and, through their humble surrender, avert massive destruction. In the wake of these decisive displays of YHWH's power and fearfulness, a lesson is given.

Apart from these general parallels in plot, there are also several unflattering, synonymous parallels between the prophet Jonah and the five kings of the Joshua account, and several antithetical parallels between the Ninevite king and the five kings that reinforce the irony involved in the depiction of the prophet's response to YHWH.

Jonah and the Five Kings. Jonah's attempt to flee from YHWH by descending into the darkness of the ship's hold and sailing over the sea is similar to the attempt of the five kings in the Joshua narrative to hide in the darkness of a cave. For both, the place of refuge becomes a prison. YHWH's men imprison the kings by blocking the cave with great stones; the sailors, working in harmony with YHWH, cast Jonah into the sea which surrounds and imprisons him (2.6-7).

In both accounts, the prisoners are brought out of their confinement: the kings are brought out at Joshua's command; Jonah is belched out at YHWH's command. The kings' emergence from their prison is only temporary and for the sake of being humiliated and killed as a sign of what YHWH will do to all Israel's enemies. Jonah is brought out of his prison as one reconciled with YHWH (2.7, 9) and who, on YHWH's behalf, is to proclaim Joshua-style destruction. However, the carrying out of his task will result in a sign of what, to quote Joshua, 'YHWH will do to all your enemies'—if they repent—but this sign of YHWH's mercy is for Jonah a source of distress[1] that will make him wish for the same end as the five kings.

The Five Kings and the Ninevite King. The five enemy kings, surrounded by the Israelites, are forced to the ground and humiliated (v. 24). In contrast, the Ninevite king, his people surrounding the lone representative of YHWH, voluntarily humiliates himself, taking off his royal robes and lowering himself from his throne into the dust (3.6).

In both accounts, a series of commands follows the royal humiliation. Joshua commands the Israelites to assume attitudes of psychological strength in view of their alliance with YHWH (v. 25). The Ninevite king commands his people to weaken themselves through fasting and, more importantly, to reform (3.7-8). Joshua commands the Israelites in full confidence of the destruction of enemies that results when one battles in alliance with YHWH (v. 25). The Ninevite king can only hope (מי־יודע 'who knows?') that the adversary's annihilating anger may give way to compassion (3.9).

---

1. חרה is translated as 'anger' in most translations, but Sasson (190: 270, 273-75) argues for translating it as 'dejection'.

In both Joshua and Jonah's proclamations, the announcement of destruction is unconditional. However, while Joshua promised that ככה יעשׂה יהוה (v. 25), Jonah found that the LORD לא עשׂה what he said he would.

After Joshua humiliates the kings, exhorts his people to strength and promises victory over their enemies, he strikes (נכה) the kings and kills them (literally: causes them to die). After the Ninevite king humbles himself and exhorts his people to do the same, Nineveh is spared. Instead of the enemy being struck down, the vine which provides comfort to the proclaimer of destruction is struck (נכה) and withers, allowing the sun—that celestial element which Joshua had so triumphantly commanded—to strike (נכה) the prophet's head and make him wish that he would die (3.8, 9).

Closure. Both accounts end with a reference to a 'great' (גדול) object which has been referred to earlier in the narrative. 'The great stones' in the Joshua account are used to seal the tomb of the five kings, and they stand 'to this day' as a witness to the great alliance of YHWH with Israel. In the Jonah account, YHWH chides Jonah for his concern over the insignificant vine in view of YHWH's concern for the 'great city', a formidable adversary turned ally.

Conclusion

Jonah is like a narrative negative of Joshua 10. The structure is basically the same, but the black and whites of the earlier narrative are reversed in the later one. Joshua and Israel run up to defend a great city in respect of its call, and they defeat their enemies through the powerful intervention of the divinity with whom they are allied. Jonah runs away from a great city in disrespect of his call, but is cut off by the powerful intervention of the divinity, who has become his adversary. Joshua ascends for battle and commands the great lights of heaven. Jonah descends and is entrapped in the depth of Sheol. In Joshua, the pagan kings are humiliated as a demonstration of YHWH's power. In Jonah, the king humbles himself but is saved as a demonstration of YHWH's grace.

This narrative manipulation of the structure and references of a battle report may be viewed as a development consistent with the transformations of the war oracle from the eighth-century prophets' insistence that YHWH was now battling against Israel[1] down to the early-sixth century transformation in which 'the primary intent of this literary mode... [becomes] the preservation of the people of Israel in the impending crisis which challenges their very existence' (Christensen 1975: 282).

However, by the time the Jonah narrative receives its final form, the crisis is not impending but realized. The people have already been swallowed up and sent to a great city. They have survived but not without anger/dejection. The Jonah narrative suggests that, though there may be dismay at the escape of the great city from judgment, it is an occasion for growing in understanding of how extensive is the grace that delivered them from the hell to which their flight from God led them.

BIBLIOGRAPHY

Alexander, T.D.
    1988   *Jonah: An Introduction and Commentary* (Tyndale Old Testament Commentaries, 23; Downers Grove, IL: Inter-Varsity Press).
Ben-Yosef, I.A.
    1980   'Jonah and the Fish as a Folk Motif', *Semitics* 7: 102-17.
Christensen, D.L.
    1975   *Transformations of the War Oracle in Old Testament Prophecy* (Missoula, MT: Scholars Press).
Grønbæk, J.H.
    1985   'Baal's Battle with Yam—A Canaanite Creation Fight', *JSOT* 33: 27-44.
Jacobsen, T.
    1968   'The Battle between Marduk and Tiamat', *JAOS* 88: 104-108.
Jones, G.H.
    1989   'The Concept of Holy War', in R.E. Clements (ed.), *The World of Ancient Israel: Sociological, Anthropological and Political Perspectives* (Cambridge: Cambridge University Press): 299-321.
Kang, S.-M.
    1989   *Divine War in the Old Testament and in the Ancient Near East* (New York: de Gruyter).
Lacocque, A.
    1981   *The Jonah Complex* (Atlanta: John Knox).

1.   'Amos has taken the earlier speech of a war oracle... and transformed it into a judgment speech against Israel' (Christensen 1975: 71-72); 'The tradition of holy-war [is] in its reversed form. The concept was so familiar in Israelite thinking that the judgment implied by its total reversal could not be missed' (Jones 1989: 318).

Magonet, J.
1976   *Form and Meaning: Studies in Literary Techniques in the Book of Jonah* (Bern: Herbert Lang; Frankfurt a.M.: Peter Lang).
Sasson, J.M.
1990   *Jonah* (New York: Doubleday).
Sternberg, M.
1985   *The Poetics of Biblical Narrative: Ideological Literature and the Drama of Reading* (Bloomington, IN: Indiana University Press).
Rad, G. von
1991   *Holy War in Ancient Israel* (trans. and ed. M.J. Dawn and J.H. Yoder; Grand Rapids: Eerdmans).
Weinfeld, M.
1984   'Divine Intervention in War in Ancient Israel and in the Ancient Near East', in H. Tadmor and M. Weinfeld (eds.), in *History, Historiography and Interpretation* (Jerusalem: Magnes).
Wolff, H.W.
1986   *Obadiah and Jonah* (trans. M. Kohl; Minneapolis: Augsburg).

APPENDIX

Structural Parallels of Joshua 10.1-27 and Jonah

	Joshua 10	*Jonah*
Setting		
a. Incitement: a fearful word	10.1	1.1
Receptor:	It was (ויהי) when the king of Jerusalem heard	It was (ויהי) the word of YHWH to Jonah
Response:	They feared greatly	—
Reason:	Since Gibeon was a great city . . . greater than Ai.	Nineveh, the great city . . .
b. Call for allied action	10.3-4	1.2
	Adoni-Zedek to four kings	YHWH to Jonah
Call to move out:	Come up to me	Get up, go to Nineveh
Desired action:	Help me	Call out against her
Reason for action:	that we may attack Gibeon	for their evil has risen before me
c. Response to the Call	10.5a	1.3
	And they gathered. . . and they went up	And Jonah got up—to flee. . . and he went down
Battle		
d. Commencement of battle	10.5b	1.3b-4a
	They attacked Gibeon. . . and fought. . .	YHWH hurled a great wind upon the sea. . .

e. Call for help	10.6	1.6
Going for help:	The Gibeonites sent to Joshua ... to say	The ship's captain went to Jonah and said
Message— Inaction is inappropriate:	Don't withdraw your hand	How can you sleep!
Move!	Come up!	Get up!
What to do:	Save us, help us	Call out to your god
Why:	for all the kings have gathered against us	perhaps God will show us favor and we will not die
f. Response	10.7 So Joshua went up... along with all his soldiers	—
g. Divine word	10.8	1.7-10
Method of obtaining:	—	They cast lots and the lot fell on Jonah
Speaker:	YHWH said to Joshua	[Jonah] said to them
Message:	'Don't fear, for I have put them in your hand'	'YHWH... I fear, the one who made the sea and the dry ground'
Response:	[Israel proceeds]	The men feared a great fear
h. Battle scene	10.9-11a	1.4-11
Confusion:	YHWH panicked them	[Several images of confusion]
Powerful attack:	They attacked them with a great attack	a great storm (vv. 4, 11, 13) ship about to break up (v. 4)
Attempted flight:	... they fled from Israel...	He got up to to flee from YHWH (v. 3)
	along the descent to Beth Horon	and descended to Joppa (v. 3) He was fleeing from YHWH
Divine cut-off:	But YHWH cast down on them great stones	(v. 10) But YHWH cast down a great wind on the sea (v. 4)
i. Death and calm	10.11b, 15	1.15-16
Miracle Report	10.12-14	1.17–2.10
Closure of Primary Battle Report	10.15 Joshua and all Israel returned to their camp	2.10 YHWH spoke... and the fish spat Jonah onto the dry land
Follow-Up and Lessons a. Don't stop!	10.19 Don't stop! Pursue your enemies... Don't allow them to enter their cities for YHWH has given your enemies into your hand	3.2-5 Get up, go to Nineveh... Call out to ('*ēl*) it... Jonah began to enter the city... He called out... 'In forty days Nineveh will be destroyed'

b. Result	**10.20** Joshua and the Israelites attacked them with a great attack	**3.5a** The men of Nineveh believed God...
c. Of royal adversaries Royal humiliation:	**10.22-25** they brought the kings they put their feet on the kings' necks	**3.6-10** the king got off his throne he sat in the dust (v. 6)
Commands:	(Joshua to Israel) Do not be afraid Do not be discouraged Be strong Be courageous	(King to Nineveh) Do not taste anything Do not eat; do not drink Cover yourselves with sacks Call out to God Turn from evil and violence
Reason:	Thus YHWH will do to all your enemies	Perhaps God will relent and have compassion God felt sorry about the destruction he had said he would do and did not do it
Final Blow:	**10.26** Joshua struck the kings and killed them	**4.7-8** a worm struck the vine over Jonah's head the sun struck Jonah's head Jonah said: 'It's better that I die'
Closure	**10.27** great stones stand to this day (as a memorial to YHWH's power)	**4.11** YHWH: should I not have compassion for that great city?

JONAH'S POEM OUT OF AND WITHIN ITS CONTEXT

Athalya Brenner

ABSTRACT

This study is addressed to the nature of the links between the Jonah narrative and the poem embedded within it (2.3-10). The poem is examined out of its narrational context, collated with its biblical intertexts, and re-examined within the framing narrative. Its compositional status vis-à-vis the prose narrative is then considered and compositional integrity argued for. The poem is read (following Miles and Carroll) as a parody and satire. Finally, the convergence of literary techniques is read as a means for producing a didactic message through humour: mercy and grace should be privileged over justice.

The problem of the function and authenticity of Jonah's poem (Jon. 2.3-10) is a perplexing one. What is it doing there, embedded in the middle of a prose narrative? Is it an insertion, or an integral part of the original composition? At any rate, what is its function within its context, especially since the pious attitudes supposedly expressed in it by Jonah are in stark opposition to his quarrelsome behaviour throughout the narrative (Carroll 1987: 12)?

Until quite recently most scholars viewed the poem as inappropriate on various grounds, a pastiche of quotations from the Psalter badly fitted into its present context. Lately, however, the trend has changed. For example, Magonet (1983: 39-54) argues that the poem is authentic and original; that its many echoes of the Book of Psalms are deliberate [mis]quotations (but see Hurvitz 1985); that the poem's apparent incongruity disappears when its 'pious' nature is perceived as ironic; and that the poem fits in well with the overall structure, intent and psychology of the book. In another recent treatment Lacocque and Lacocque (1990: 94-113) once more affirm the authentic status of the poem and analyse it as a journey of Jonah's self 'From Nothingness into Being' (the name of the chapter dealing with the Jonah poem, p. 94). In view of this change in scholarly opinion, and because of the convincing reassessment of the book of Jonah as a parody/satire (Miles 1976; Carroll 1990), I would like to explore the poem once more.

The Poem out of Context

It is evident that, overtly, the poem is a prayer, orthodox in tone, beseeching God for a metaphorical 'rescue from a pit' (Miles 1975). The praying subject-in-the-text describes his situation (or hers—there are no gender markers in the text, which is delivered in the first person singular). She/he was desolate: desolation and despair are expressed metaphorically in terms of abyss—'Sheol', death and water imagery. No specific source for this despair is voiced, apart from the centrally placed and unmetaphorical complaint—the subject's spatial separation from God's place of worship, whose exact location is unspecified (v. 5). In spite of the physical separation between God and worshipper, the prayer reaches its destination (v. 8). Now it seems that the subject is inside the Temple, grateful for the present release and promising to repay the previously unmentioned vows to YHWH.

The Sheol and drowning-in-water images stand in spatial and qualitative opposition to God's place of worship. The reunion of worshipper and worshipped effects a solution to the former's problem. Therefore, both (metaphorically expressed) problem and setting seem to be cultic rather than physical or social. By the end of the poem the real complaint has become apparent through the effected solution: the ability (in the present, for the Hebrew tense system allows the interpretation of the verbs in v. 10 in the present tense) to be near God once more ends the crisis. Verse 9 too, although problematic (see below), suggests a cultic *Sitz im Leben* for Jonah's psalm.

The Poem and its Intertexts

It is in Psalms 69 and 84 that one finds characteristic water and pit imagery in the Psalter. Miles (1976: 174-75) shows that even in those psalms such imagery is not nearly as dense as in the prayer attributed to Jonah. Generally speaking, then, Jon. 2.3-10 offers the most articulate and extravagant use of water and pit imagery in biblical poetry.

A more detailed analysis of expressions and combinations produces the following observations. Disregarding the problematic v. 9 for the time being, each verse of the Jonah poem has an identical or closely parallel counterpart in the Psalms. Here is a list of correspondences which is by no means exhaustive:

Jonah		Psalms
2.3	=	22.3, 5; 31.23; 118.5; 130.1
2.4	=	42.8; 88.8, 18
2.5	=	31.23
2.6	=	113.3; 69.2
2.7	=	30.10
2.8	=	42.7; 77.4, 12; 107.5; 142.4, 23-31; 143.4
2.9	=	31.7
2.10	=	107.22; 116.17

To these individual parallels we may add Psalm 18 = 2 Samuel 22 on grounds of similarity in imagery, tone and choice of metaphors. For the problem of v. 9, as well as the shifts in the so-called quotations, one should consult Magonet's work, where it is claimed that the shifts are deliberate and methodical, in the service of charting Jonah's road towards accepting his mission.

Turning from imagery to other intertextual matters, what can be gleaned from other biblical poems similarly and dissimilarly embedded within a narrational prose context? The embedded Song of Miriam (Exod. 15) and Song of Deborah (Judg. 5) are indeed poems of thanksgiving and praise for divine salvation too. Both link up with their contexts by subject matter; they contain quasi-historical accounts of events previously narrated in prose. Jonah's psalm, however, has no direct dimension of historicity or personal history; thus its link with the surrounding prose context is less apparent. Another difference is the following: the Song of Deborah does not contain specific cultic elements. The second part of the Song of the Sea, like Jonah's poem, does have affinities with a cultic shrine; however, its affinity with the prose account is problematic (Childs 1974: 243-53).

What about the Davidic psalm embedded in 2 Sam. 22 (= Ps. 18)? Placed within the context of addenda (2 Sam. 21–24) that are only loosely connected to the narrational context (2 Sam. 20 on the one side and 1 Kgs 1–2 on the other side), David's psalm has no overt biographical significance—just like Jonah's 'psalm'.

The next intertext is Hannah's prayer (1 Sam. 2.1-10), which is perhaps the closest parallel to Jonah's. Significantly, *Yalkut Shim'oni* even quotes Hannah's prayer within the treatment of Jonah's prayer. In both instances the poems constitute a plot break. The link between prose and poem is thematically, overtly, problematic, in that the occasion invites thanksgiving *after* (see above) an event of salvation, the change in style introduces variety, and a suspension of tension occurs on the plot level. The contents of the poem, nevertheless, do not correspond closely to that of the prose narrative. The similarity, inasmuch as it exists, lies in the correlation between poetic imagery and story event. Thus the correlation is overt but superfluous, in both cases based on catch-phrases rather than on true congruity. Finally, the language of both poems differs from that of its prose surroundings and is more akin to that of the Psalms (cf. Hurvitz 1985). It is therefore not surprising that scholarly debates concerning the integrity and dating of Hannah's prayer vis-à-vis its prose frame closely parallel those concerning Jonah's prayer.

The Poem within its Framing Narrative

The Jonah poem certainly breaks the ongoing movement of the plot advanced by the (prose) narrative. The embedding of a poem is obviously a change in style. As in the passages cited above and others, the change is first and foremost a multifunctional literary device. It enhances the tension while allowing for a respite. It introduces a variety of poetic expression. In short, it is a 'filler'. Beyond this, does the poem do anything for the story line apart from functioning as an orthodox intermission?

Isolated from the narrational flow that surrounds it, the poem can hardly be perceived as related to the narrated situational context (the belly of the male/female fish) in which Jonah finds himself. The problem was noticed already by the ancient Jewish sages and exegetes. They went to great lengths in order to tie details of the poem with the foregoing narrative of 1.1–2.2. The borderline between *peshat* and *derash* is perforce trodden here, as for instance in the case of the difficult v. 9. The verse is linked to ch. 1: 'the preservers of vanities' are understood to be the heathen sailors who, after seeing YHWH's glory, 'forsake their former attachment'—so even Rashi, Kimhi and Ibn Ezra. In short, the attempts to relate the poem biographically to Jonah are more than a trifle forced.

Ibn Ezra, however, raises another important question which has been referred to briefly earlier. Whereas the superscription of the poem has Jonah pray inside the belly of the female fish (2.2), and the conclusion states that God made the (male!) fish spout him out after the prayer had been uttered and heard (2.11), the language of the poem enclosed by these two statements expresses the joy of the praying subject at a salvation effected in the past/present rather than the future. In other words, there is no correlation between the situation of the fictional Jonah and the language of the praying 'I' which is put into his mouth in the psalm; and the seams connecting prose and poetry (2.2, 10) exacerbate the incongruity.

Ibn Ezra indeed explains this as an apparent incongruity only, since the prophetic mind regards the prayer as having been answered even before salvation is accomplished. The same argument often crops up in modern biblical scholarship too: for instance, in order to explain peculiarities of the Hebrew tense system in the so-called prophetic style and genres. Within the framework of the present discussion, the usage of the perfect *tense* for designating future *time* is thus excused. Needless to say, such explanations are not truly inspired by linguistics as much as by ideology, by the wish to harmonize and gloss over extralinguistic difficulties. In the case of Jonah's prayer, the 'tense–time' question emphasizes the alienated position of the poem within its context.

The Compositional Status of the Poem

The arguments for the poem's independent status within the framing narrative can be summarized as follows.

1. The *Sitz im Leben* of the poem is cultic and linked to a specific, although unnamed, place of worship.
2. The water/pit imagery is motivated by genre and conventionalized metaphorization, not by Jonah's actual situation in the story.
3. Other instances of embedded psalms, notably Hannah's prayer, exhibit the practice of linking a general psalm of thanksgiving to a specific narrational context by overt verbal means and through superficial content associations.
4. The incongruity of the prose–poem links is poignantly expressed in the incompatibility of the verb tenses in the poem, as against those in the verses that frame it.

What, then, is the 'original' nature of the poem? On the one hand, it can be viewed as an insertion from another and older source, an import from the stock of a well-known genre (cf. the parallels in the

Psalms). Accordingly, Jonah's prayer should be classified as an addition, a pious interpolation whose value for the plot *per se* does not exceed the literary considerations outlined above. I find this evaluation difficult to accept, since the unquestioning piety and orthodox ideology of the poem are in stark contrast to Jonah's behaviour outside it. Let me be frank: if the poem is indeed an addition conditioned by piety and the convention of embedding poetry at seemingly appropriate spots, this particular poem is not well chosen. It damages the credibility of the book and its anti-hero, Jonah the *refusenik*. Why would an author, or an editor, thus interfere with his/her own literary creation? Was not she/he aware of the incompatibilities, and the superficiality of the seams combining poem and prose narrative? Or was he/she willing to forgo the difficulties simply for the sake of introducing a multifunctional literary device? Once more, such a hypothetical solution, such a presumed authorial or editorial choice, has serious flaws.

On the other hand, if the poem is regarded as a compositionally and originally integral part of the story line, another view emerges. Then the questions a reader may pose shift slightly. Assuming that an author/editor has deliberately created the prose/poem contradictions, what aims were in mind? In other words, why did the author switch genres and religious attitudes in midstream, so to speak? Personally, I prefer this perspective, for I tend to turn to a solution based on authorial or editorial naivety only as a last resort, and there is no compelling reason to resort to that in the present case. At the very least, the incompatibilities here seem too pronounced to be explained away. Hence, authorial intentionality should be reconsidered.

Let us return to the language of the poem. Unlike the language of the prose narrative, it is free of Aramaisms and highly conventional. Consequently, should it be characterized as relatively *archaic* or just *archaistic*? Does the language of the poem predate that of the prose narrative? Methodologically, both evaluations of the linguistic data at first appear to be equally valid. Convention implies conservatism and makes dating, even relative dating, uncertain—contra Miles (1975) and others who postulate a relatively earlier date for the poem. Drawing on a contemporary, not necessarily older, stock thesaurus of a genre explains the linguistic difference between poem and prose narration as adequately as a theory of an earlier dating for the poem. In short, viewing the poem as a conscious imitation of genre and religious attitude seems to be a cogent possibility. I will therefore explore this possibility in the hope that such a viewing will plausibly account for the poem's status within its framing (prose) word context and situational (plot) context.

The Poem—A Parody and a Satire

Let us assume that the poem in Jon. 2.3-10 is not only a conscious imitation but also a humorous, self-conscious one. In that case, it should be classified as a parody of its generic kind. I believe that this interpretation clarifies some of the poem's central features and fits in with the tenor of the prose sections.

The imagery of the poem is extremely extravagant. The water metaphors finally add up to an inflated hyperbole, quite removed from the poem's central issue (separation from God and the cultic shrine). And yet, they finally amount to an inadequate aping of Jonah's actual situation. *Sheol*, referred to in terms of a monster, is more horrific than the male/female/male fish of the prose narrative, a primaeval sea-dragon. The abundance and concentration of both metaphors constitute a veritable flood (Miles 1975) of primordial images. Such a concentrated cluster (note how many psalms were listed for the purpose of comparison with this one!) exceeds ordinary poetic convention, or naive generic correspondence. The conventions are all there, but are overdone to the point of absurdity. Hence, the result is parody—a conscious (!?) imitation of a literary genre which conveys, through exaggeration, comedy, and humour, criticism of the source genre and the accepted literary and ideological norms that inform it.

Miles (1975: 174-75) makes an additional sound point. Water and abyss imagery is ordinarily just that—imagery. It refers to situations by metaphorizing them into something else, into some equivalents. In Jonah's case, however, the metaphors are no metaphors. Read within the framing prose, they refer to the (extralinguistic) 'real thing'. Jonah *is* in the monster's belly; turbulent water *is* all over his head. Unlike the imagery in similar psalms, the metaphors in Jonah's prayer are rendered invalid because, within the story, they cease to function as metaphors. Factuality and image cancel each other out. The result is a ludicrous parody of the true believer's complaint: will the same metaphors still be meaningful when the metaphorized situation materializes?

Returning to the frame narrative that immediately follows the prayer, it is worth noting that God does not answer Jonah's prayer by word of mouth. The silence towards Jonah is especially conspicuous, since God communicates with the fish (a male fish once more; the Jewish exegetes made much of the frequent changes of the fish's gender). Is this not ludicrous? Jonah has spoken so eloquently, delivered a speech replete with erudite knowledge of conventionalized prayer, yet that is not deemed worthy of a direct divine reply!

In obedience to the divine word, the fish 'vomits' Jonah onto dry land. 'Vomit' is a strong word, evocative, derisively imaginative in its reference to the digestive tract. Can we really claim that we feel sympathy towards the unfortunate messenger Jonah at this juncture, or do we laugh at him? Imagine the filth, to quote the Jewish sages again! It is plain that the man is satirized, the folly of his behaviour exposed, his just deserts meted out to him.

Let me repeat. The possibility that the poem is a parody—critical and humorous, a comical presentation of genre and fictional character—could not have been so defined in isolation. Had there not been other indications of genre parody (the prophet's call, the reluctance to comply, the conflict between prophet and king, the God and prophet dialogue) and satire (the angry prophet, his unusually pliant foils and target audience—foreign sailors, foreign city, foreign king), I would have been happy to consider the prayer as an imagined sincere expression of a person in distress. A little incongruous perhaps, a convention borrowed for the purposes of insertion into a specific fictional context from a more general one but, nevertheless, well grounded in biblical traditions and biblical attitudes. As things stand, though, such an interpretation seems to me less than plausible.

Medium and Message

Stylistically, the poem introduces a variety of form into the Jonah story. Compositionally, it allows for a break and heightens the dramatic tension (Jonah remains in the belly of the fish for the duration; we readers remain in suspense). Hebrew genres of poetry and prophecy are parodized. Angry Hebrew prophets, together with quick to repent foreigners and, by implication, the famously obstinate 'Hebrews' who seldom listen to their prophets' call to repent—all are satirized. The question we finally face is: what is the didactic aim of the entertaining Jonah story? What message does the humour serve apart from entertaining?

Jonah is a reluctant messenger, albeit, and despite himself, a successful one. As it transpires (ch. 4), his reluctance stems from a rigid
sense of justice. He does not want the foreigners to escape their fate,
the consequences of their wicked behaviour. Jonah, apparently, has a
precise legal mind and believes in divinely meted retribution. It transpires that he is more extreme, more legally 'just' than the God who
dispatches him. In contradistinction, YHWH is extremely merciful
towards all creatures. The conflict between the two coexistent divine
attributes, justice and mercy/grace (Hebrew *ḥesed*; cf. Exod. 20.5-6 =
Deut. 5.9-10; Exod. 34.6-7) is the subject matter of the story. In the
Jonah story, the two attributes are split between the two literary
personae. Jonah embodies the attribute of plain (absolute) justice; God
embodies the attribute of (relative) mercy/grace. In the last verse of
the book God says something like 'How can I not forgive the Ninevites
(= everyone) when they are so lost, when they are so numerous, when
they are (like) cattle?' In other words, human folly is recognized by
God (or so our author claims) for what it is. YHWH therefore makes
allowances. He is prepared to forgive, to be on the side of life rather
than rigid principle when life is at stake. The flimsiest excuse—even
repentance motivated by threat, the kind of repentance whose sincerity
is questionable—suffices for God to abandon his 'Seat of Justice' and
proceed to his 'Seat of Mercy' (*Yalkut Shim'oni*, after *Pirke deRabbi
Eliezer*).

In the book of Jonah, God's word is the final word. In the end Jonah
is rendered silent. I find it difficult to agree with the Lacocques that
Jonah has acquired a 'self'; his selfhood is one of expediency, it seems,
rather than ideology and recognition. Jonah does, however, learn to
keep quiet when all else fails. Thus the end is possibly an open end; he
who appealed to God directly only when threatened by fish and water,
who sorrowed so energetically when the *qîqāyôn* plant died and could
protect him no longer, perhaps remains unconvinced when God applies
to him the same treatment that would have awaited the equally
frightened gentiles.

So, by the end of the story, human folly is once more exposed.
Within the narrative, no person has been immune from it: prophet,
sailors, foreigners, the Hebrew community that created the story and
adopted it into its literary canon, any reader and any writer of the
established genres utilized. Only God, whose superior wisdom dictates
benevolence rather than human (sometimes hypocritical) justice, is

depicted as unperturbed by personal and seemingly theological considerations. And therein lies a lesson. To be truly human is to partake of divinity not only through orthodox sentiment (see the poem). To be in God's image (Gen. 1.26-27; 5.3), to be sanely judgmental, is to forsake legalism and become understanding and merciful. Jonah, prayer and all, remains the butt of the story. His example is certainly not one to be followed. We readers, do we mostly behave like the messenger or like his dispatcher? Let us ponder this, but not without smiling.

BIBLIOGRAPHY

Brenner, A.

1979 'The Language of Jonah as Criterion for the Dating of the Book', *Beth Miqra* 79: 396-405 (Hebrew).

Carroll, R.P.

1987 'Lampooning the Prophets: Two Burlesques on Prophecy' (unpublished paper read at the SBL International Meeting, Heidelberg, 1987).

1990 'Is Humour also among the Prophets?', in Y.T. Radday and A. Brenner (eds.), *On Humour and the Comic in the Hebrew Bible* (Bible and Literature Series, 23; Sheffield: Almond Press): 169-89.

Childs, B.S.

1974 *The Book of Exodus* (OTL; Philadelphia: Westminster Press).

Hurvitz, A.

1985 'Originals and Imitations in Biblical Poetry: A Comparative Examination of 1 Sam. 2.1-10 and Ps. 113.5-9', in A. Kort and S. Morschauser (eds.), *Biblical and Related Studies Presented to Samuel Iwry* (Winona Lake, IN: Eisenbrauns): 115-21.

Lacocque, A., and P.-E. Lacocque

1990 *Jonah: A Psycho-Religious Approach to the Prophet* (Columbia: University of South Carolina Press).

Magonet, J.

1983 *Form and Meaning: Studies in Literary Techniques in the Book of Jonah* (Bible and Literature Series, 8; Sheffield: Almond Press [1976]).

Miles, J.A.

1975 'Laughing at the Bible: Jonah as Parody', *JQR* 65: 168-81 (= *On Humour and the Comic*, 203-15).

THE REDACTIONAL SHAPING OF NAHUM 1
FOR THE BOOK OF THE TWELVE

James Nogalski

ABSTRACT

This paper introduces a seldom recognized catchword phenomenon in the Book of the Twelve as one clue to understanding its unity and its growth. Nah. 1 is then discussed as an example of how the recognition and evaluation of this technique both aids the interpretation of the text and furnishes insight into the growth of the Book of the Twelve.

1. *The Unity of the Book of the Twelve*

Ancient sources provide incontrovertible evidence that the Book of the Twelve was not only transmitted on a single scroll, but counted as a single book, not twelve. Jesus ben Sirach, LXX, Qumran, Josephus, *4 Ezra* 14, *Baba Bathra* 13b-15a and Jerome all attest to the common transmission of these writings.[1] Sir. 49.12 supplies the earliest concrete reference to 'The Twelve', meaning that they were already considered a corpus by the beginning of the second century BCE. *4 Ezra* 14 relates Ezra's inspired role in the restoration of the 24 canonical books, and Josephus (*Apion* 1.40) counts 22 books. While this discrepancy creates some uncertainty over the precise identity of these books, neither total can be reached unless the Book of the Twelve is counted as a single book. Jerome states this unity explicitly in the introductory remarks to his translation of the prophets.[2] *Baba Bathra*

---

1. See further the discussions in Dale Schneider, *The Unity of the Book of the Twelve* (PhD dissertation, Yale University, 1979), pp. 1-4; J. Nogalski, *The Use of Stichwörter as a Redactional Unification Technique in the Book of the Twelve* (ThM Thesis, Baptist Theological Seminary, Rüschlikon, Switzerland, 1987), pp. 2-3.

2. 'Incipit prologus duodecim prophetarum', *Biblia Sacra Vulgata*, II (Stuttgart:

13b-15a categorizes the Twelve differently from the remaining books in the Old Testament with regard to the space between the writings, and when listing the order of the biblical books, it refers to 'the Twelve', and does not refer to the prophecies contained within by name. The remainder of the evidence is more indirect, but nevertheless helps demonstrate conclusively that the minor prophets have a long history which places them in a common transmission.

Modern scholarship has for the most part ignored this evidence, or merely given it token acknowledgment. The few who do treat the question tend to regard the writings as though they had entirely separate transmission histories, implying that only the final form of the individual writing was incorporated into the larger corpus.[1] Only a handful of scholars treat the growth of the individual writings in connection with the context of the Book of the Twelve.[2]

Württembergische Bibelanstalt, 1969), p. 1374. Jerome says 'unum librum esse duodecim prophetarum'.

1.   See, for example, the theories of H. Ewald, *Die Propheten des Alten Bundes erklärt* (Göttingen: Vandenhoeck & Ruprecht, 2nd edn, 1868), pp. 74-82; F. Delitzsch, 'Wann weissagte Obadja?', *Zeitschrift für lutherische Theologie und Kirche* 12 (1851), pp. 92-93; U. Cassuto, 'The Sequence and Arrangement of the Biblical Sections', *Biblical and Oriental Studies*, I (Jerusalem: Magnes, 1973), pp. 5-6; C. Kuhl, *Die Entstehung des Alten Testaments* (Bern: Francke, 1953), pp. 217-18; H.W. Wolff, *Dodekapropheton. II. Joel und Amos* (BKAT, 14/2; Neukirchen: Neukirchener Verlag, 1977), pp. 1-2; W. Rudolph, *Haggai—Sacharja 1-8—Sacharja 9-14—Maleachi* (KAT, 13/4; Gütersloh: Gütersloher Verlagshaus, 1976), pp. 297-98. See also the dissertations by Schneider and A.Y. Lee, *The Canonical Unity of the Scroll of the Minor Prophets* (PhD dissertation, Baylor University, 1985). Most recently, the work by P. House (*The Unity of the Twelve* [JSOTSup, 97; Sheffield: JSOT Press, 1990]) applies a 'New Literary Critical' approach, and makes the assumption of one literary form programmatic for his treatment.

2.   C. Steuernagel (*Lehrbuch der Einleitung in das Alten Testament* [Tübingen: Mohr, 1912], pp. 669-72) believes sections of Nahum and Zech. 9-14 were added after other sections of their respective writings were already part of the canon. Two scholars attempted redactional hypotheses to explain common transmission which affected the shape of the writings in the Twelve: K. Budde, 'Eine folgenschwere Redaktion des Zwölfprophetenbuchs', *ZAW* 39 (1921), pp. 218-29; and R.E. Wolfe, 'The Editing of the Book of the Twelve', *ZAW* 53 (1935), pp. 90-129. However, the efforts of both Budde and Wolfe were seriously marred by the assumptions of the old source-critical school, and have not received favorable treatment in subsequent commentaries. More promising are the observations of Blenkinsopp, Weimar and Bosshard: J. Blenkinsopp, *Prophecy and Canon* (Notre Dame: Notre Dame Press, 1977), pp. 106-108; P. Weimar, 'Obadja: Eine redaktionskritische Analyse', *BN* 27

A phenomenon in the Book of the Twelve exists that has not yet been given the attention it deserves, namely, the presence of words at the end of one book that reappear at the beginning of the next. Occasionally, scholars have noted that catchwords play a role in the order of some of the writings, but the definition, extent and implications of these catchwords remains virtually untreated. The extent of these catchwords is considerable. Anywhere from five to twenty-five words appear in tandem between adjacent writings. The consistency of this phenomenon is even more intriguing, in that those places where it breaks down (Jon. 4; Zech. 14) illumine other phenomena. Jonah 4 does not exhibit the catchwords like the endings of the other books, but the long noted secondary hymn in Jonah 2 does contain catchwords to Micah 1. Additionally, If Jonah is removed from consideration, a strong connection exists between Obadiah and Micah 1. The end of Deutero-Zechariah presents a second inconsistency in this catchword phenomenon. Yet while Deutero-Zechariah does not exhibit the phenomenon, the end of Proto-Zechariah manifests a strong word connection to Malachi 1. Both of these inconsistencies therefore raise the question whether these sections were placed into an existing connection.

Three possible explanations can be offered for the *Stichwort* connections. Each option must be evaluated for every 'connection' separately, although some generalizing helps to clarify the character of the connections. The three options are:

(1985), pp. 94-99; E. Bosshard, 'Beobachtungen zum Zwölfprophetenbuch', *BN* 40 (1987), pp. 30-62. Blenkinsopp notes that a number of the writings have received substantial additions with an eschatological character. Blenkinsopp is not unique in noticing these additions, but he describes them as a common characteristic in the literary history of the Book of the Twelve. Blenkinsopp lists several of these additions, including Amos 9.11-15, Obad. 16-21 and Zeph. 3.9-20. Weimar briefly considers the question of the growth of the Twelve from the perspective of Obadiah. He argues that Obadiah must be viewed in light of several redactional levels across the Book of the Twelve which point to a common history. Weimar mentions one progressive level of redaction on the prophetic collection which produced literary *'Querverbindungen'* through the aid of *'Stichwortentsprechungen'*. He suggests that at this level the 'collection' took the shape of a 'book'. Bosshard documents a strong correlation between the ordering of the writings in the Book of the Twelve and the structuring themes and motifs of Isaiah. His observations most certainly point in the direction of a common tradent, and, taken *en bloc*, present a striking phenomenon that should be considered carefully.

1. *Accident.* This option is the least satisfying in most instances, because the phenomenon appears too frequently, and because the existence of broader organizing principles (chronological order of the superscriptions, similarity to Isaiah) demonstrates a thoughtful ordering of most of the writings.

2. *Collection.* This option argues that a compiler recognized the similar wording, and placed the completed works next to one another. This model represents the model traditionally espoused or presumed for the growth of the Book of the Twelve. It is difficult to exclude for every catchword, since one editorial technique appears to have incorporated previously existing material into new contexts. Nevertheless, close analysis of the text often leads to the conclusion that one or both of the books received significant additions in light of the neighboring book, or in light of themes and motifs within the larger corpus. Many times the most significant words in a connection appear in passages long noted as 'secondary' or 'tertiary' in their respective contexts. One logical assumption is that the secondary portion was added to unite two or more works.

3. *Redaction.* This option provides the best model for treating the texts as a whole. It asks whether the appearance of these catchwords, particularly in those passages which are literarily suspect, should be approached as deliberate changes to the text in view of the context of the Book of the Twelve. Indeed, significant catchwords often take on considerable importance when viewed as part of larger, programmatic work on the prophetic texts. The intentional reworking of material from an expanded literary context often provides a plausible explanation for troublesome syntax and pericopes. The recognition of various techniques for uniting these texts helps to explain a large number of the common words. Such techniques include redactional notes within existing contexts, incorporation of pre-existing material, free composition, redactional frames and superscriptions. Many words and phrases traditionally treated as text-critical problems take on greater significance when viewed from a redactional and literary perspective.

2. *Nahum 1 as Example*

A cursory treatment of Nahum 1 will exemplify this catchword technique. The phenomenon itself is readily demonstrable, since Nahum 1 shares at least thirteen different words with Mic. 7.8-20.[1] The words, both nominal and verbal, range from those which are relatively common, such as 'river', to those which are quite uncommon, particularly in prophetic literature, such as Bashan and Carmel in the same context.

The chapter may be safely divided into three sections: the superscription (1.1); the semi-acrostic theophanic hymn (1.2-8); and the remainder of the chapter (1.9-14). Close inspection of the Hebrew suffixes and addressees in the last section make it difficult to view these verses as an inherent unity. The remainder of the chapter can be further divided into four subsections: the literary transition from the poem to the Nineveh material (1.9-10); the accusation against Nineveh that originally opened the corpus (1.11); a reworked oracle of relief for Zion (1.12-13); YHWH's announcement of the imminent burial of the king of Assyria (1.14).

There are good reasons for arguing that a redactor has expanded earlier material in 1.11-12a, 14. Recent studies on the composition of Nahum arrive at the conclusion that Nahum did not obtain its final form until the postexilic period.[2] There is strong evidence that the poem (1.2-8) and its transition (1.9-10) are postexilic accretions. The remainder of the chapter (1.11, 12-14) blends with 2.1-3 (Eng. 1.15–2.2)

---

1.   Those words in common between Nah. 1 and Mic. 7.8-20 are: 'enemies' (Nah. 1.2, 8; Mic. 7.8, 10); 'anger' (Nah. 1.3, 6; Mic. 7.18); 'dust' (Nah. 1.3; Mic. 7.17); 'sea' (Nah. 1.4; Mic. 7.12); 'rivers' (Nah. 1.4; Mic. 7.12); 'Bashan' (Nah. 1.4; Mic. 7.14); 'Carmel' (Nah. 1.4; Mic. 7.14); 'mountains' (Nah. 1.5; Mic. 7.12); 'land' (Nah. 1.5; Mic. 7.13); 'inhabitants' (Nah. 1.5; Mic. 7.13); 'day' (Nah. 1.6; Mic. 7.11); 'passing over' (Nah. 1.8; Mic. 7.18); 'darkness' (Nah. 1.8; Mic. 7.8).

2.   See especially J. Jeremias (*Kultprophetie und Gerichtsverkündigung in der späten Königszeit Israels* [WMANT, 35; Neukirchen: Neukirchener Verlag, 1970]), who argues there was a pre-exilic core to Nahum which received a postexilic expansion; and the more radical views of H. Schulz (*Das Buch Nahum: Eine redaktionskritische Untersuchung* [BZAW, 129; Berlin: de Gruyter, 1973]), who views the entire book as a postexilic composition. Most recently K. Seybold (*Profane Prophetie: Studien zum Buch Nahum* [Stuttgarter Bibelstudien, 135; Stuttgart: Katholisches Bibelwerk, 1989]) dates the units differently than Jeremias, but agrees with him insofar as he also finds evidence of a pre-exilic core and exilic and postexilic additions.

and expands an earlier structure. The earlier structure included a
parallel core inside a redactional frame. Chapters 2–3 manifest a well-
documented parallel structure. The role of 1.11, 12a and 14 as redactional frame for the early corpus has not been noted, yet its function
as *inclusio* with 3.15b-17, 18-19 is readily demonstrable as noted in
the following chart (where A = the early redactional frame and B =
the parallel core):

A^1		1.11-12a: The numerical strength of Nineveh will not deliver it from destruction
A^2		1.14: The preparation of the grave of the king of Assyria
	B	2.4-14: (Eng. 2.3-13) First description of Nineveh's destruction
	B$'$	3.1-15: Second description of Nineveh's destruction
A^1		3.16-17: The numerical strength of Nineveh will not deliver it from destruction
A^2		3.18-19: Mocking funeral dirge at the grave of the king of Assyria

The later accretions (1.12b, 13; 2.1-3) blend allusions and quotes
from Isaiah 52 as promises to Zion and Judah.[1] Similar Isaianic allusions in the literary transition in 1.9-10 raise the likelihood that the
redactional hand responsible for these allusions is the same one that
incorporated the semi-acrostic poem in 1.2-8.[2] All of these observations, when taken together, reinforce the belief that the semi-acrostic
poem in Nah. 1.2-8 was a pre-existing hymn that has been redactionally incorporated into the corpus. The fact that the catchwords to
Mic. 7.8-20 appear in the hymn deserves consideration.

The semi-acrostic poem is broken in four places. Each of these
places contain significant words, which also appear in Micah 7, raising
the question of whether this repetition is intentional. Recent literature
tends to relativize the acrostic elements. A general consensus exists
that regards the hymn as never having extended beyond the first half
of the alphabet. A reaction to earlier theories of radical emendation
attempting to reconstruct the entire poem along acrostic lines, as well
as an increasing respect for the integrity of the MT, has caused textual
corruption to all but disappear as an explanation for the break in the
acrostic character of the poem. The textual corruption model has

---

1.   Nah. 2.1 quotes Isa. 52.7. In addition to the herald formula of Isa. 52.7,
Nah. 1.12-13 contains other allusions to Isa. 52 as well. There Zion is admonished
to shake her bonds from her neck (Isa. 52.2; cf. Nah 1.13), and reference is made to
the oppression/affliction of Assyria (Isa. 52.4; cf. Nah. 1.12).

2.   Compare Nah. 1.9-10 with the anti-Assyrian polemic in Isa. 10.15-19.

virtually been replaced by a widely attested opinion that the hymn should be understood as only loosely semi-acrostic in nature.[1]

The presuppositions of this relativization should be challenged. The presuppositions, which are sometimes stated explicitly, concern the style of the poem and the nature of composition. Proponents believe the acrostic technique is only one of several stylistic devices Nahum uses, and that he was so creative that he was not slavishly bound to one single device such as an acrostic pattern. This relativization assumes the acrostic poem as it stands in the MT represents the author's work in its pristine state. In response to these assumptions, it should be noted that the first assumption treats the creation of acrostic poetry too casually. The creation of such poetry requires considerable deliberation and creativity. It is highly improbable that a poet would deliberately choose to write a poem that is *nearly* acrostic. By contrast, an acrostic once recorded is a subtle device which could readily be overlooked or ignored by someone desiring the poem for another purpose. The second presupposition does not consider fully the possibility that the inconsistencies in the acrostic are deliberate changes to the poem. Indeed when viewed from this perspective (within the frame of the catchword phenomenon), these inconsistencies take on considerable significance.

In the case of Nah. 1.2-8, this relativization is unwarranted. The breaks in the acrostic pattern can be explained plausibly as deliberate alterations to a pre-existing poem. The easiest disruption to explain is the presence of the ו in the י line. Someone incognizant of the acrostic nature of the poem would have readily added the ו to conform the text to more typical syntax.

The addition of the two bicola between the א and ב lines can be explained from the context of the Book of the Twelve. Nah. 1.2b-3a introduces thematic elements that run counter to the main body of the acrostic poem, namely the delay of YHWH's vengeance. This delay functions meaningfully when one understands Nahum's position in the Book of the Twelve. Nahum functions as representative of the prophetic message during the Assyrian oppression. In addition to the

1. Such as J. De Vries, 'The Acrostic of Nahum in the Jerusalem Liturgy', *VT* 16 (1966), pp. 476-81; and R. Smith, *Hosea–Micah* (WBC, 32; Waco, TX: Word Books, 1984), pp. 71-72. By way of contrast, see D.L. Christensen, 'The Acrostic of Nahum Reconsidered', *ZAW* 87 (1975), pp. 17-30. Christensen offers a reconstruction based on syllable count that too nearly approaches the old emendation attempts.

basic theme (destruction of Nineveh), its position following Micah and preceding Habakkuk is appropriate for this function. The delay in 1.2b-3a by no means reflects the lack of faith that YHWH would overthrow Assyria. On the contrary it is better understood as a theological reflection upon historical reality. YHWH will ultimately bring judgment upon his enemies. In addition, the phrases in this expansion quote and adapt Joel 2.13 and 4.21.

The redactor has worked differently in the ד line. Those not opting for the flexibility of a loose acrostic device have been satisfied with either one of two suggestions for emendation, but both pose considerable difficulties.[1] It makes good sense to suppose that a redactor either changed the first half of the ד line on the basis of Mic. 7.14 or inserted an entirely new line into the context. The pairing of Carmel and Bashan is not common, appearing only twice elsewhere (Isa. 33.9; Jer. 50.19), both times in the context of Assyrian oppression. This makes it difficult to believe that the two words appear accidentally in adjacent passages in the Book of the Twelve, particularly in light of the fact that Nah. 1.4 breaks the acrostic pattern. Other stylistic observations distinguish this half-verse from the remainder of the poem.[2]

1. The presence of אמלל breaks the acrostic, leading to the argument that דללו was original. However, LXX never translates דלל with ὀλιγόω, but does use ὀλιγόω with אמלל (Joel 1.10, 12). The second verb, ἐξέλιπεν, does not necessarily imply another text, since it can be used for אמל (cf. Isa. 38.14). The Vulgate likewise uses two different words ('infirmatus' and 'elanguit'), but this likely relates to the two different subjects. Some, e.g. D.L. Christensen (*Transformations of the War Oracle in Old Testament Prophecy: Studies in the Oracles against the Nations* (HDR; Missoula, MT: Scholars Press, 1975], pp. 168-69), have suggested that the verb was originally דאב, but it is difficult to perceive how these consonants could have been confused to the point of becoming אמלל, and it could not easily explain the reading in LXX.

2. In addition to the acrostic interruption, several observations set this line apart literarily, making plausible the suggestion that this entire line has been substituted for one that did not adequately serve the redactor's purpose. First, this line is the only line in the entire poem containing no reference to YHWH. Secondly, the entities Carmel, Bashan and Lebanon are not intrinsic to Old Testament theophanic material. Thirdly, the passive use of אמלל stands out from the active verbs elsewhere in the hymn, giving this line a *situational* character, rather than one that depicts the reaction to YHWH's appearance. Fourthly, the reference to the withering of Bashan, Carmel and Lebanon take up literary traditions appearing elsewhere. Scholars typically interpret the withering of these three areas only via traditions associating these regions with fertility. However, this interpretation ignores two essential elements of the metaphor: the political and the literary.

Three possible explanations present themselves for the ז line. The most common explanation argues for the presumed dislocation of לפני from elsewhere in the sentence. Simultaneously most argue that the form was originally לפניו. The problem with this proposal is that it offers no real explanation as to how the word became transposed. More likely is a grammatical correction. The verb עמד in the qal can take a direct object without a preposition, and be used in the sense of 'to stand before'.[1] A later hand unaware of the acrostic could very conceivably have added the preposition to conform to more common constructions of עמד. A third alternative suggests the insertion of the phrase 'all its inhabitants' in the preceding line could have accounted for the dislocation and the change from לפניו to לפני. The deletion of the phrase, and the change to לפניו, improves the parallelism.[2] The presence 'all its inhabitants' can be explained in light of Mic. 7.13, where the phrase appears in similar form. This suggestion is less probable than the simple grammatical change, but still well within the realm of possibility.

Thus, not only can all four interruptions of the acrostic be explained as deliberate changes, but at least two and possibly three are best understood as the work of a redactor operating from a broader literary perspective. This broader perspective demands brief treatment.

3. *The Function of Nahum within the Book of the Twelve*

A brief survey of Nahum's structure and literary history confirm that its position and function in the Book of the Twelve has been created with considerable deliberation. The selection of Nahum in its current position, as already noted, coincides well within the historically oriented literary framework of the Book of the Twelve, even though it does not contain the typically Deuteronomistic superscriptions stating the chronology, which themselves probably represent an earlier corpus.[3]

---

1. For example, Gen. 19.27; Jer. 48.11; Hab. 3.11; Exod. 33.9; Josh. 20.4. Many of these constructions also have theophanic elements present in the context.

2. The phrase would then have read originally, 'And the land is lifted up before him (מפניו), and the world before him (לפניו)'.

3. Compare Hos. 1.1; Amos 1.1; Mic. 1.1; Zeph. 1.1. Similar Deuteronomistic superscriptions that lack reference to the ruling king(s) appear in Joel 1.1, Jon. 1.1, Hag. 1.1 and Zech. 1.1 are related stylistically to one another, and probably

The structure of Nahum in its expanded form, which incorporates the semi-acrostic poem, fits a structural pattern beginning in Micah and extending through Habbakkuk. This pattern helps explain the selection of the theophanic hymn in its current position. Micah, in its latest structural development, begins with a theophanic portrayal (1.2-5), and ends with a lament (7.1-7 [8-20]). Nahum also commences with a theophanic portrayal and concludes with a woe oracle and mocking lament. Habakkuk starts with a compositional lament and finishes with a theophanic portrayal which shares vocabulary and outlook, to a certain extent, to Nahum 1.

The inserted redactional allusions to Joel in Nah. 1.2b-3a coincide with the same phenomenon in Nah. 3.15ab, 16b, and indicate a considerable probability that Nahum entered the corpus simultaneously with, or subsequently to, Joel. The dating of Joel in the Persian period (at least in the form containing Joel 4) suggests that the Nahum corpus entered the larger corpus after 400, and not closer to the time of Deutero-Isaiah.

In summary, the catchword phenomenon is one facet that should be borne in mind when treating the writings of the Book of the Twelve. In the case of Nahum, this phenomenon simultaneously affords a rationale for the presence of the acrostic poem and unlocks insights into the interruption of the acrostic pattern.

experienced similar transmission histories. They also date the prophet's message by reference to the reign of a specific king.

INDEXES

INDEX OF REFERENCES

OLD TESTAMENT

INDEX OF AUTHORS

JOURNAL FOR THE STUDY OF THE OLD TESTAMENT

Supplement Series

DATE DUE

NOV 10 1997		
DEC 31 1998		
APR 19 2002		
MAY 18 2001		
MAR 31 2003		
DEC 30 2008		